THE HIDDEN LAWS OF EARTH

THE HIDDEN LAWS OF EARTH

BASED ON THE EDGAR CAYCE READINGS

by Juliet Brooke Ballard

A.R.E. PRESS • VIRGINIA BEACH • VIRGINIA

ACKNOWLEDGEMENTS

The author wishes to thank the following persons for their invaluable assistance in the preparation of this book: Mary Ellen Carter, editor and author of publications concerning the Edgar Cayce readings; Margaret H. Gammon, editor and author of the booklet *Astrology and the Edgar Cayce Readings;* Roberta Mueller, professional astrological consultant and lecturer; Alica W. Platt, lecturer and psychic therapist; Rolf Schaffranke, author and scientist; and Mary Ann Woodward, lecturer and author of publications concerning the Edgar Cayce readings.

ISBN 87604-117-9

9th Printing, May 1995

Cover design by Richard Boyle

Printed in the U.S.A.

FOR MY DEAR HUSBAND,
WHOSE UNSWERVING SUPPORT HAS MADE
THIS BOOK POSSIBLE

CONTENTS

THE HIDDEN LAWS
OF EARTH

THE NEED TO UNDERSTAND

A most arresting concept was presented to me when I was still a child.

My aunt and I were looking at a fire on our family hearth. I was basking in the warmth, enjoying the beauty of the ascending flames but being careful not to go too close and risk being burned.

"You have learned about fire," my aunt remarked. "You know that if you put your hand in it, it will burn you. It will burn anyone, even a person who doesn't know any better. The fire does not care whether or not you know.

"When you grow up, you will find there are laws of the universe that operate as the fire does. As long as you proceed within their structure, you can obtain advantages from them just as you can obtain warmth and beauty from the flames. But if you go against these laws, you will be hurt just as a person who puts his hand in the fire will be burned. The laws do not care. The world was set up this way.

"So you should try to learn what the framework is. Remember this when you are grown."

I did remember. After I was grown, again and again this conversation came back into my mind. My aunt's thinking was logical. Intuitively I knew that she was right.

The nub was to discover the structure of the laws. That they existed was obvious. Seasons came and went with regularity. Celestial bodies moved in certain orbits. The operation of gravity was a fact. Even though scientists could offer no explanation for this phenomenon, people everywhere utilized its effects. Without fully understanding some great force, any person could go along with it, *reaping the benefits, avoiding the hazards.*

3

The goal of living, whatever it might be, could be pursued and attained more readily if one acted in accordance with the laws and therefore realized optimum potential. If one did not do this, he would be poorly prepared to achieve his objectives and would be constantly getting into difficulties.

I needed to know the answers to two questions: What was the purpose of life? and, How did the world work?

A number of years after that conversation by the fire, my search ended. I came upon a huge fund of information, some of which perfectly answered my two questions.

I was introduced to the Edgar Cayce readings.

There are a number of volumes based on these readings which clearly show that the purpose of life is spiritual development.

There are many thousands, probably millions of people in this land and others, striving to advance on the spiritual path. They rely on a variety of teachings, for truth is the same the world over. Often these seekers are so engrossed in their search that they scarcely consider the framework in which they are functioning.

This book is concerned with that framework. The author has assembled material from the Edgar Cayce readings which shows the structural features. Much of this material is at variance with accepted scientific thinking today. Since one scientific fact after another which appeared fantastic at the time the readings were given has now been shown to be true, there is reason to believe that this other information will be proved correct also; and science will finally catch up with Edgar Cayce. Those readers schooled in today's scientific thinking may have to clear away preconceived ideas in order to comprehend fully what is given. Only when they comprehend it, can they use it to good effect.

For the scientifically minded another hurdle also exists. Science and religion are considered separate fields. Yet the readings see them as one.

This the entity may take in its study of this and understand why the spirit of life, the spirit of light, of hope, of desire to know the truth, must be greater than that man has called scientific proof, and yet it is the science of light, of truth, of love, of hope, of desire, of God. Study these well . . .

Science and religion are one when their purposes are one.

5023-2

Those who have not thought of these two as one may find it hard to adjust to this idea, continually expressed in the readings.

The author believes that most persons desirous of ascertaining the readings' viewpoint will have enough mental courage to shake off the shackles of past misconceptions and face up to what these transcripts have to say about the framework of this world and how it operates.

For those not burdened with prior notions, it should be a joyous experience to delve into the mysteries of our human existence. It is not necessary to understand the subject completely to *reap the benefits, avoid the hazards* of the laws. The readings bear this out. The members of a prayer group were advised to use certain techniques and were told that these could be effective without their understanding the whole tremendous subject of vibration. (281-7)

This book is offered in the hope that its contents may be a help to many readers in their everyday living and thus prepare them more adequately to continue their spiritual search and development.

THE PLAN

Creation

To understand anything really perfectly one must first ascertain its general plan. For this study to have any validity, the purpose of creation, creation itself and the general structure arising from it seem to be points of departure.

The Edgar Cayce readings are very specific as to the reason for creation. They start with the statement that there is a force which in this book we will call "God" or "the Father." This force is responsible for activity in our material world.

For Life is the expression of the Father-God, the Creative Force itself . . .   1587-1

Then life, or the manifestation of that which is in motion, is receiving its impulse from a first cause.
What is the first cause?
That which has brought, is bringing, all life into being; or animation, or force, or power, or movement, or consciousness, as to either the material plane, the mental plane, the spiritual plane.
Hence it is the force that is called Lord, God, Jehovah, Yah, Ohum [Om?], Abba and the like. Hence the activity that is seen of any element in the material plane is a manifestation of that first cause. One Force.   254-67

The readings go on to say that God created all souls in the beginning to be companions to Him. Later, after the fall into matter, a way was arranged for them to return to Him, perfected. This way involves regular stages of development.

All souls were created in the beginning, and are finding their way back to whence they came.   3744-4

The evolution of life as may be understood by the finite mind. In the first cause, or principle, all is perfect. In the creation of soul ... the portion may become a living soul and equal with the Creator. To reach that position, when separated, must pass through all stages of development, that it may be one with the Creator. 900-10

In what fashion was God able to create the heavens and earth? By mind. It is interesting to note that we, the children of God, share in the attribute of mind.

In the beginning God created the heavens and the earth. How? The *Mind* of God *moved,* and matter, form, came into being.
Mind, then, in God, the Father, is the Builder. How much more, then, would or should Mind be the Builder in the experience of those that have put on Christ or God, in Him, in His coming into the earth? 262-78

The method of return is specified—a growth upward.

... man's evolving, or evolution, has only been that of the gradual growth upward to the mind of the Maker. 3744-4

Although God created the world through mind, it was because of love that He did so. The world is a place in which all souls can attain companionship with the Father.

... the gifts that have been made his [man's] through the love that the Father would show, in that he [man] might be a companion, one with Him; not the whole, yet equal to the whole, able in that realm to magnify, glorify ... that love the Father bestowed upon His sons. 254-68

The next question is: How does the soul return to God? The readings tell us that this can be accomplished by will.

The soul, then, must return to its Maker: the *will* being that factor which may be used to carry the entity, the soul, back to the First Cause, to identify itself as being an entity worthy of acclaiming the name that makes it *one with* the Whole yet known to be itself, a part of the Whole. 633-2

In the developing, then, that the man may be one with the Father, necessary that the soul pass, with its companion the will, through all the various stages of development, until the will is lost in Him and he becomes one with the Father.
900-10

Hence, will is given to man as he comes into this manifested form that we see in material forces, for the choice.   262-52

In man's progress he uses his own mind to gain a consciousness of the many forms of life about him.

So as ye contemplate, as ye meditate, as ye look upon the Mind, know the mind hath many windows.   262-78

Life is the manifestation of *Creative* forces in a material world, in whatever form we may become conscious of it in. For, there are within the material experience of man many forms of life; even matter, even in the various strata of activity about the individual that man is not conscious of. And in *obtaining* the consciousness of it, through the applications of individuals, how many lives have been lost?   262-39

When the mind of the soul becomes capable of expressing itself in the physical and mental, thus erasing restrictions, the body of the entity will take on immortality.

For when those activities become such that the Mind of the individual, of the soul, finds itself expressing itself in the physical, in the mental, the body will take on what? Immortality! In the earth? Yes; reflecting same that it may bring what is as the tree of life in the garden, that its leaves are for the healing of the nations; that are the leaves that may fall from thy lips, from thy activities to thy fellow man, in whatever sphere or realm of activity. Why? Because of thine own self, because thou art grounded in the water of life itself . . .   262-78

To achieve such soul development an individual must learn to make his will one with the Father's.

Blessed, then, are they that make their wills one in accord with Him, as they seek to know, "Love, what would Thou have me do!"   254-68"

What is the Father's will? The following passage tells us that it is contained in the Golden Rule.

For, the whole law, the whole gospel that has been proclaimed from the beginning, is "Love the Lord thy God with all thine heart," and, as the Master added, "thy neighbor as thyself." *This* is the will of the Father. This is that He would have ye do.   254-71

9

First, we should love God with all our hearts. Then, we should learn to love ourselves and give the same measure of love to others.

The Extent of the Universe

In order to provide for the various stages of development through which souls may pass, God created a universe completely related to man's needs.

... to meet the needs of man, for which there was made all that was made ...   3744-4

... "Subdue the earth." For all therein has been given for man's purpose, for man's convenience, for man's understanding, for man's interpreting of God's relationship to man.   262-99

The earth is the Lord's and the fullness thereof. The universe He called into being for purposes that the individual soul, that might be one with Him, would have, does have, those influences for bringing this to pass or to be in the experience of every soul.   1347-1

A glimpse into the magnitude of this structure is afforded by information as to the dimensions represented by earth and other planets. Earth represents three dimensions, but actually there are eight. All are related to one another.

Man is three-dimensional in his aspects and study of what he finds within and without, and as to its source and its end ...   1580-1

Earth, in this solar system, merely represents three dimensions. Then how many dimensions are in this solar system? Eight! What position does the earth occupy? Third! What position do others occupy? That relative relationship one to another.   5755-2

Since there is a relationship between the various planets in this system, it is natural that they should be governed by the same laws.

There are, as were set in the beginning, as far as the concern is of this physical earth plane, those rules or laws in the relative force of those that govern the earth, and the beings of the earth plane, and also that same law governs the planets, stars, constellations, groups, that constitute the sphere, the space in which the planet moves. These are of one force, and

10

we see the ma   of the relation of one force with
another in the   us phases as is shown . . .   3744-4

The early Atla   following passage tells us, inquired
into these laws   them. (According to the readings,
the Atlanteans   ble living on a continent now
submerged in the   cean.)

As the peoples [lantis] were a peaceful peoples,
their developmen   rather that form—with the
developing into tl   material bodies—of the fast
development, or to   of the elements about them to
their own use; rec   emselves to be a part *of* that
about them.   364-4

We, too, can use th   the glory of God.

Spirit that uses m   uses every influence in the
earth's environ for th   e Creative Forces, partakes
of and is a part of the   Consciousness.   3508-1

Time   *Patience*

What are the three di   verning this earth? Time,
space and patience, the   ngs say.

So man's concept of the   's three-dimensional . . .
The communication or the   the motivating force . . .
is three-dimensional--time,   and patience.   4035-1

Concepts of time and space are ones with which we are
familiar. "Patience" is another matter. Here are some
comments on it.

Time, space, and patience, then, are those channels through
which man as a finite mind may become aware of the infinite.
For each phase of time, each phase of space, is dependent as
one atom upon another. And there is no vacuum, for this, as
may be indicated in the Universe, is an impossibility with God.
Then there is no time, there is no space, when patience
becomes manifested in love . . .
Passive patience, to be sure, has its place; but consider
patience rather from the precepts of God's relationship to
man: Love unbounded is patience. Love manifested is patience.
Endurance at times is patience, consistence ever is
patience . . .   3161-1

Not in selfishness, not in grudge, not in wrath; not in *any* of
those things that make for the separation of the I AM from the

11

Creative Forces, or Energy, or God. But the simpleness, the gentleness, the humbleness, the faithfulness, the long-suffering, *patience!* These be the attributes and those things which the soul takes cognizance of in its walks and activities before men. Not to be *seen* of men, but that the love may be manifested as the Father has shown through the Son and in the earth day by day. 518-2

The following excerpt points out that to pursue patience properly we must comply with its laws, working with love, purpose, faith, hope and charity and expressing these in daily life; then waiting with faith for the certain outcome.

Learn again patience, yet persistent patience, active patience—not merely passive. Patience does not mean merely waiting, but as it does for those that would induce nature to comply with nature's laws. So with patience, comply with patience' laws, working together with love, purpose, faith, hope, charity; giving expression to these in thy daily associations with those ye meet; making thy daily problems as real as real life-experiences, purposeful in every way.

And let not thy heart be troubled; ye believe in God. Believe in His promises, too, that as ye sow, so in the fullness of time and in material experience these things shall come about.
1968-5

The Way of the Return

The nature of the three dimensions implies that the framework in which we may return to the Father is an extensive one, laid out to encompass a long and perhaps difficult journey. Yet the lifetime of man is very short. Moreover, how could an entity or being attain in one short lifetime the perfection that would enable it to be a companion to the Father?

The answer is very simple. Multiple lives give us one chance after another. Alternating with them are sojourns under the specific planetary influences needed to round out our soul qualities. A beautifully designed system, devised by Infinite Mind! Through continuity of life the soul can at last attain the perfection needed.

The Edgar Cayce readings use the term "reincarnation" for this succession of lives and explain that the opportunities for them are continuous.

The reincarnation or the opportunities are continuous until the soul has of itself become an *entity* in its whole or has submerged itself.

Q-8. If a soul fails to improve itself, what becomes of it?
A-8. That's why the reincarnation, why it reincarnates; that it *may* have the opportunity. Can the will of man continue to defy its Maker?   826-8

How can we use these earth lives to the best advantage? By learning from our errors, as King David did, and not repeating them. Obviously in time such a policy would produce a person who would choose only the good and right.

What is righteousness? Just being kind, just being noble, just being self-sacrificing; just being willing to be the hands for the blind, the feet for the lame—these are constructive experiences.
Ye may gain knowledge of same, for incarnations *are a fact!* How may ye prove it? In thy daily living!
Using the experience of David the king as an example, what was it in his experience that caused him to be called a man after God's own heart? That he did not falter, that he did not do this or that or be guilty of every immoral experience in the category of man's relationship? Rather was it that he was sorry, and not guilty of the same offense twice!
Well that ye pattern thy study of thyself after such a life!
                                                  5753-2

During the sojourns in the environs of the planets, the soul is subject to *their* influence.
Mental effects differ according to the individual planets. We will find later that every soul needs to be subjected to all of these influences to become perfectly developed. After death there is an ensuing time in which the entity rounds out its recent earth life on an astral level. (5756-4) Then the soul is given an opportunity to draw on whatever specific planetary influence it especially needs by a stay in this planetary environ. It will be attracted at one time to one planet, at another time to another planet, depending on what has been gained and/or lost in the prior earth life. In due course the soul will have been under all the planetary influences. If it does not benefit from its stay near a particular planet and repeats the errors it needs to avoid when it has returned to earth living, then it will have to revisit this planetary environ. Eventually the influence will become effective.

... the planets about this earth's sun ... And yet with those influences about same by the variation in what is called in the earth the effect of the various influences shed from solar systems, suns and so forth.
For, much might be given respecting those environs and as to

how or why there have been and are accredited to the various planets certain characterizations that make for the attractions of souls' sojourns in that environ.   541-1

In the sphere of many of the planets within the same solar system, we find they [individuals] are banished to certain conditions in developing about the spheres from which they pass, and again and again and again return from one to another until they are prepared to meet the everlasting Creator of our entire Universe ...   3744-3

Vibration

How do the influences in our earth lives and our interim planetary sojourns affect us? Chiefly by vibration.
As living beings, we manifest vibration.

Life in its manifestation is vibration.   1861-16

The world about us is, also, in a state of flux, as physicists have learned. Under such circumstances it is readily understandable that rays, waves and various other forms of vibration can institute changes in our pulsing bodies and minds. Because of free will we can meet such situations and control the effects.
There are *many* influencing vibrations. Since each soul has been made so that it is a little different from the others, a very large number of these vibrations are needed for *all* the souls to utilize on the way back.

. . . the sons and daughters of God are personal, are individual, with their many attributes that are characteristics, personalities or individualities ...   254-68

... it is not by chance that each entity enters, but that the entity—as a part of the whole—may fill that place which no other soul may fill so well.   2533-1

But hast thou conceived—or canst thou conceive—the requirements of the influence to meet all the idiosyncrasies of a *single* soul?   5755-2

14

ASTROLOGICAL INFLUENCES

The Heavenly Bodies

Foremost among influencing vibrations are those emanating from the environs of the planets. Their positions in regard to one another constitute a vast system of permutations and combinations. The soul after death is attracted into the spot in their environs by which its needs can be best satisfied.

After spending an interim absorbing these influences and in the light of them assessing the losses and gains of the previous life, the soul returns to an earth life, in which it will generally be affected by what it has fed on mentally. Just what this is can be ascertained to a large extent by the position of the stars at birth. It would seem that the soul proceeds from these vibratory influences when they are striking earth most acutely, as though fortified at this time by greatest help and impelled by the tremendous activity.

There are a number of passages in the readings which infer that when the specific planets are again in position to beam strongly on the earth, the individual will be affected by their influence even more than usual. Logically, therefore, it would seem best for him to learn not only his natal aspects (in order to know his strengths and weaknesses) but also the times when certain of these aspects will reoccur.

Thus we find that the sojourns about the earth, during the interims between earthly sojourns, are called the astrological aspects. Not that an entity may have manifested physically on such planets, but in that consciousness which is the consciousness of that environ. And these have been accredited with certain potential influences in the mental aspect of an entity.   2144-1

15

. . . there is the influence of the planets upon an individual, for all must come under that influence . . .   3744-3

Thus as the soul passes from the aspects about the material environs, or the earth, we find the astrological aspects are represented as stages of consciousness; given names that represent planets or centers or crystallized activity.

Not that flesh and blood, as known in the earth, dwell therein; but in the consciousness, with the form and manner as befits the environ. And the judgment is drawn as to the mental attitudes.   1650-1

Each planetary influence vibrates at a different rate of vibration. An entity entering that influence enters that vibration; not necessary that he change, but it is the grace of God that he may!   281-55

This last selection explains how all vibration affects us. We are caught up in a strong force and adjust to it. We find some of it left in us later.

It is of interest to note that, according to the readings, planetary effect is confined to the special influences we have experienced between earth lives.

. . . it is not so much that an entity is influenced because the Moon is in Aquarius [now] or the Sun in Capricorn or Venus or Mercury in that or the other house, sign, or the Moon and Sun sign, in that one of the planets is in this or that position in the heavens, but rather because those positions in the heaven are [important to the entity] from the *entity* having been in that sojourn as a soul. This is how the planets have the greater influence in the earth upon the entity, see? For the application of an experience is that which makes for development of a body, a mind, *or* a soul.   630-2

This last sentence points out a very important fact—that only in the earth can we consolidate and make part of ourselves what we have learned mentally in planetary sojourns.

The readings agree with modern astrologers as to the exact time on which to base a natal chart.

Q-5. Should an astrological horoscope be based on the time of physical birth or the time of soul birth?
A-5. On time of physical birth; for those are merely *inclinations* and because of inclinations are not the influence of will.   826-8

The use of the geocentric system in astrology is, also, endorsed by the readings.

Q-2. What is the correct system to use in astrology—the heliocentric or the geocentric system?

A-2. . . . the Persian—or the geocentric—is the nearer correct. **933-3**

(The geocentric system uses the earth as a center from which to calculate, while the heliocentric uses the sun.)

With this data in mind, we need to remember, however, what the readings repeatedly emphasize—that the will of the individual is paramount in determining *how* astrological forces will affect him.

As to the application of self respecting the astrological forces—these . . . are only urges. As to what one does *with* and about same depends upon choices made.

Hence the needs for each soul, each entity to have a standard, an ideal by which the patterns of the life, of its associations with its fellow man, may be drawn.   **1710-3**

By proper use of astrological aspects in earth lives, an individual can eventually reach a point in development where he is no longer affected by such aspects.

In giving the influences that arise in the experience of the entity, it will be . . . found that little of the astrological sojourns has an influence upon the entity. For those tendencies as characteristics are not merely from the astrological aspects but what the entity has done *about* those aspects in the sojourns in the earth.   **2542-1**

Yet may this entity be set apart . . . For through its experiences in the earth, it has advanced from a low degree to that which may not even necessitate a reincarnation in the earth. Not that it has reached perfection but there are realms for instruction if the entity will hold to that ideal of those [at] whom it once scoffed [Christians at the time of Nero] . . . Astrological aspects would be nil in the experiences of the entity . . . No such may be necessary in the experience again in the earth-materiality . . .   **5366-1**

Astrology as a Tool

The importance of astrological study is pointed up by the fact that both Jesus' nurse and His mother undertook this study—in His best interests, we infer.

Thus, this entity, Josie, was selected or chosen by those of the Brotherhood—sometimes called White Brotherhood in the present—as the handmaid or companion of Mary, Jesus and

Joseph, in their flight into Egypt . . .

The period of sojourn in Egypt was in and about, or close to, what was then Alexandria.

Josie and Mary were not idle during that period of sojourn, but those records—that had been a part of those activities preserved in portions of the libraries there—were a part of the work that had been designated for this entity. And the interest in same was reported to the Brotherhood in the Judean country . . .

When there were those beginnings of the journey back to the Promised Land, there were naturally—from some of the records that had been read by the entity Josie, as well as the parents—the desires to know whether there were those unusual powers indicated in this Child now . . .

Q-2. *What was the nature of the records studied by Josie in Egypt?*

A-2. Those same records from which the men of the East said and gave, "By those records we have seen his star." These pertained, then, to what you would call today astrological forecasts, as well as those records which had been compiled and gathered by all of those of that period pertaining to the coming of the Messiah . . .   1010-17

Astrology was a subject included in the curriculum planned by the teacher Judy for Jesus Himself.

Q-18. *Tell about Judy teaching Jesus, where and what subjects she taught Him, and what subjects she planned to have Him study abroad.*

A-18. The prophecies! Where? In her own home. When? During those periods from His twelfth to His fifteenth-sixteenth year, when [after which] He went to Persia and then to India. [He was] In Persia, when His father died. In India when John first went to Egypt—where Jesus joined him and both became initiates in the pyramid or temple there.

Q-19. *What subjects did Judy plan to have Him study abroad?*

A-19. What you would today call astrology.   2067-11

The exact nature of astrological influences is summed up in a reading.

Q-29. *Please give a definition of the word astrology.*

A-29. That position in space about our own earth that is under the control of the forces that are within the sphere of that control, and all other spheres without that control. That is astrology, the study of those conditions.

In the beginning, our own plane, the Earth, was set in motion. The planning of other planets began the ruling of the destiny of all matters as created, just as the division of waters was ruled and is ruled by the moon in its path about the earth;

just so as the higher creation as it [was] begun is ruled by its action in conjunction with the planets about the earth. The strongest force used in the destiny of man is the Sun first, then the closer planets to the earth, or those that are coming to ascension at the time of the birth of the individual; *but let it be understood here, no action of any planet or the phases of the Sun, the Moon or any of the heavenly bodies surpass the role of man's will power,* the power given by the Creator of man, in the beginning, when he became a living soul, with the power of choosing for himself. The inclinations of man are ruled by the planets under which he is born, for the destiny of man lies within the sphere or scope of the planets.   3744-3

The true value of astrological study is indicated in the same reading.

Q-35. Is it proper for us to study the effects of the planets on our lives in order to better understand our tendencies and inclinations, as influenced by the planets?
A-35. When studied aright, very, very, very much so. How aright then? . . . in the influence of the knowledge already obtained by mortal man. Give more of that into the lives, giving the understanding *that the will must be the ever guiding factor to lead man on, ever upward.*
Q-36. In what way should astrology be used to help man live better in the present physical plane?
A-36. . . . the position of the planets give the tendencies in a given life, without reference to the will. Then let man, the individual, understand how *will* may overcome, for we all must overcome, if we would, in any wise, enter in . . .
Q-38. Are the tendencies of an individual influenced most by the planets nearer the earth at the time of the individual's birth?
A-38. At, or from that one which is at the zenith when the individual is in its place or sphere, or as is seen from that sphere or plane the soul and spirit took its flight in coming to the earth plane. For each plane, in its relation to the other, is just outside, just outside, relativity of force, as we gather them together.   3744-3

The Spheres of Influence of the Planets

Now we need to know just what is the scope of these planetary influences. A summary of their characteristics is an excellent introduction to more detailed study.

Q-3. Does the soul choose the planet to which it goes after each incarnation? If not, what force does?
A-3. In the Creation we find all force relative one with the other, and in the earth's plane that of the flesh. In the

19

developing from plane to plane becomes the ramification, or the condition of the will merited in its existence finding itself through eons of time.

The illustration, or manifestation in this, we find again in the man called Jesus:

When the soul reached that development in which it reached earth's plane, it became in the flesh the model, as it had reached through the developments in those spheres, or planets, known in the earth's plane, obtaining then One in All.

As in Mercury pertaining of Mind.

In Mars of Madness.

In Earth as of Flesh.

In Venus as Love.

In Jupiter as Strength.

In Saturn as the beginning of earthly woes, that to which all insufficient matter is cast for the beginning.

In that of Uranus as of the Psychic.

In that of Neptune as of Mystic.

In Septimus as of Consciousness.

In Arcturus as of the developing.

As to various constellations, and of groups, only those ramifications of the various existences experienced in the various conditions.

Q-6. Name the planets in order of the soul's development and give the principal influence of each.

A-6. These have been given. Their influences, their developments may be changed from time to time, according to the individual's will forces, speaking from human viewpoint. This we find again illustrated in this:

This man called Jesus we find at a Oneness with the Father, the Creator, passing through all the various stages of development; in mental perfect, in wrath perfect, in flesh made perfect, in love become perfect, in death become perfect, in psychic become perfect, in mystic become perfect, in consciousness become perfect, in the greater ruling forces becoming perfect. Thus He is as the model, and through the compliance with such laws made perfect, destiny, the predestined, the forethought, the will, made perfect, the condition made perfect. He is an ensample for man, and only as a man, for He lived only as man, He died as man.   900-10

A soul must experience all these "stages of consciousness" (1650-1) to be able to develop the correct vibration.

For, without passing through each and every stage of development, there is not the correct vibration to become one with the Creator . . .   900-16

Mercury

Now let us consider the effects of the various planets according to the placement just given in 900-10.

We will commence with Mercury, the planet concerned with mental activities.

... what is termed the dimensional environ of the mental capacities expressed by Mercury enables an entity or soul in the earth's environs to give a manifestation of high mental abilities, high mental capacities. Thus we may observe that such an one is enabled to obtain what we call knowledge, as pertaining to mental faculties, much more easily than those whose environs or indwellings previous to the earthly manifestation at present have possibly been in Saturn, Mars, Venus, Uranus, Pluto or the Moon. But what meaneth these? That these abilities are such as termed good or bad. These *exist* as conditions. And it is what a soul does *about* such conditions, or what it uses as its standard of judgment, that produces what is called in man's environment Cause and Effect. The same may be said of each of the other spheres or experiences or phases of the indwellings of the entity; in Venus, Mercury, Mars, Jupiter, or all such that have been the experience of the entity, producing those elements within the *mental* which is of the body or entity a part.
    Then, for this entity, we find:
    Mercury makes for the high mental abilities.   945-1

In the astrological influences, then, that find activities in thine own consciousness of mind, we find:
    Mercury—high minded; a thinker; deep.   2823-1

    Then, the influence from Mercury in *this* entity's experience we find making for rather the enquiring mind, the delving into the varied activities of others and their experiences with same—as to what their delving produced as mental reactions. And the entity in itself tends to draw conclusions from experiences of others. Not that the entity shuns its responsibility in such, but draws upon those influences that have been in the experience of others as well as how they may weigh with self's own experience.   1037-1

    From Mercury we find the high mental ability, the necessity for reasoning things out—within thy own mind, that of reaching conclusions by the entity.   2144-1

    These four preceding passages emphasize high mental ability, an inquiring mind which draws conclusions from what it discovers, and deep thinking, all varied aspects of Mercury. There are other facets, too. When this influence is combined with that of Uranus, the individual affected may read character easily, become a good executive, a banker or insurance man.

The influences from Mercury, with Uranus, make for the high mental abilities; and an individual . . . who may read character easily; thus adapting self—in the mental, the associations and the environs of associations—towards an executive, or as one who may direct the activities of others in their associations with individuals, especially as to such things as *collecting*—whether money or things, or those things that would deal with the individual life or affairs of individuals—even moneys. As insurance, banking, or the like. All of these come under these influences.   630-2

Mercurian keenness of perception may make it easy for a person to solve mathematical problems. It may, also, bring about order in his personal life, promptness and a reluctance to forgive deception. He may be interested in the response of the young to mathematics.

By the sojourn in Mercury, there is the influence of a keenness of perception in mental things; adaptable easily to some forms of mathematical problems, and for order or symmetrical activity in association with those in the activities of self; prompt in keeping the appointments to self, to others; slothful in forgiving those that would in any manner *willfully* attempt to deceive; especially interested in the minds of the young in their response to the association of things or numbers, as to their development.   553-1

An individual under the influence of Mercury may have a phenomenal memory and may function much like a computer.

The influences in Mercury show a great mental ability, and a memory that if it is kept in a developing way and manner becomes rather unusual—as to data, as to facts or figures, as to statistical developments in any field in which it may be applied.   1252-1

However, the influence of this mental planet can be detrimental if it is not directed properly.

. . . this influence in Mercury will make for a high *mental* development. With the experience as has been indicated this must be directed. For if these tendencies are turned from the right *mental* attitudes *as* to choices, these may be as detrimental as they are beneficial. For the entity will be, as it has been, an extremist—in *all* of its associations. And what it wants it will *want now!*   1208-1

Mercury brings the high mental abilities; the faculties that at times may become the developing for the soul or at others be turned to the aggrandizement of selfish interests.

For the entity is among those who have entered the earth during those years when there was the great entrance of those who have risen high in their abilities; and who are then passing through those periods when there must be application of the will, else the very abilities that have been maintained in the Sun and Mercurian influences will become as stumbling blocks . . .   633-2

These selections emphasize that a person should not use cleverness or mental ability to advance himself in a purely selfish way and that, if he does, his character will deteriorate.

Mars

The name Mars was originally applied to the Roman god of war. Designation of a planetary influence as Mars implies it carries a tendency to anger or violent action.

The Edgar Cayce readings bear this out. A person with strong aspects from Mars is easily aroused to anger. However, anger is a correct emotion if it is governed. Learning to control anger is an important first lesson in experience.

From Mars we find a tendency for the body-mind at times to be easily aroused to anger. Anger is correct, provided it is *governed*. For it is as material things in the earth that are not governed. There is *power* even in anger. He that is angry and sinneth not controls self. He that is angry and allows such to become the expression in the belittling of self, or the self-indulgence of self in any direction, brings to self those things that partake of the spirit of that which is the product or influence of anger itself.   361-4

Q-3. In reading of July 24, 1932, what was meant by "Be mad but sin not"? . . .
A-3. One that may control self in anger is beginning the first lessons or laws of experience. One that may control self in anger, that must come as resentment in the speech of individuals, may make for that which disregards the words said; disliking that which would produce such a feeling within self, yet able to love the soul of one that causes or produces such a state of feeling. This is patience, and love, and hope, and meekness, and pureness of heart. The meek shall inherit the earth, said He—the pure in heart shall see God. They are promises! Believest thou Him? Then [to] be angry and sin not is to know that these are thine *own* promises—to thee—to thee!
                                                262-25

If a person has been able to master the lesson provided by Mars, then he can go on to help others master it. This is another step in self-development.

From Mars also we find a benevolent influence, so that in the entity's experience it may be found that oft upon the activities of others in disputes, in wrath, in anger, there may come from the entity's own attitude—as to its mental influences—conditions and experiences even in the *material* world that are beneficent influences in the entity's activity.   1037-1

Martian influence can, also, result in a good opinion of oneself. This condition is desirable if not carried too far.

We find in Mars a high, exalted opinion of self; which is well, but abused—as it may be in Pluto, or in Mercury—may become a stumbling stone rather than a stepping-stone to advancement in this present sojourn.   3126-1

The individual affected by Mars should check himself for anger, animosity, covetousness and hate. If he can rise above these detrimental forces, he can advance in purposes and ideals.

In Mars we find anger, animosity, covetousness becoming the influence or force for detrimental activity in the experience.
But being forewarned, and applying that which has been and may be given in the experience, as has been and will be a part of the entity, the entity may so pattern its policies, its activities with its fellow men as to make such experiences stepping-stones rather than stumbling stones in its advancement in its development for its purposes and ideals through this material sojourn.   1797-1

Mars indicates the abilities to hate as well as to love.
                                                        2902-1

When Mars and Mercury join influences, emotion is involved. This may show itself in mental aspects. The emotion may drive the person to match wits with others. However, if he holds fast to an ideal, he will be able to meet the conditions.

There is a great deal of emotion, as in Mercury with Mars, indicated in the mental as well as in the desire for expression of same in the entity's experience.   3664-1

In the relationships as influences found in that of Mercury and of Mars, brings those conditions of mental abilities, mental felicity, in the experience of the entity with others; *forcing,* as it were, at times—through social *and* business relationships—to often match wits, as it were, with others. Will the entity hold fast to an ideal, and the *ideal* being set in

24

Him— who *is* the way, and the truth, and the light—the entity may ever be able to *meet* those conditions as they arise in the experience of self and self's relationships to others. **6-2**

This same combination of planets can, also, bring quick judgments as well as a sense of humor (a saving grace).

Mercury and Mars bring the *mental* abilities and the quick judgments, as well as a sense of humor, that has oft been and oft will be the saving grace, in which many escapades of a nature have been a part of the experience and escaping at times only through the sense of the ability to see the ridiculous as well as the sublime. Hence that pronouncement, that there should be a tempering of the too-quick judgment of others. **2051-5**

Mars adverse to Jupiter can on a physical level bring dangers from fireworks and firearms, which should, therefore, be avoided.

As to warnings: Beware of fireworks and firearms, of allowing the entity to play with or to carry same; though there will be the inclination for the entity to desire such things in the experience. For, Mars is adverse to Jupiter in the experience of the entity, and as will be seen—there have been experiences when these have brought disturbing influences in the experience of the entity in the earth. **3340-1**

This reading goes on to consider other Martian inclinations. Stubbornness should be directed. The urge to activity insures that the entity will not be lazy. This urge, of course, is an underlying feature of all the Martian characteristics cited previously.

In Mars we find this activity. The entity will never be called lazy. May be called stubborn at times, but this, too, may be directed—not by undue punishment but by reasoning with an appealing to the entity—in a manner as to bring much better influences. Not that there should be a prize for goodness, but remembering that virtue has its own reward, even in those attempting to direct or train children. **3340-1**

Mars and Vulcan (Pluto) together, also, bring dangers from fire and firearms as well as explosive passions in self. There is a warning against wrath and grudges. The individual is directed toward the love force.

In the influences that bring for warnings, as seen in Mars and Vulcan—beware of fire, and especially of firearms, or explosives that take the form of body in same . . . Beware of wrath in self, and in grudges as may be builded through wrath's influence in the relationships of the fellow man . . . Keep self attuned to that love force . . .   1735-2

Earth

Among the planetary influences listed in 900-10, A-3, earth is the third and is interpreted "as of flesh." In the readings there is no mention of earth influences *per se* that this author can find. However, we are told that the first vibration needed in our development is that of spirit quickened with flesh, a condition which is found on earth's plane.

Q-1. Explain the various planes of eternity, in their order of development, or rather explain to us the steps through which the soul must pass to climb back into the arms of beloved God.
A-1. These . . . must be manifest only as the finite mind in the flesh. As in the spirit forces, the development comes through the many changes, as made manifest in the evolution of man.
In the development in eternity's realm . . . a finite force as made of creation may become one with the Creator, as a unit, atom, or vibration, becomes one with the universal forces. When separated, as each were in the beginning, with the many changes possible in the material forces, the development then comes, that each spirit entity, each earth entity, the counterpart of the spirit entity, may become one with the Creator, even as the ensample to man's development through flesh, made perfect in every manner . . . without passing through each and every stage of development, there is not the correct vibration to become one with the Creator, beginning with the first vibration, as is of the spirit quickened with the flesh, and made manifest in material world (earth's plane).
                                                              900-16

The nature of this basic vibration is made a little clearer as the passage continues.

Then, in the many stages of development, throughout the universal, or in the great system of the universal forces, and each stage of development made manifest through flesh, which is the testing portion of the universal vibration. In this manner then, and for this reason, all made manifest in flesh, and development through the eons of time, space, and *called* eternity.   900-16

This reference points out that on earth we have to prove our development. It reinforces the excerpt previously quoted on application (under the section "The Heavenly Bodies").

For the application of an experience is that which makes for development of a body, a mind, *or* a soul.   630-2

The logical way to consider earthly influence is as that of a laboratory in which individuals put theoretical knowledge to a practical test. This theoretical knowledge consists of mental urges coming from interim planetary sojourns. On earth they are subjected to test conditions set up by emotional urges coming from former lives on earth. If what has been assimilated mentally can be made to stick under such pressure, then real development results and the basic or foundation vibration is established. It is one of strength, an insurance against vacillation.

If we think of earth's planetary influence simply as one of application, we cannot go far wrong.

Venus

A Venusian sojourn results most often in a tender, loving nature, well equipped to carry out the Christian principles.

One of a tender, loving disposition; that may be ruled or reasoned with through love, obedience or duty; yet may not be driven . . . through sheer force or fear of corporal punishment.

In this influence also we will find then, that sympathy—or the activities in being able under any circumstance to make for the alleviating of hardships, pains, or such conditions in the experience of others—will ever be *appealing* to the entity.

To be sure, these traits come from not only Venus' sojourn but as relative influences in the experience of the entity through earth's sojourns, also.   309-1

Appreciation of the niceties of life also comes from Venus.

In Venus we find the nicety of things, of conditions . . . the appreciation of influences and forces; yet demure, quiet in its manner, because of the relationships same *has* borne through the application of that very force in other sojourns in the material plane . . .   2144-1

It is readily understandable that this love influence should foster home-making.

The associations in Venus make for an affability in its associations in self as related to friendships and the social side of the self; and as at the home in every environ, provided there is not a fuss or turmoil in or among those that are present; hence the home life for the reason of its affability of self, as well as the necessary congenial life by associations of individuals and their minds' reaction.   553-1

Venus encourages beauty of expression.

In the astrological aspects we find that, through influences from sojourns in the Venus environs, the entity is a lover of beauty; especially of song.

And there should be given training and development, and the awakening for the entity in those influences pertaining to a knowledge of, and the channel for the expression of, the abilities for the use of the entity's voice in *praise* and in thanksgiving—rather than in those pertaining to the emotions of body or the arousing of those influences that would direct same in such channels.

Hence all things that have to do with phases of man's ability of expression in beautiful ways and manners will be of interest ... whether pertaining to nature, to voice or song, or even to art subjects.   1990-3

Combination of home-making and of artistic expression may result in the greatest career of all.

As Venus is the ruling influence in the experience, we find that the home will be, should be, the channel through which the greater abilities, the greater expression of those influences and powers may be made manifest.

Not that there are not abilities in music, in art, in those things pertaining to sources that make up what might be called a career life; yet these ... would not be the channels in which the entity may succeed the best in this experience.

But making an artistic home, making a home that is the expression of beauty in *all* its phases, is the greater career of *any* individual soul. This is the closer expression of that which has been manifested in the experiences of man's advent into materiality.   2571-1

The ability to make friends readily is a Venusian attribute.

Those influences in Venus make for an open, frank, loving disposition; making for friends in most any walk or every walk of life. These if they are kept upon that basis as indicated of sincerity in every activity will make for associations of pleasant natures, yet if these become too pleasant or irrespective of the spiritual life they might become detrimental.

But these kept in their reason and activity from the spiritual or constructive aspect become the helpful influences.

For as the entity indicates in the present, *all* may be

benefited by the closer associations and the sincerity of the
entity in its activities.   1442-1

Mercury and Venus together may bring about a feeling of
duty.

Venus makes for the emotional side of the body or entity in
the present, that becomes at times rather lacking but at others
makes for the great motivating influences and forces in the
experience of the entity; that it holds as a duty to self, as a duty
to its relationships in its various spheres of activity in a
material world. For its environs and activities from this
association in Venus have made for not sentimentality, but
sentiment is a portion; yet as Mercury is the ruling influence
this is done from reasoning rather than from sentiment alone.
                                                             945-1

The Edgar Cayce readings tell us that the body-form in
Venus itself is near to that in our three-dimensional plane. This
is because of the nature of love, which in its larger sense is
giving. In Venus beauty, love, hope and charity all blend
together.

The entity as Bainbridge was born in the English land under
the *sign,* as ye would term, of Scorpio; or from Venus as the
second influence.
We find that the activity of the same entity in the earthly
experience before that, in a French sojourn, followed the
entrance into Venus.
What was the life there? How the application?
A child of love! A child of love—the most hopeful of all
experiences of any that may come into a material existence;
and to some in the earth that most dreaded, that most feared!
(These side remarks become more overburdening than what
you are trying to obtain! but you've opened a big subject,
haven't you?)
In Venus the body-form is near to that in the three-
dimensional plane. For it is what may be said to be rather *all-*
inclusive! For it is that ye would call love—which, to be sure,
may be licentious, selfish; which also may be so large, so
inclusive as to take on the less of self and more of the ideal,
more of that which is *giving.*
What is love? Then what is Venus? It is beauty, love, hope,
charity—yet all of these have their extremes. But these
extremes are not in the expressive nature or manner as may be
found in that tone or attunement of Uranus; for they (in Venus)
are more in the order that they blend as one with another.
                                                             5755-1

On our own plane the Venus influence may bring about sex attraction.

We find in Venus that unusual attraction that the opposite sex will have for the entity, and the entity for the opposite sex. Hence those relationships in such should be the problems as well as the studies and the guidance through the periods especially in the next cycle—or during the next seven years . . .   2890-2

The Moon and Venus together may bring troublesome forces in the sex life.

One whose forces in the Moon and Venus are in opposition to that of good in this entity's sojourn in this plane, and those forces are those which the entity must overcome here now, for there have in other spheres been those conditions that this entity is now meeting to overcome; giving then of the spiritual insight, as this entity has in this sphere . . .
As to those influences in the life of the present plane's forces, as exercised in the force of the Moon and Venus we find this brings many of those troublesome forces to all conditions relating either to the physical or bodily love, and of the strange marital relations that may exist in the present plane.
2553-8

Those especially affected by Venus should all try to avoid being imposed upon—a situation not good for themselves or others. In early years they might attempt to develop qualities of leadership.

Venus makes for an easy disposition, very easily imposed upon. Yet the self-assertion that should be taught or given should be from the reasoning and spiritual promptings in the activities. And especially in those trainings as to spiritual promptings for a moral or religious life or experience, not for its own sake but for that in which and through which the entity may gain in the abilities to serve and be a channel of expression of the divine in its relations to others; else too easily may it be led into being imposed upon in every phase or manner to maintain friendships.
Hence its companionships through the developing years should be with an eye single in purposefulness that the entity may become more the leader than relying upon others to take expression, that there may be given into the activities that are latent and need expression, the abilities in the directions as indicated.   1206-3

One person was told that Venus was both a constructive and a confusing influence on her. It brought appreciation of beauty of character in others but at times self-condemnation—obviously because the entity felt she was not living up to that same beauty of character herself. She was advised to condemn neither herself nor others.

In Venus we find both constructive and confusing influences. For, there is in the entity's experience the appreciation of the beauty of character in others, and also at times self-condemnation.
These should not be conflicting. Condemn not self. Neither condemn others. 2487-1

Jupiter

In Roman mythology Jupiter, the king of the gods, exerted an all-powerful influence on earth dwellers. The planet named after him has a benevolent effect and fosters universal consciousness. It may even result in a good speaking or singing voice.

In Jupiter there is the greater impelling force. This the benevolent influence, the universal consciousness for one sojourning in the earth. This makes for those experiences as would direct towards harmony in relationships with others; and gives the entity a good speaking, a good singing voice. These abilities, to be sure, need to be cultivated but cultivated in that direction as a message of divine or spiritual import, ever ... 3188-1

Sincerity is a Jupiterian trait. However, this should be seasoned with appreciation of the lighter side of life.

We find in Jupiter the universal consciousness, the sincerity of the entity. For, when the entity gives expression to its feelings, one may be sure that it is the entity speaking. For, as indicated, the entity is deep, sincere. Though the entity may be called by others the plodder, it may arrive, it may attain to that peace, that understanding which comes only from true sincerity.
Cultivate, though, those truths as may be attained or gained through the expression of the joking side of life; though the entity cares little for the practical joke or the practical joker. Yet see not the seamy side, but truths. For remember—even in the last hours, He made light of His suffering, and gave expression of those things that are the deep feelings in the emotions of man in the present. 2571-1

A person strongly affected by this planet may be a good leader—on the basis not of fiery emotion but of excellent judgment. He may well become a teacher or a public servant or go into a healing profession.

From Jupiter the abilities are in a pleasing personality, as in relationships to groups, individuals, or in associations with large bodies or groups of people. While never one considered as a leader from the aspect of being fiery in the activities of the individual, yet one—in groups or masses—that controls rather through better judgment; and has those tendencies or abilities to move groups or individuals for the consideration of any activity, whether pertaining to those things in the secular or material life or as to controlling the mental aptitudes or attitudes of groups, as respecting *their* associations or relations in either mental or physical activity.

Hence, as an instructor, a teacher, or preferably in alleviating sufferings—or in a political field, as one controlling some great movement—would the entity make a name or place for self; or as an active practitioner in the alleviating of physical ills.

These urges all come under the aspect of Jupiterian influences . . .   309-1

If the Jupiterian is in charge of large amounts of this world's goods, he should always remember that these are lent for him to use properly.

In Jupiter we find the associations making for those tendencies for large groups to be in relationships with the entity. This makes also for those inclinations that in the experiences of the entity will be great amounts of this world's goods. May the training also then not only in its teenage but throughout its developments be as to the use of same, as being lent from Creative Forces and energies and not as for self-indulgence or aggrandizements.   1206-3

The readings point out that Jupiterian aspects make a good executive.

In Jupiter we find . . . the broad-mindedness, the ability to consider others . . .   2890-2

We find Jupiter making for the experience in the present of the entity [a 30-year-old woman] being an excellent executive . . . And especially will the entity find, from that sojourn in the present experience, there will be brought marital life in the latter or middle portion of this experience; and in relationships with one whose dealings are with (or should be) wheat, grain, cereals, coffee, tea, or those things that have to do with the body-functioning of individuals, groups, masses, classes or nations. In this environ will the entity gain the better in such relationships . . .

As a leader, as a director . . . in the commercial, the teaching, or the mental relations.   630-2

The broadening influence of Jupiter may result in travel and study of people and things from other lands or ages.

In Jupiter we find a widening, a broadening influence; so that things pertaining to travel, to people of other lands, to things of other ages and other climes, make for that upon which the entity may dwell; and which also may be used as a stepping-stone for understandings.   1037-1

While Jupiter with Venus may bring enjoyment of the beautiful according to a universal consciousness, the adverse in Mars, added to it, may add wrath, which will result in a reversal of this enjoyment.

From the Jupiterian sojourn, we find not only the benevolent, but the adverse forces. For while Venus *with* Jupiter brings enjoyment of the beautiful in ways that pertain to a universal consciousness or activity; the adverse in Mars indicates that wrath . . . may bring those things that will cause the influence to be in a reverse manner . . .   1990-3

A way to overcome certain adverse inclinations from Jupiter was clearly shown to [826]. He could avail himself of the influences innate within himself from Uranus, Saturn and Venus, and when his period of testing came in the ten years following the reading, he would be able, if his heart was in it, to rise above the temptations of power and material advancement. He could then utilize opportunities to help others. This would bring him peace, harmony, love and understanding.

In the astrological aspects we find the entity coming under the adverse influences of Jupiter, yet *with* those influences in Uranus, Saturn, Venus, that are innate within the entity—and which planets are in a conjunction in the coming year and years. These should in the next ten years make for the greater advancement for the entity, in the material positions, the trust by others that will be placed in the entity, material power that is not only given by position but by worldly means. Yet these must necessarily, with such opportunities, carry with same that same period of test. And unless they are . . . [motivated] by the spirit of truth, the spirit of service, the desire to show forth the glories of the Lord rather than of self, the glories of help, aid, understanding, brotherly love, good fellowship, faith and hope in the minds and hearts of individuals, they must come as to naught in the latter portion of the experience in this sojourn. But if these opportunities, that begin within the present year, are used in that way and manner as to make for the greater developments in the minds and hearts of others, then may the entity find that peace, harmony, love, understanding in the earth as the Lord hath given, "He that loveth me and keepeth my commandments may ask in my name, believing, and it will be done unto him" ' .. And greater and greater may be the opportunities of the entity in this experience to do good unto his fellow man; not only in high places, not only in material conditions and experiences but in all walks, in all ways of man's experience in the earth.

826-2

Saturn

According to the Edgar Cayce readings, Saturn institutes changes. It is because of lack of spiritual development that the entity has been banished to this sphere. Here he may be remolded in such a way that he will now be able to pass satisfactorily through the other planetary conditions. It is in them he must show his gained development.

Q-1. Explain and illustrate, "In the sphere of many of the planets, within the same solar system, we find they [individuals] are banished to certain conditions in the developing about the spheres from which they pass, and again, and again, and again return from one to another, until they are prepared to meet the everlasting Creator of our entire universe, of which our system is only a small part." [From 3744-3, A-30]

A-1. In this condition we find much ... in relativity of force ... when such conditions are shown in the body that the spiritual entity is banished unto Saturn, that condition in the earth's solar system to which all insufficient matter is cast for the remolding, as it were, for its passage through the development in earth's plane, or in the spheres to which the earth's relations adhere in the development of a spiritual or physical body ... we find the relations ... from those spheres in the earth's sphere; that is, as in Mercury, as in Venus, as in Mars, as in Jupiter, as in Earth, as in Uranus, as in Neptune, and the chancing or changing, as it were, from one development to another, until the entity passes from that solar system, or sphere, through Arcturus or [from] Septimus as we see. As would be illustrated in this: We find in the earth's plane that entity that manifests such hate, such aggrandizement of the laws of the flesh, in any desire made unnatural—these find their reclamation, their remolding, their beginning again, in the spheres of Saturn's relative forces. Hence again pass through those spheres in which the entity (spiritual) must manifest, that it (the entity) may manifest the gained development through the earth's plane. For in flesh must the entity manifest, and make the will one with God or Creative Force, in the universe, and as such development reaches that plane, wherein the development may pass into other spheres or systems, of which our (the earth's) solar system is only a small part . . . the entity must develop in that sphere until it (the entity) has reached that stage wherein it may manifest through the spiritual planes, as would be called from the relation to physical or fleshly plane.   900-25

How does this remolding come about? Saturn brings longings for change. They are so potent that when other planets exert a special influence on an earth life, these longings augment their power and *strong changes can occur,* directed by the other influences but given greater power by the urges. These changes are generally basic in nature since they arise from a desire to alter the mainsprings of activity.

We find also Saturn having been an influence that has made for experiences within the entity's activities in the present in which it has continued to long for changes in its associations. This has caused the entity at times to find itself . . . having daydreams . . . by longings for that building up . . . an ideal relationship or condition that would be . . . the greater activity in which it might engage itself; either for the satisfying of the material desires or to create the character of environment in which the mental and soul forces might find the greater expression. More often have these considered rather the *material* things. But as these changes have gradually passed, more and more does there come now . . . that as sought from the mental and the spiritual expression rather than from the purely material.
For the earth and Saturn are opposites, as it were; for to Saturn go those that would renew or begin again, or who have blotted from their experience much that may be set in motion again through other influences and environs that have been a portion of the entity's experience.   945-1

Saturn combined with Uranus brings extremes.

In Saturn we find the sudden or violent changes—those influences and environs that do not grow, as it were, but are sudden by that of change of circumstance, materially, or by activities apparently upon the part of others that become a part of self in the very associations. And yet these are testing

35

periods of thy endurance, of thy patience, of thy love of truth, harmony and the spirit that faileth not.

From the combination of this with Uranus, we find the extremes; the environs materially or mentally in which the very opposites may be expected. Remember, only in Christ, Jesus, do extremes meet. 1981-1

The longings do not always terminate in real improvement.

From Saturn, we find the tendency for the starting of new experiences, the starting of new associations in the activities; and unless these are tempered with the mental influences they are rarely carried to their full termination. This again would be as a warning ... When thou hast chosen that direction, that activity thou would take, know that thou art kept in a balance that is of the material, mental and spiritual influences near to right. Then lay it not aside until it, the activity, has borne fruit in thine mental and material experience. 361-4

The desire for change can even result in muddling.

In Saturn we find the inclinations for changes, as to this, that or the other; and to muddle a great many things together in the activity.

Hence that injunction as given by the sages of old, "The merchant is never the student; neither is the student ever the merchant," should be as a part of the entity's program in its choice of its activity in this experience. 1426-1

A tendency toward too many new starts may be offset by consistency and persistency.

While the Venus influences are latent, these should find the greater expression; else the urges as from Saturn would make for the entity having *many* homes, or many marriages—and these are *not* well in the experience if there are to be the developments.

For consistency and persistency are the sister[s] of patience; patience the entity needs to learn as its lesson in this experience.

Patience naturally makes for turmoils for an individual or entity so strong under the influence of the Uranian forces, but these periods of benevolent activities in the Uranian, the Venus[ian] and the Jupiterian, when in adverse influence to Saturn, will make for periods when decisions had best be made. 1431-1

The role of Saturn is vital. It gives us a chance to begin again, as has been so well brought out in the excerpts from readings 900-25 and 945-1, cited before.

Afflictions of Mars and Saturn can make an individual slow to anger but also secretive in carrying out plans.

One with the afflictions of the forces as given in Mars and Saturn will and does make one slow to wrath, but subtle in the ultra extent in carrying out purposes, good or bad.   221-2

Advice is given to those discouraged because of the changes brought on by Saturn: Minimize the disheartening influences; magnify those that would remove the discouragement.

We find in Saturn the changes that come—those periods in which the entity may become easily discouraged, and weep. But remember, He gave expression in such a manner; weeping with those who wept, rejoicing with those who did rejoice.
Minimize in the experience, then, those influences that are discouraging and disheartening; magnifying the glory of those influences that may remove such far from the feeling or comprehension of the entity.   2571-1

Uranus

Uranus impels a person toward extremes. It is, therefore, important that he should be trained to weigh the value of every different kind of experience of body, mind and soul and be aware of the purpose or need for each one.
Uranus may, also, bring intuitive influences, which can result in the development of psychic perception.

From the Uranian influences we find the extremist...Hence the necessities in the trainings for this entity as to the value of experiences of every nature ... [whether] pertaining to body, to mind, or to spiritual things. And nothing should be given the entity merely as rote or routine, but as purposefulness in every phase of its experience. These make for also the intuitive influences and the abilities for the development in the very psychic forces of the entity.   1206-3

Interest in the occult, stemming from intuitive influences, should be balanced in the spiritual nature.

In Uranus we find the extremes, and the interest in the occult—or the mystical. This is well, if it is balanced in the spiritual nature—not of an ism or a cult but of the truth that is expressed in Him.   2571-1

Lack of such balance, coupled with anger and the Uranian urge to extreme action, may break down self-control. This, in turn, can wreck spiritual development.

There are the tendencies from Uranus towards the occult and the mystic forces; as visions, hearing, seeing and knowing without having the physical contact with experiences in the *mental* body. These also must be tempered with not only justice but the spirit of truth, for they may become experiences that—with anger, with the accentuations of the activities from the Uranian experience—bring periods when uncontrol of self may wreck self in its better endeavors.   361-4

It is easy to understand why the influence of Uranus can result in tidiness, methodical habits, even directness. A person with such characteristics may sometimes feel urged to chide those not possessing them.

In those influences in the Uranian, makes for that often called the extremist in the niceness of things, in the tidiness of self, of things about which the entity has a particular interest; often chiding others for their actions or activities in not being methodical, or being as nice or as direct in their activities as they should be or as viewed by the entity.   282-2

Uranian moods of optimism and pessimism should be controlled in such a way as to help others the most.

The influence from Uranus brings the extremes, or the periods when ye are very hopeful and periods when ye feel very pessimistic. At other periods the optimism is quite enlightening and quite given to create courage in the minds of others. And thy *pessimism* may be just as depressing. Keep that in mind!   2823-1

The individual may turn from great activity to solitude and self-examination.

Thy sojourns in Uranus, my brother, make for the mental interest in things that are hidden; and an extremist at times in all of the other influences, so that—though there may be periods of extreme motion from association—the desire for self and to be alone comes as the periods of experience or expression in the mental self; also the interest in occult or mystic influence. And the spiritual life is the yardstick or standard of the mental self, no matter to what *extremes* the associates or others may go.   553-1

In the swing from being definite to indefinite, the Uranian may be able to keep others guessing. This is an asset for a real executive.

And as the psychic forces are manifested from the Uranian experience, it makes for . . . one that may be called very definite, yet at times very obstinate and at times very *indefinite* as to whether it will or whether it won't in whatever the relationships may be! Hence it often keeps not only the friends but the family, and even the male associates, *guessing* as to what will be the activities or the relationships; but this is an ability for a real executive, *provided* the entity or soul—in such relationships—knows *itself* what it is after—and the entity in its experience usually does!   630-2

Uranian forces coupled with those of Mercury may in other ways, also, qualify an individual to become an executive. He may read character very easily and thus be able to adapt himself. He may be able to *collect* easily and for this reason go into the fields of insurance and banking. (See the selection from 630-2 included under "Mercury.")

Excessive talking may stem from Uranus with a strong Mercury influence.

Easily might the entity become one who would talk of self too much.

While the entity will ever be a good listener, do direct the entity so that there is always the consideration for others.

Astrologically, we find Uranus (the extremist, of course, in same), Mercury (the high mental abilities; for at least eight to ten experiences have been through the Mercurian consciousness— thus, quick in the varied fields will the entity in material happenings find ways and means of expression).
                                                        2922-1

These same two planets may foster selfishness as well as graciousness. The former should be controlled.

Thus those experiences from Mercury indicate mental abilities, and yet these in the realm of Uranus make for extremes—in which the entity may be very gracious at one time and very dictatorial, very selfish at other times. These must be (selfishness, dictatorship), eliminated entirely from the entity's application of relationships with others, replacing them with the fruits of the spirit . . .   3656-1

Benevolent influences in Mars and Uranus may bring about abilities as a peacemaker.

. . . benevolent influences in Mars and Uranus . . . bring . . . exceptional abilities as respecting intuitive forces for the body, and as for the abilities for the entity . . . to quiet those who would show wrath or unkindly feeling toward another.

Oft will the entity—if trained, especially in this formative period—be able to act as oil upon troubled waters, as that interbetween which will make for beauty in the lives of those the entity contacts, making for a bond of sympathy, of union, that will be exceptional for the entity's experiences *in* the earth's plane, as well as that which may be trained for an awakening of abilities within self that will bring for one that may be the peacemaker, not only among individuals but in groups, in classes, in States, in masses.   1911-1

Jupiter and Uranus together may promote exceptional abilities, including exceptional abilities to err.

One that, with Jupiter and Uranus influence, will be found to be exceptional in abilities toward those arts, or elements of life that go to make up the characteristics of the developing personality as manifested in the present experience . . .
. . . exceptional abilities with Uranian influence may be *well* said also to mean exceptional abilities to err, or to be led astray, in the direction not best for self or self's development.
                                                        38-1

The tendency toward extremes may have an effect on an individual's losses or gains from games of chance. He may experience both winning and losing streaks. He, therefore, needs to control himself in this area especially.

Uranus is the greater influence for the present experience.
Hence we will find an individual that will oft be called an extremist; either very active or very dull or lazy; inclining to be in the position of over enthusiasm about any association or activity, or not caring or paying much attention to same. Yet the abilities in the mental plane will tend to make for the mental understanding. As to whether this is expressed or not will depend upon the entity, as to whether the influences become active or subjugated by the entity . . . There will also be made experiences or periods when the entity would be called lucky at any game of chance, yet there will be periods when—from the influence—it would be practically impossible for the entity to gain through games of chance. Hence there will be the necessity of controlling self as to any games of chance, whether these be with the ordinary associations with cards, with races, with stocks, or what, as the entity develops.
                                                        406-1

The Uranian may have recently passed under the influence of Saturn.

As in Saturn—that to whom all insufficient matter is cast for its remolding, its changing into the various spheres of its

40

activity, either re-entering through those of the Uranian—
which makes for the accentuations of very good or very
bad . . .   311-2

It is well to remember that extremes meet only in the Christ.

In the Uranian influence we find the interest in the spiritual
things, as well as the awareness of that which is sordid. The
extremes, ye know, meet only in the Christ, who came unto His
own and they received Him not. So in thy extremes, when ye
become discouraged, disconsolate, when ye become in such an
attitude as to wonder what is the way, know that He *is*
listening—listening! As ye *call,* He hath said, "I will hear and
will answer speedily."   1968-1

Neptune

Spiritual forces and mysticism are associated with Neptune.
Ennobled by Jupiter and the Sun, they can be used toward the
developing of others.

. . . that plane from which the soul and spirit took its flight to
the present earth plane . . . that far away force as exercised in
Neptune. Hence we have an entity that to self and all others,
for many, many moons—present sphere's conditions—will be
peculiar to other people, rarely ever being understood; yet one
with the spiritual insight of the developing in earth plane, and
one whom others would be, could be, benefited by, by being in
contact with this entity.
One that will give much toward the developing of many in
the earth's plane.
One whose greatest forte lies in developing others toward
the spiritual forces, and those things mysterious to earth plane
dwellers who understand little of the spiritual forces.
One whose forces are exercised to such an extent that those
who come in contact with this entity and trample under foot
those spiritual forces as exercised do so to their own souls'
detriment. Many such cases are in this body's life.
As to those forces in the astrological effect received for this
entity: Those in Neptune, with that force of Jupiter and the
Sun's rays, as the Gemini, that gives of the better and
ennobling forces to this entity.   2553-8

Neptune in conjunction with the Sun brings the inclination
to be open-minded about higher influences of the mystical
nature.

*Q-3. What are the effects of Neptune, in conjunction with the
Sun, in one's horoscope?*

A-3. Neptune, of course, is the water sign, and is of the farther distance; and in conjunction with the Sun in the sign of the individual is that inclination . . . of being open-minded to spiritual or higher influences of the mystical nature—as represented in the figure of the body through those particular periods.   1100-27

Water may affect Neptunians in various ways. Proximity to expanses of it kept one person free of hate.

In Neptune, we find always mysterious to self as relation to others, and especially as to the environs, and *innately* have the waters often called to the entity as a place of abode . . . *never* on or very *close* to waters does the entity experience that of hate, yet inland, on mountain, this would be a different experience to the entity.   99-6

Sometimes salt water is preferable.

. . . those influences of Neptune bring . . . the *mystery* in the experience of the entity; the associations in many peculiar circumstances and conditions . . . as, by others, would be misunderstood . . .
In those influences seen in Neptune . . . the entity will gain most through the experience, has gained and will gain, through sojourn near, or passing over, large bodies of water, and *salt* water is preferable; for in the experiences will be seen, fresh hasn't *always* meant for living water.   243-10

This last comment would indicate that pollution had commenced some time back.
Preoccupation with water may lead to desire for travel. However, the excitement of travel should not cause a person to lose sight of ideals.

In Neptune we find the inclinations for things that have to do with water and over water and to be on waters and upon waters. These then give an urge again, as through Saturn, for change of scene and change of environment—and the desire for travel; desire for those things that are exciting, and those things that pertain to the heroic and hero worship. This urge must ever be tempered, then, with directing the entity to the character of ideals that should be held by the heroes that the entity follows in the very activities of its study and its progress.   1426-1

Any associations with water may be helpful.

In Neptune, again we find the artistic temperament . . .
And any of those influences where water or decorations for

things that float on water, or those things across bodies of water, associations with individuals who have to do with things pertaining to water, will all be a part of and a helpful force in the experience of the entity; if there is *ever* kept the use of constructive forces in having an ideal that *is* grounded in spiritual import.   1771-2

The creative influence from Neptune may be used to revive or give life to things. Could this at times account for the "green thumb" attributed to gardeners?

We find in Neptune the power of water, or of the influences about same; the creative expression, the ability to aid in reviving or in giving life to things. And most anything that would be planted in the earth by the entity would live. And flowers and those things that are cut from nature blossom or give off *better* perfume by being about or on the body of the entity (and there are few of which this could be said).
                                                            2641-1

This facet of Neptunian influence may explain one person's bent toward biology and horticulture.

Hence we will find also the influence of Neptune; not so much as that ordinarily seen from the activities of waters, but rather as these become associated with the realities in the experiences in the earth.
Hence those things that have to do with the kingdoms of the earth . . .
As the animal kingdom, or the agricultural, or the combinations of these become as a part of the innate desires of the entity.
Hence as a biologist, or as one active in the horticulture or agriculture as combined with its relationships for the better influences in the experience of many, may the entity find the field of activity in which greater developments are apparent.
                                                            1442-1

Interest in detective stories may stem from Neptune.

. . . the entity comes under the influence of Neptune and Uranus, with those influences in Jupiter and in Mars . . .
One loving mystery, and every condition as regards . . . a mystery of the sea, and of the sleuth or detective nature . . .
One who will find the entity's greatest abilities in the present earth's plane in the study of the occult forces.
                                                            2213-1

Neptune can attract a person toward a study of psychology.

. . . we find . . . in Neptune an interest in psychological and spiritual things.   3126-1

Neptune can incline an individual toward a methodical life.

In Neptune we see something again of the methodical life, in a *mystic* manner. Do not be too mindful of mysticism, unless weighted well *with* those influences in love and in nobleness.
255-5

Jupiter and Neptune together may bring the desire for study and loneliness as well as an interest in people and things. The people will be valued for their character and worth.

Those influences in Jupiter and in Neptune bring for the entity those desires of study, those desires of loneliness, yet the life filled with those conditions that have to do with people. People and things, *both,* interest the entity. The barter and sale interest little . . . Rather those of character, and . . . that that builds for an individual . . . worth, and their worth to the entity meaning their ability to aid in . . . [giving] direction, or in giving to individuals or groups that which will aid them in making life either easier or more profitable—whether for moneys or for pleasures, or for own development.   256-1

Ability in construction work can come from Neptune. Tied in with this may be a forcefulness in the field of law and order.

In Neptune we find the construction, the building, as well as water, as well as law and order, all as parts of the experience in which the entity has had and may have force or power with others, or influence upon others.   2051-5

The readings contain a warning against allowing oneself to be dominated by the occult forces of Neptune. One should dominate them.

As in Neptune, with Uranus and Aries influence, will make for those influences that waters, and those of mystic forces, or occult influences, will ever have (as in suggestion) an *influence* in the experience of the body. Allowing self to become subject to, rather than dominating the influences or suggestion, would make the entity a subject of, rather than being able to . . . *dominate* that which is harmful in the experience of the entity.
279-4

Septimus, Pluto or Vulcan

Prior to 1930 there were a few references in the readings to the planet Septimus, including reading 900-10. (See the section on

"The Spheres of Influence of the Planets.") The word "septimus" means "seventh" in Latin. After the discovery of Pluto, the seventh[1] planet outward from the earth, in 1930, no more references to "Septimus" occurred. Instead "Pluto" was mentioned. It seems reasonable to assume that the term "Septimus" was used by Edgar Cayce to identify Pluto before it was named. The following section, based on this assumption, correlates readings on the two.

In addition, there were a few references to "Vulcan," definitely identified as being Pluto. Doubtless this was the ancient name. These, also, are correlated.

Q-17. Is there a planet anciently known as Lilith or Vulcan?
A-17. Pluto and Vulcan are one and the same.   826-8

The Plutonian influence, presently and in the future, was assessed in a reading given December 2, 1939.

. . . a development that is occurring in the universe or environs about the earth—Pluto. Not as some have indicated, that it is gradually becoming dissipated. It is gradually *growing,* and thus is one of those influences that are to be a demonstrative activity in the future affairs or developments of man towards the spiritual-minded influences, or those influences outside of himself.

These are in the present . . . merely the becoming *aware* of same. Rather within the next hundred to two hundred years, there may be a great deal of influence upon the ascendancy of man; for it's closest of those to the activities of the earth . . . and is a *developing* influence, and not one already established.
1100-27

The few references to Pluto in the Edgar Cayce readings do not explain clearly how it will contribute to man's spiritual advancement. There are hints, however.

. . . self-centeredness in Pluto, and earthward in application of self.   3126-1

Later in this reading there is reference to "a high exalted opinion of self" being "abused . . . in Pluto." (See excerpt 3126-1 under the section dealing with Mars.)
Another reading throws more light on this situation.

---

[1] Pluto's eccentric orbit carries it at times closer than Neptune to the sun and the earth. Hence Pluto can be said to be seventh in position from the earth.

In astrological associations, these would appear adverse in their first appearance, coming much under the influence of the Dog Star and Vulcan [Pluto]. These make for that influence as has been of sudden changes in the social affairs, the relationships as respecting those of kinship, and those changes as respecting physical or business relations; yet these *adversities* may be used and applied in the experience of the entity as stepping-stones for soul's development, as well as of a mental and material change in the experience of the entity... one in Mercurian forces as has brought for a development of a mentality that becomes necessarily pecuniary in its aspect...   1727-1

It would seem that the self-centeredness of Pluto, on a very earthly level, may bring the adversities. [1727] was evidently of a mercenary mind. It is a reasonable supposition that this may have gotten him into trouble.

Adversities, when used properly as stepping-stones, can advance a person. Just as Saturn brings an opportunity to begin again, Pluto may hasten the process of facing the worst in oneself and then rising above it.

There is further mention of the tie-in between Pluto and financial affairs.

Those... financial [affairs] through the position of Aries and Septimus [position of Septimus with regard to Aries] give the force through financial plane which will be in the ascendancy to the last days on this plane, and for some generations to come its effect will be there unless the will cut this short.   5717-1

The next reading for this individual contained the same warning as to the necessity for exercising self-control.

As to the financial reached through Aries and Septimus, these... deal with those... governed by the force and will, and the natural tendency for all other forces to become the elements necessary to bring financial gains to the individual, and its force as brought will be felt throughout many generations unless the will of this individual (see, it is outside of the spiritual realm), sets it differently, see. In Aries... the force... governed through the head, that of Septimus as those through digestion—each comes back to physical forces of gain, see.

The will refers to the condition as is brought to bear in the body, as to whether its appetites are governed for its head, physical forces we are speaking of.   5717-2

Certainly dealing with money is one of "the activities of the earth." (1100-27)

A warning against the use of firearms and explosives and holding wrath in self may be found as applying to both Vulcan (Pluto) *and* Mars in the section under Mars (reading excerpt 1735-2). It is understandable that this earthly (Plutonian) influence would bring with it a propensity for anger.

It may be concluded that the self-centeredness of Pluto precipitates situations from which the only escape is upward. The individual finally faces reality. "Septimus as of consciousness" (900-10) is an apt appraisal.

Arcturus

In the list of planetary influences which the readings give as being important in man's spiritual development (900-10, A-3), Arcturus is the final one.

The reason for this may be partially explained by a statement as to Arcturus' relative position.

> Arcturus is that junction between the spheres of activity as related to cosmic force, and is that about which this particular environ or sphere of activity rotates, or is a relative source of activity.   263-15

This source can be used for strength in the development of the soul's mental and spiritual attributes.

> Also we find the Sun and Arcturus, the greater Sun, giving of the strength in mental and spiritual elements toward developing of soul and of the attributes toward the better forces in earth's spheres.   137-4

How this supply operates is explained in detail.

> In the harmony of strength or might the entity falters...In a word *much* has been made of the *present* experience, and it will lie within the own desire of the entity as to whether the return in earth's experience becomes necessary or not; for in Arcturus' forces, these become all magnified in will's force, and the conquering of self is truly greater than were one to conquer *many* worlds, and *is* conquering those of *our*, or of our *sun's* own attributes.   115-1

Apparently magnification of tendencies brings about a tremendous trial for our wills and if we can conquer self under these conditions, we have *really* progressed.

Once such progress has been made, it seems that the soul has a choice as to whether it shall return to earth's sphere or go on to a greater one.

Edgar Cayce was told he had returned from Arcturus.

And we find that the experience of the entity before that, as Uhjltd, was from even without the sphere of thine own orb; for the entity came from those centers about which thine own solar system moves—in Arcturus.   5755-1

It was made plain that others, also, had returned from Arcturus, though this was not the general pattern.

Q-6. The sixth problem concerns interplanetary and inter-system dwelling, between earthly lives. It was given through this source that the entity Edgar Cayce . . . went to the system of Arcturus, and then returned to earth. Does this indicate a usual or an unusual step in soul evolution?
A-6. . . . Arcturus is that which may be called the center of this universe, through which individuals pass and at which period there comes the choice of the individual as to whether it is to return to complete there—that is, in . . . the earth sun and its planetary system—or to pass on to others. This was an unusual step, and yet a usual one.   5749-14

This statement is supplemented by references to other persons who have returned from Arcturus.

But beginning with Mercury, the entity has run the gamut even unto Neptune and Arcturus, and then returned to earth.
                                                                         3637-1

[Regarding urges from astrological aspects:] And Arcturus! For the entity has gone out and returned, purposefully.
                                                                         5259-1

A statement that there is Arcturian influence affecting many persons on earth, seems to imply that *many* have returned from the environs of this celestial body.

Keep rather that as is of the idealistic; for the entity, in form, in mind, in manifestations of its, the entity's, personality—and, most of all, the individuality—shines through in that influence gained in Arcturus, the power and influence over many in the earth's plane.   2686-1

There is an exquisite description of this power.

. . . in its (the entity's) dwellings in the hills and plains of Persia, also in Egypt, the beauties and music of the spheres sang and brought into the experience of the entity its studies of the light by day, the joy of the voices of the night, and the star that led the entity—that source from which and to which it may gain so much of its strength in the present; *Arcturus,* the wonderful, the beautiful! As the bright and *glorious* light from same set afire, as it were, its meditations in the plains, so may the illuminations do the same in the lives of those the entity contacts through its gentleness and kindness and service.

827-1

Arcturus' contribution to a broader consciousness is also stressed.

Arcturus comes in this entity's chart, or as a central force from which the entity came again into the earth-material sojourns. For, this is the way, the door out of this system. Yet purposefully did the entity return in this experience.

As to appearances—these are so varied, as may be indicated from the entity's appearance in the earth from Arcturus, or from the changes that come.

Hence the entity may be expected to experience, to be associated with, to be connected in some form or manner with not only unusual experiences for an individual entity, but with many who have had, who will have, much to do with the changing of policies—local, state, national and international. For, these are as a part of a universal or broader consciousness to which the entity will in great measures contribute in this sojourn.

2454-3

Arcturian influence, combined with that of Mercury, may bring a mental force primarily spiritual, rather than earthly. Therefore, the purely physical will not impel the individual to the fullest extent.

. . . we find here that with the variations in the entity's experience using that of the experience in Mercurian forces to Arcturus brings an innate force in the present experience that of not only high mental force, yet as measured with Arcturian experience, an excellency above ordinary, yet without the full innate force to impel when hindrances arise from the purely physical side . . . to the extent that carnal mind, carnal or earthly forces shadow so many of the ideas and ideals . . .

105-2

It is interesting to note that Arcturus was to strengthen one person's bent toward chemical forces, gained from Mercury.

One whose forces from that of Mercury will turn in the middle portion of life to those elements pertaining to the chemical forces, with that of Arcturus' forces giving strength to the elements as is directed in the entity.

4228-1

The power of Arcturus, combined with Venus, may be applied in either mental or spiritual activities.

Those influences also in Venus, with those of the Arcturian influence—bring a power that may be applied in either the mental or the spiritual influence of the activities as may control those of the material natures.   957-1

The combination of Arcturus and Uranus tends to stimulate interest in scientific, semi-scientific and mystical subjects.

... that of Arcturus with Uranus [gives] a delving into those of the scientific or semi-scientific nature ...   358-3

The aspects and sojourns in Uranus and Arcturus bring those interests in the mental expressions in a varied line of endeavor; yet there may be seen throughout the associations and the developments in this the material plane that methodical manner—even in mental, occult or mystical subjects these find their influence and affinity in the very activities of soul-entity's developments in the sojourns throughout space or time, or in the earth for the material expressions. Hence ... there are variations in experiences that come from afar; things that are hidden to many become a portion of the entity's activity or sojourn. Unexpected happenings that may deal with the emotions or with even the relationships of individuals become a portion of the material experience of the entity throughout this sojourn. Relationships that deal with mystical subjects—not only of gases, chemistry, the elementals of the earth, the elements of space, of the universe, those sojournings into such fields of activity—make for particular interest in the mental sojourn. Also the delving into the realm of the questionable scientific subjects, whether it be in regard to explorations in the material far corners of the earth or the sojourning or delving into the ether, these are subjects that become of special interest to the entity; making for abilities in certain directions that will be seen by the material applications of these experiences of the entity in specific or direct directions in its relationships with others.   757-8

The influence of the visionary Neptune, combined with that of the mental Mercury, can be augmented by Arcturus to produce an individual of excellent judgment, who is a dreamer and yet is associated with those of worldly interests. By presenting those persons with truth in well-chosen words he may shatter their earthly illusions and start them on the road to self-development.

Hence, in those influences through Neptune with Arcturus, the entity has swung far from the earth's influence and at times—with these visions of the inner self, or the dreams ... lost ... the import of the material activity or the material upon the activities of a soul; yea, of a body, in its expressions in materiality. Hence at times do those about the entity call the entity the dreamer, the visioner of dreams, the one lost to those things save of the superlative degree in their expressions; and as to the manners or means of showing the beauties that are found in self becomes questioned by others as to its choice. Yet in itself, as from the Mercurian influence, the entity oft finds judgments in the material bringing for self *temperamental* assocations in the material plane. Hence there may be numbered among the entity's associates, yea even the entity's friends, those that are wholly spiritual-minded; those that are turned to the cause and effect in the material things, those of the scientific turn of mind, and yet those that are worldly for worldly sake that there may be the satisfying of the longings of the flesh for the fleshpots of the gratifyings of material desires. Yet all gain, as does the entity from such associations oft, that which makes for the turning in their own selves for the looking-glass of self-expression. For as the entity oft in its visions passes from realm to realm of its visioning, so do those that contact the entity find in the expressions or the moods of the entity that which enables them—in meeting their own problems, in seeking in their inner quests for those fields of expression, of activity—to bring to life that which to them becomes as the next stepping-stone in their experience.

So may we find from these experiences and from these sojourns the entity using the earthly words, endowed with that which may break men's bodies, which may aid men to mount to their higher selves, which may make for the arousing in the individual and in the group the seeking to use self in service; yea for those that find in those very expressions that which may take away from them that little footing that had been as their hope among men.   764-1

It can be truly said that Arcturus brings finishing influences, the effects of which will be felt in earthly life if the entity chooses this again.

Also those influences from Arcturus, where the finishing influences may be said to have been and to be an expression in activities when brought to materiality ...   1032-1

If the choice is other than a return to earth, where does the entity go? To other realms of consciousness, the readings tell us.

... Arcturus, or that center from which there may be the entrance into other realms of consciousness.   2823-1

Passage After Arcturus

After the entity has passed through Arcturus on into various spheres, it may still return to earth to manifest the development it has attained. It does this, however, in the form known in the dimensions of the plane it occupies.

...an entity passes on...from...*this* solar system...passes through the various spheres...first into that central force... Arcturus—nearer the Pleiades...on and *on*—through the *eons* of time...or space—which is *One* in the various spheres of its activity; even passing into the inner forces, *inner* sense... after a period of nearly ten *thousand* years—may an entity enter into the earth to make manifest those forces gained in *its* passage. In entering it takes on those forms that may be known in the dimensions of that plane which it occupies, there being not only three dimensions—as of the earth—but there may be seven, in Mercury—or four, in Venus—or five, as in Jupiter. There may be only one as in Mars. There may be many more as in those of Neptune, or they may become even as nil— until purified in Saturn's fires.   311-2

Could those entities who come to earth in forms known in the dimensions of their own planes include so-called "visitors from outer space" and also others whom we cannot see but whose influence is keenly sensed? It is possible.

This partial category of the dimensions of the planets is of particular interest as we look back upon the influence of each. The statement that different "forms" exist on them gives a tantalizing glimpse of the onward passage of life.

Another excerpt provides a few more details.

We find Jupiter, then, as the greater ruling force; or the entity's sojourn in that environ. Not as a physical body as known in the earth, but as a body adaptable to the environs of Jupiter; for there's life there (not as known in earth), as there is in Saturn, Sun, Moon, Venus, Mercury, Uranus, Neptune, Mars; all have their form—as about the earth, the inhabitants of the air, fire, water—in and out of the earth. The elements about same are inhabited, if you choose, by those of their own peculiar environment.   630-2

The above would appear to make direct reference to elementals about the earth.

The Signs of the Zodiac

An individual is affected by the positions of the Sun and the Moon at the time of his birth. These positions are indicated by the zodiacal houses in which the natal Sun and Moon are found. Knowledge of these twelve houses through which the Sun and Moon pass and of the lessons to be learned in them was, according to the readings, included in the culture and teachings of a prehistoric Egyptian civilization (10,500 B.C.). There are many extracts describing this era, in which Ra Ta, the High Priest, tried purposefully to help mankind toward spiritual development. One of the means was a Temple of Sacrifice. Apparently the twelve stations in it were those of the zodiacal signs.

Before that the entity was in the Egyptian land, when the activities of the entity brought about much of that experienced in the present through intuition, or the ability of the mind to control matter, in its dealings with others in their biological development.

The entity gained through the activity, aiding in the temple service. When there were the various positions set in the Temple of Sacrifice, the entity was among the few that went through the whole course—or that occupied what today would be termed the seat of learning in the various twelve houses through which it was learned that the Sun passed, that might apply to the individual in the material world.   3474-1

Each of these zodiacal houses represents a center of consciousness of which an entity must be aware.

For in patience ye become aware of thy own soul, and thy own abilities. Think not that He in the flesh found not stumbling in the mind and in the experience of each of those He chose, even as His representatives in the earth.

As each of the twelve Apostles represented major centers or regions or realms through which consciousness became aware in the body of the earth itself, so did He find—as in thine own self ye find—those twelve stumbling stones, those twelve things that oft not only disgust but disappoint thee—as to the reaction and way people and things react. These are the price of flesh, of material consciousness, and are only passing. Know deep within self that these, too, must pass away, but the beauty, the love, the hope, the faith remains ever.   2823-1

The zodiacal signs bear on the activity of the individual and are characterized by parts of the body.

The study of the meaning of Aries, Sagittarius, Pisces, Libra, or any or all of such phases, would indicate the activity of the individual. For, remember, it is body manifestation—some the feet, some the head, some the thigh, some the groin, some the bowels, some the breast—some one and some another, see? These indicating the *activity* of the individual.   5746-1

These zodiacal signs more often serve as warnings with reference to illness, accident or changes.

In those influences as are ordinarily termed the zodiacal, Moon and Sun, these—from an astrological viewpoint—may be more often termed the warnings as respecting either illness or accident, or the changes as may be apparent in the entity's experience . . .   1737-1

In general a natal Sun in one of these houses indicates strength in the activity, a natal Moon change and sometimes weakness. Other planetary factors, however, should be taken into consideration before assessing the total situation.

The Sun indicates strength and life, while the Moon indicates change . . . [From a reading on aura charts] 5746-1

Being under the influences of Moon and Sun, also, we find in the Sun the strength and in the Moon, the weakness. 2990-2

The following extracts deal with the scope of the various zodiacal signs or houses. The material on this in the readings is much more limited than that on the planets. An evaluation of each zodiacal sign according to modern astrological thinking, precedes the evaluation found in the readings. The characterizations are on the basis of the natal Sun, not Moon.

Aries

The Edgar Cayce readings and current astrology agree on Aries as the sign ruling the head.

In Aries the forces governed through the head . . . 5717-2

In Aries—an entity that uses the head and the mental abilities, rather than the brawn or physical exertions, to accomplish that as would bring those returns for self in any material affairs. Naturally, the mental is builded likewise.
                                                         426-2

. . . the entity under Aries makes for one headstrong, headwilled . . .   517-1

. . . under the influence of Aries, Uranus, Jupiter, Neptune and Venus . . .

Through Aries associations, there are the abilities of a high *mental* development, yet there are rather those warnings for this entity regarding accidents to the head. Injuries of some nature may come in the experience of the entity, either during the next four months or early portion of '34. These warnings are from influences that come from Aries or head associations with Mars.   406-1

In entering we find the influences astrologically in Aries—which will require in the present experience the use of the mental abilities of the entity in making its choice. Hence the particular reference [care] that should be taken . . . through the formative period of the mental developments . . . that the basis of thought is well founded, or grounded, should be the thing *most* to be considered by those who are responsible for this period.   276-2

Taurus

The neck is generally accounted to be the part under the dominance of Taurus. The Taurean may be thought of as bull-necked and obstinate. An Edgar Cayce reading bears out this obstinacy.

Q-13. Why does the body feel such an indecision about this?
A-13. As it does in changing in any one thing. It's natural tendency, or the hardheadedness as would be better expressed, of the body—it's April! [Born 4/22/1893] 257-170

Gemini

It is thought that Gemini governs the shoulders, arms, hands and lungs and that Mercury or the mind is its ruler.
The following extract may possibly support this position with its reference to "influences of the head and of Gemini."

From the astrological aspects, then, we find rather a confusing—as taken from the ordinary angle. For those influences of the head and of Gemini become a portion of the entity's experience.
Hence we find one, as indicated from the manner or type of birth in the present, that is a "sensitive" to spiritual import.
                                                        325-63

The sign of Gemini or the Twins is thought to denote a double influence. (Note that there is a pair in each part of the body governed by it.) The Edgar Cayce readings agree.

In the astrological aspects, we find these as rather confusing. Naturally, coming under those signs as well as the expressions in the material plane of the double sign, or Gemini, there are two natures within the urges of the entity. One is to seek to know; that may oft be upon very questionable things or conditions, even in the experience of the entity. The other is the innate and manifested spiritual seeking for a greater, better, more perfect relationship. And these as may be seen in the experience are more combative one with another in the experience of the entity than as may ordinarily be experienced. Yet these become, then, rather choices that are to be made in the experience of the entity.   674-3

It would seem that the underlying reason for this dual personality is the need to be in a position to make choices—ultimately the correct ones. The following extract shows this in greater detail.

Then, as to the appearances in the earth as the manifested body or individual in flesh, that make for experiences in the present sojourn, these must be constructive. Build not upon the shells of former activities, but use rather those experiences for the stepping-stones to those things that may make for—in thine association among thy fellow men—the life becoming more and more worthwhile. Failures in the sojourns in the earth have brought—as for all of Gemini children—the experience of becoming morose, melancholy; speaking quick without taking thought of other than to give vent to self's own spleen. In same must patience be manifested. Hence that as given first and foremost, learn to be patient, not only with self. For that [which] one cannot endure within itself it finds as a fault in others. That thou findest as a fault in others is thine own greatest fault, ever!   815-2

A Gemini influence combined with that of Mercury can result in immediate analysis of events, the basis for which may not be clear to the individual.

Coming under the astrological influences when Gemini becomes very close to its activities, we find the entity often wondering within self if there is not a double personality within self; yet the high mental abilities from the Mercurian influence produce the attempt to often analyze. Yet many of the things the entity *thinks* he would *like* to analyze, he finds them analyzed for him—as it were—in the experience. Hence confusion, and the lack of the entity's realization that thoughts *are* deeds—and as their currents run through the experience of the entity they become either miracles or crimes. And the entity, from the very impulse or the emotions of self, often gives thoughts power, an influence.   1107-1

To others a Gemini mind may appear unstable even though the possessor feels perfectly sure of it in its different expressions.

These arise from those associations of Gemini, or a two-way mind; that which often appears as not stable, yet the entity is very sure it is very stable in those things it wishes, those things it desires, those things that it would carry on. 1173-4

Others may misinterpret the current intent of Gemini.

Being under Gemini gives the air, as it were, not exactly of deceitfulness but of being too often taken literally when only an illustration may have been meant, or taken in the abstract when only the concrete was the intent and purpose; not taken seriously enough at times and at others taken so when not intended to be serious at all!   2058-1

A Gemini inclination to change may result in a person's becoming speculative. One individual had fought this tendency in the past but had now developed to the point of being favored in this field.

For while in Gemini children there are those influences that make for the double-mindedness, in this entity it finds expression in its inclinations at times to change and to become speculative. And this has had to be curbed in the experience of the entity.
Yet the entity would do well in any of those environs where there is the speculative influence. For the entity is, as might be termed, a favored one through those experiences in the earth and the astrological influences.   962-1

The objective should be to grow *out of* this dual nature.

Hence we find the two natures as indicated in the astrological aspect of Gemini. Yet, as indicated, the entity has grown from and not toward these. These developments have been and are in the grasp of the entity, *now today!*   1991-1

Cancer

Cancer is believed to govern the breast and stomach and to induce great sensitivity. One person, born June 21, was told in an Edgar Cayce reading:

From the astrological aspects we find the entity almost *exactly* upon the cusps [of Gemini and Cancer]. Hence we will find two influences . . .

Coming under those influences of Gemini and Scorpio, as are indicated, there will be tendencies for weaknesses in the early developing; requiring that those caring for the body be mindful as to the digestive forces and that there is kept an equal balance—else there may come, of course, those experiences of an early change in the activity, or in the sojourn . . . precautions should be taken, that there are the proper relationships and that there is the proper balance kept between those things that produce acid and those that keep an alkaline balance in the digestive forces of the body.   1208-1

The weakening influences would attack the stomach area. Sensitivity seems to be touched on in the following:

We have afflictions in Cancer with the relationships in the Jupiterian forces. These make for those conditions where the strength of the body in its relationships to others has been and is spoken of rather in terms of that which is hushed in the manner of its greater expression.
In its associations with individuals, then, the entity becomes as a [source of] *helpfulness;* being a confidante, of many; one to whom many come for their *own* instruction.   325-63

Leo

Leo is supposed to rule the heart and spine. Because of the heart involvement, the individual is apt to be emotional.
An Edgar Cayce reading speaks directly of the mental forces in Leo as being of the heart.

. . . in the sign of Leo, that has much to do with the worries mentally of the body in the earth's plane. That is, the mental worries of the present entity have to do more with conditions that are of the mental, or head forces, as in Leo, and of the heart than other conditions . . .   4313-4

This emotional viewpoint may make for quick changes.

One that has exceptional abilities, then, in many lines, and these may be turned into either good or bad . . . though the influence in Leo gives the quick change in the entity's attitude towards conditions.   4840-1

The demanding attitude of Leo brings out the truth.

Q-1. Is there a special problem of karma causing certain members of my family, for at least four generations (including myself), to be Leo-born?
A-1. Not necessarily. Yet one who has in this family so lived

that he wants to be or desires to be, can be. For remember, the soul is co-creator with God and Leo demands, and if you keep on demanding you will keep on having to face the truth.

5259-1

Another reading refers to the willfulness of Leo. It also explains a most interesting condition—that a person born under one sign may be influenced by another if the person absorbed enough of those influences in the past.

Astrologically we find urges, not because the Moon or the Sun or Leo or Pisces may have been in this or that position when the entity was born [March 29]. But the entity as a consciousness experienced those activities or awarenesses in those environs. Thus these become part of the soul experience. As will be found, Leo—or the consciousness of that mind will be a part of the entity's awareness. Thus at times the entity will appear headstrong, willful; yet, as has been indicated, there are other influences of the benevolent nature.   2905-3

Virgo

The intestines are considered the province of Virgo.
An indirect reference to this occurs in the readings. The individual had been born under Pisces, which governs the feet. He was warned of weaknesses in the feet and also the digestive tract, particularly the caecum region (intestines). Since the natal Sun of a Piscean would be in opposition to Virgo, it is understandable that a weakness might occur in the part assigned to Virgo.

In entering astrologically, we find the entity coming near the cusps and under the influence of Pisces—in its latter portion. Hence we will find, while the entity has altered much of that ordinarily termed as astrological, these are as innate and as conditions to be warned concerning in the *physical* body:
In the latter portion of the Moon's phases, especially in June, September, December, be mindful of injuries to the feet. Especially beware of disorders with the digestive system, and at all times *do not* overtax same with condiments, strong drink, nor with those conditions that make for the digestive forces becoming clogged—especially in the caecum region. These tendencies are innate, yet—with care taken—the body may *use* the condition rather as a stepping-stone than being submerged by same.

282-2

So it is obvious that an individual should be on the watch for physical weaknesses in two parts of the body—the one

59

corresponding to the zodiacal sign in which his Sun is found and the one corresponding to the opposite sign.

In addition, one should be cautious when influences beneficent or detrimental to him are arising or ceasing.

Q-13. What month and years should the body be on his guard?
A-13. Those opposite from those that are, or in conjunction with those that are to be, the better influences; as they are passing in or passing out. One should be on guard when they know they enter or leave those environs that make for betterments.   452-6

Libra

Libra is thought to govern the kidneys and lymphatic system and to be the sign of balance.

A reference in the readings to Libra confirms the idea of balance. Mention is made of the priest Ra Ta and his followers being sent to Libya (Libra) after the physical had been emphasized to the detriment of the spiritual. There in exile the spiritual was developed. Recalled to Egypt, these people sought balanced development for all.

This building [the Great Pyramid] ... was formed according to that which had been worked out by Ra Ta in the mount as related to the position of the various stars, that acted in the place about which this particular solar system circles in its activity, going towards what? That same name as to which the priest was banished—the constellation of Libra, or to Libya were these people sent.   294-151

Scorpio

The sex organs are assigned to Scorpio. One reading excerpt seems to agree.

As to the physical, as created in the present plane ... in the circulation, overtaxed through Scorpio, which is as the seat of the central portion of the body, see?   2895-1

Sagittarius

Sagittarius is believed to rule the thighs. There is agreement in the readings.

... we find the afflictions come in that of Sagittarius, Saturn afar off, and the Moon in the wane. Hence the afflictions have been to the body of the digestion and the thighs.   4219-3

Capricorn

Capricorn is identified with the knees. The author could not find any data in the readings on it.

Aquarius

Aquarius is thought to govern the lower legs and ankles. It is considered the sign of the astrologer.

The readings tell us it *is* a sign of mental application.

Aquarius—making for the application of the mental self.
1265-1

Aquarius and Pisces together may touch off mental sprees.

Those influences in Aquarius and Pisces make for those periods when the body is unlike its normal self; not that as may be called sprees, but as sprees in the direction of the mental attitudes assumed or taken. **5463-1**

Aquarius is a very suitable sign for an astrologer or a numerologist according to one reading. (Excerpts from this, 256-1, have been given before under "Neptune.") In the following portion of the reading the mental influence of Aquarius is noted with reference to the entity's abilities as an architect dealing with the elements of water (Neptune) and air (Aquarius). He is also encouraged to master numerology and astrology.

In the abilities as come through the influence in Aquarius, we find the entity could, or would, be able to apply self in influencing those that have to do with mathematical calculations, especially regarding aeronautics or boat building. The entity may become an architect beyond compare, provided these have to do with those elements that have to do with water or air ...

In the mathematical end of developments may the entity gain much, especially in study that has to do with the mystic, and the mysticism of numbers. These to the entity may be made much worthwhile. The entity may aid self, aid others, in the study of not only astrology but astronomy, and numbers as associated with same; aiding individuals in that, through that, that may be builded from character as related to individual development, and the entity may then find that which will, may become, in *this* individual application of truths ... the astrologer ... through numbers. Not through astrology alone. Rather numbers and ... numerology in its *deeper* sense. These

61

are the elements that interest the entity. These may be worked out with mathematical precision in *many* individuals, yet applied with ... the application of the individual towards life ... in its own individuality, these may aid much in the establishing of truths in these directions.

... will the entity apply self in that direction, the entity may become that one that may aid much in having individuals understand numbers, mysticism of numbers; also in the relationships of *astrological* effects (without the application of will) in the lives of individuals.   256-1

(In a former life this person had been one of the Wise Men and had brought frankincense to Jesus.)

Pisces

Pisces is concerned with the feet. One Edgar Cayce reference has already been cited (under the "Virgo" section), bearing this out. Another is included now.

From Pisces there are those conditions at certain periods when the lower limbs and feet cause some uneasiness, and the greater accidents (minor as they may have been) were through those same extremities.   539-2

There are a number of references indicating that a Piscean is interested in religion, spiritual matters, the astral, the occult and the psychic.

This entity, then, we find coming under those influences of Pisces (in the astrological); so that water and religion or spiritual imports have an untold influence; depending upon the manner in which the entity responds in the experience, for these have played an important part or been innate in the experience of the entity through many, many sojourns in the earth.

Pisces means that which is naturally ... representing those influences that are of the higher soul or spiritual import. In *this* entity it has been the experience in the present to judge same the more often from the physical than the spiritual reaction; yet there has been in this experience the continual seeking—seeking—for *something* in the spiritual nature of some influence that would answer that which is innate within the experience of the entity. Such answers may come only in the greater environs of waters, or those elements that make for the activities of same in the mental and spiritual imports.   816-3

... as indicated by the Piscean influence—is sensitive to influences of the spiritual or astral as well as of the material natures.   1158-2

62

. . . the period indicated under the Piscean . . . giving a religious or a routine thought.   2339-1

. . . that influence in Pisces—which makes for the occult.
                                                              2137-1

Pisces may influence an individual toward "good works."

Coming under the influence of Pisces, or that making for a spiritual attunement, we find this—with the sojourns of the entity—is a portion of the entity's whole being.

For more than once has the entity in its sojourns in the earth come under the influence of this same astrological aspect.

Hence it is one that ever *will* and does judge the experience and the expressions of individuals according to the ideal of the entity in spiritual things, and its relationships to spiritual experiences, more than that ordinarily termed the moral relationships. Yet these, too (the moral relationships), must be a portion of the entity's judgment according to the activities of individuals with whom the entity becomes associated in any way or manner.

Also we find these make for those expressions of the entity in what may be termed material things; being a contributor to good works in *every* form or manner.

It is one then that aids those who have the ideal, then, for the benefit of the fellow man; in their activities to bring peace, harmony and understanding in the activities of such individuals.   1007-1

A desire for security and the companionship of others may be a Piscean characteristic as well as that of holding close to friendships.

From the astrological sojourns we find rather the Piscean influences . . . The *tendency* for security, the *tendency* for the companionship of others, the tendency for an interest in those things that are mysteries and that are of a mysterious nature—or that arise from out of the metaphysical or psychical force to the inclinations for the creating of hope, the holding about self of those friendships that are near and dear.   1232-1

A Piscean may exaggerate or overdraw on his imagination in an attempt to establish himself as an authority. He should remember that his intuitive urges are of spiritual origin. If he does not magnify what he knows to be true, he can use this in helpfulness to others.

For the natural inclinations as from the Piscean influences have been at times to exaggerate, to overdraw upon the imaginations or upon the desires to become the spoken self...
                                                              1009-4

... under the astrological aspects of Pisces; making for a very intuitive force—and this is well, but do not magnify same in letting the imaginations oft override the better judgments in thy relationships to others. If such intuitive urges are kept in a spiritual import, they will grow to be helpful rather than antagonizing influences.   2082-1

After the Piscean has conquered self, he may exercise the ability to direct and become a leader.

... of the Piscean [influences] that make for the mystic, for the leaderships, for love and beauty, for the abilities to direct; especially when self has been conquered.   1346-1

Pisces may bring the need for definite decisions, which will result in a changed situation.

Pisces' influence brings those conditions ... where definite decisions must be made by self, that alter not only the surroundings and environs but the adaptability of self to those sudden changes that come in the experience of the entity.
2115-1

The Cusps

The readings note that a person born on the cusp of two zodiacal signs—or with the Sun in the degrees at the end of one sign and the beginning of the next—is subject to both influences.

In entering the present experience, we find the entity is indeed one who may be said to be under the influence of ... the cusps ... those who are near to the rising of one influence and the submerging ... of another, are oft in those experiences where ... they are in a strait ... as to what should be the activity.   801-1

Such a person may need special help from those rearing him.

From the astrological aspects we find the entity almost *exactly* upon the cusps. Hence we will find two influences, and the entity oft needing, requiring, a consideration by those making the choice of environs for the entity during the early portion of its developments.   1208-1

During the formative period the cusp child will respond well to guidance. He will, however, be rebellious against domination, then and in the future.

This entity comes upon the cusps; thus we find at times conflicting emotions with the entity. During the formative period of mental and physical developments, we find that the entity may be easily led.   2411-1

Through the cusps, or that changeable influence in the variations as are experienced, felt or known as conscious innate feeling—these will *always* bring that of rebellion to the others [who] would dominate.   220-1

Inclinations coming from the cusps can result in many changes.

. . . with the influences of the cusps having much to do with the many changes and variations.   1101-1

The Effects of the Natal Sun

It is time to review and condense the information from the readings with respect to the effects of a natal Sun in the various zodiacal signs.

The Sun signs indicate the activity of the individual and show two phases: the physical, involving that part of the body which may be subjected to stress; and the mental or character of the mind. This last point was clarified by the first excerpt included under Leo—"the mental, or head forces, as in Leo." These were classified as "of the heart."

According to the readings, the type of mind stemming from the various Sun signs might be described as follows: Aries, developing or basic; Taurus, headstrong; Gemini, ambivalent; Cancer, sensitive; Leo, emotional; Virgo,——; Libra, balancing; Scorpio,——; Sagittarius,——; Capricorn,——; Aquarius, comprehending the total picture; Pisces, combining the spiritual with the material. There is a definite order in this series, designed to develop a fully functioning mind.

The correlation between the type of mind and the part of the body affected is now apparent. Basic mind (Aries) requires the brain, therefore the head; strength of mind or obstinacy (Taurus), a strong neck to support the head. A mind that can explore both sides of a question (Gemini) needs double implementation. Through the right and left sides of a person flow positive and negative currents, respectively, symbolizing the masculine or active and feminine or receptive. The shoulders, arms, hands and lungs receive these currents and carry impressions to the brain on the basis of which it acts.

Sensitivity (Cancer) can certainly be symbolized by the breast, a very sensitive part of the anatomy. Moreover, to properly apprehend and, therefore, be sensitive to any subject an individual must receive it and relate it to his own consciousness. In the same way, the stomach receives food and acts upon it. A mind that considers emotions as well as facts (Leo) requires the heart (emotions) and the spine (facts). Without an Edgar Cayce reference on the mind of Virgo, we can only conjecture. Virgo is commonly supposed to indicate a precise person, attendant to details. It rules the intestines which extract the food values of the material going through them and pass these on to the circulatory system to be used in feeding the body. The intestines evacuate the waste. Precision and detail are required, functions which characterize a discriminating mind.

A balancing mind (Libra) again requires, as does Gemini, two tools. The kidneys and the lymphatic system are both constituted in two portions. Moreover, in their excretory function, they help to balance the body. Eliminations as well as assimilations are required for its health. Scorpio is commonly supposed to indicate force and energy. Now that the mind has evolved to this point, it needs energy to carry out its decisions. This, physically, corresponds to the sex force usually ascribed to Scorpio and also to "the seat of the central portion of the body" noted in the readings. Sagittarius ordinarily indicates the philosopher and student and also the traveller. Now that the mind has readied itself, it is in a position to receive more impressions and it goes in search of them. Again it can go in different directions. There are two thighs, and they carry the body onward.

Capricorn is generally supposed to denote tradition and common sense. It would seem that the mind, progressing ahead, as in Sagittarius, needs some brakes, some past experiences to guide it. The knees bend with a forward-backward motion, which could be described as braking, and there are two of them to allow greater flexibility. A mind that comprehends the total picture (Aquarius) could well be embodied in the lower legs and ankles, which rely on the total instructions presented by the parts of the body above them. Again both sides are represented. A mind that combines spiritual and material (Pisces) is well expressed in the feet, which rest on the earth but also receive the Spirit forces which course through the entire body. Again, two directions are possible.

From his head to his feet man is a mental and physical being.

Astrological Effects of the Moon

References have been given previously on the general effects of a natal Moon as indicating change and sometimes weakness (5746-1 and 2990-2). Before exploring the Moon's astrological effects in a more detailed way, it might be well to examine three passages concerning individual sojourns *on* the Moon. From the first excerpt it would appear that these were in advance of those in material form on earth.

As it has often been presented by one school of thought, the dwellers upon the Moon (the satellite of the earth) preceded the abilities for matter (expressed in a form that is known as matter in the earth). And this entity was among those that so dwelt, and is influenced by two sojourns there.

Hence there have ever been in the experience of the entity periods that are governed by the influence of not only the satellite's drawing upon the earth and the elements of same, but of the mental, in such a manner as to make for physical as well as mental and material changes in the affairs of the entity; when the mental being of the entity allows the influence to dominate rather than dominating the influence.

264-31

The Moon was [represented] a sojourn of the entity. Hence oft in the developing years, though beautiful in body and in manner of expression, in its association, the entity was called fickle—or changeable. This is a part of the entity's experience, and yet—as the entity would express self—it never intended to be such. But there are the emotions and the activities. Hence there are the needs for the entity to make for the finding of self and the purpose and the desire within.

1620-2

From the astrological aspects we find there was a sojourn upon the Moon.

Hence the Moon is an active influence of the entity, and *do not* ever sleep with the moon shining upon the face!

In the sunshine, much; for the Moon and the Sun are the ruling of the emotions, and these are—as from the sojourns of the entity in Venus—a greater portion of the experiences as will be had.

1401-1

These references further emphasize the influence of the Moon toward change. The advice to counter lunar emotional effects with solar ones would seem to underline the weakness coming from the Moon. (Sun, positive; Moon, negative or receptive.)

There are, however, other lunar effects. These will now be taken up with respect to a natal Moon in various zodiacal combinations.

The Moon may bring great development. An ensuing interest in spiritual matters, mysticism and rites should be handled constructively and not allowed to deteriorate into rote.

The Moon in its effect gives that of the great increase in the physical, and also in the development of the entity toward the mark of the higher calling, as is set in Him; the Sun's effect leaving the afterglow of the relations as have been effected upon those whom this individual has and will contact. 288-1

Those influences in Neptune and the Moon make for the interests in those of spiritual influence, mysticism and rites. These governed, or guided properly, may be made to manifest in material influences in the experience of the entity, in such a manner as to become more and more constructive. These misapplied or the acts themselves as in rote . . . may become detrimental . . .   355-1

The Moon rules sex so it is natural that it should affect marital relationships. When this influence is adverse, it may be subdued by will.

. . . other environs are manifestations of the influence that controls centers in the human body—as . . . sex, the Moon . . . as the centers through which activity manifests in the five senses of the body, and the centers that manifest same.   2608-1

. . . the Moon's elements . . . bring the forces in love affairs to deter these conditions. One that is given to thinking lightly of the heart's forces—and should only be in domestic relations late in life, see?   900-6

From another and later reading for the same individual:

Q-5. Are there particular times when Moon's influences are particularly strong, and thereby counteract the good influences of Jupiter and Neptune, to bring worldly goods to body's possession? How may he use will to avoid these adverse influences?
A-5. Moon's influence in this entity has particularly to do with the earthly satisfaction of desire toward opposite sex . . . These we find are at times adverse to ennobling forces, and may be made to appear in self to coincide with mysteries of life; using will then to know that each and every such condition must be brought under those forces of Jupiter and Neptune, that this influence, through will, will be turned into that which will bring the better conditions in the life's plane . . . Will used directly. Warding against such conditions becoming detrimental to the body's development.   900-14

One who through the Moon's forces may bring that in the marital relations, that that will be detrimental to developing in a period of two to three years, unless the conditions are corrected through will force. They will appear in the life present in the coming year, on the new of the Moon, after passing the meridian that brings the place of dwelling at that time below the constellation of Gemini, and the will must be exerted to overcome these conditions.   2495-1

Being under the influences of Moon and Sun also, we find in the Sun the strength and in the Moon, the weakness. These have brought experiences also in the marital relationships or quite variations as to whom the entity would say it loves the most—itself, its husband, its children, or its friends. These become entanglements in part, and much is kept submerged in the physical reactions of the entity.   2990-2

The Moon does often indicate a weakness.

This brings the forces that give the greater elements in the life, yet with the undue influence by the Moon's forces, when square to Saturn and Mars, brings doubts within the body's mental forces. In will's realm then must the entity bring the better forces when such conditions arise.   137-4

From a later reading, asking for clarification of the above:

These conditions . . . are of the earth's relation to the refuse forces as are cast unto Saturn, and the Lunar forces of earth's relation, that has to do with the forces, particularly, of the night shade conditions, which bear more on the mental than in destructive forces, meaning night shade. With Saturn's forces, then, may be the elements of the spiritual, or mental, or material forces. Hence the doubt through which the body enters in the material plane, the mental plane, the spiritual plane, manifested in earth's plane . . . Hence the injunction for the body . . . through the mental and spiritual forces, [to] receive and apply those projections of the Universal Forces to self to overcome doubt of every nature.   137-12

. . . with adverse Moon, the entity changes almost as the Moon does. Not in purpose; not in intent; not in mien, but as to those expressions that *others* obtain of the entity's abilities, and the entity's desire.   39-2

These may be expected—that is, the off periods, when there is the closer conjunction with Saturn in Aries, with the *Moon* on the wane. So, these periods will not be for more than sixty to ninety days at a period, though they may come more *often* at some years than others.   340-15

... with the often [frequent] change in the Moon's influence in the life ... as to those conditions ... of the home, of the marital relations, and ... those that would build in the purpose of the bringing into the life that which would build in the dependence of others in the labors, and in the giving of self for a purpose.   4286-3

(In a former life the children of this person had burned to death, and now she was afraid to bear children.)

One that is ever ... being controlled by ... Jupiterian influence ... high and ennobling conditions are the criterions to the entity in every action, yet with adverse influences as appear in Moon's influence ... these are ... at times overshadowed, and hence ... with the greatest purport of self to accomplish the good, many speak evil when no evil intent or purpose is meant by the entity ...
One that has in present plane found that often, on account of adverse conditions apparent when none meant, the entity tends to appear to others as secretive in actions, when to the entity such conditions present ... an element of safety, rather than ... attempting to be of the undermining or secretive nature.   943-2

From the Moon we find the tendencies towards the love of social life, which might easily become a failing—because of its greater abilities as an individual. For ... the entity's personality will stand out in groups and among its associates in such a manner that all will seek companionship with the entity.   2459-1

In the afflictions of the Moon, with the earth forces, we bring that of self-aggrandizement through Venus' afflictions with the Moon's position at time of birth. Hence, the affairs of the heart are many, but should be balanced in this coming year, 1924, in Mars' and Neptune's forces ...
One who could through the better elements of such, *using will*, make for its success when self was controlled, and those things that so easily beset through Saturn and Moon's forces and Mercury element ... controlled and used rather than *allowed* to control daily walks.   257-5

In entering astrologically, we find the entity coming under the influences—from sojourn—of Mercury, Venus, Jupiter, Uranus, with those of the Scorpio and the Moon in the adverse. These only as innate, but manifestedly as conditions in physical attributes ...
In the influences as seen from the warnings in the adverse forces, these make for a tendency—under seasons and periods, especially when Moon is in that constellation—to be afflicted

in the central portion, or in the region of the digestive forces as make for the body building portions of the system; yet these are merely tendencies ...   261-5

An adverse condition of the Moon at birth may lead to unfortunate investments if the will is not properly exercised. The same adverse condition may affect the pursuit of evening pleasures.

The Moon being in that adverse condition ... the entity has found that there are apparently periods in which everything ... is lucky that the entity touches; other periods wherein everything "goes to pot" ... These are especially ... pertaining to investments, and if the entity were to take the time he will find these are ... any conditions that have to do with pleasure seeking in the evenings. These have been failures. The influences ... then are that, at certain periods when Moon is at variance with the various elements that enter from the astrological viewpoint into the life, the entity tends toward investments of that nature. Will's force and more of that *ennobling,* rather than that of obtaining dollars for the pound of flesh, or irrespective of the result that is to come to other hands.   2855-1

It is also possible, however, for the Moon to be a favorable influence with regard to speculation, provided this is in the field of the "earth's storehouse," over which the moon has influence.

... Moon's forces being earth's spheres. Hence the entity's ability to handle those forces in nature that come from earth's storehouse, and any of the elements of this nature become the speculative forces for financial returns to this body in the earth plane.   221-2

Perhaps this matter of earth's storehouse explains the fact that the Moon rules the division of waters.

In the beginning, our own plane, the Earth, was set in motion. The planning of other planets began the ruling of the destiny of all matters as created, just as the division of waters was ruled and is ruled by the Moon on its path about the earth ...   3744-3

The connection between the Moon's influence and water was pointed out to one person.

... and about large bodies of water may the entity find the greater development ... experienced especially in the Moon's influence.   282-2

Sun and Moon at variance produce an unusual situation. Problems arising in the evening may be analyzed in the day among a crowd, those arising in the day, analyzed in the evening, alone.

. . . in the influences in Sun and Moon . . . for being in at variance with the experience of the entity, when troubles, consternation or distresses arise *in the day*, they may be easily understood or analyzed in the moonlight; when troubles arise in the *evening*, these may only be analyzed or understood when the entity *studies* same in the day—and among the crowd; yet those in the evening must be alone.   99-6

Another influence coming from both Sun and Moon may result in a person's being always the same in impulse—morning, noon and night.

From the astrological influences . . . called Sun and Moon's influence upon the entity, an unusual aspect presents itself; not only from the time and the day of week, but from the astrological aspects the entity may be truly said to be . . . the same morning, noon and night in impulse! and this can be said about very few!   338-2

Two references give a somewhat comprehensive picture of the roles of Sun and Moon respectively and together.

. . . the Sun is the source of life in materiality in the earth . . . the Moon indwellings from which individual or soul experiences . . . travel in the planets within this same realm, *all* are a portion of the entity's . . . soul experience in its passage. Why?
That the soul . . . might find expression, the souls of men and women came into being; that there might be that which would make every soul, then, as a fit companion for that realm [of companionship with God]. There is the necessity of fitting itself through the experiences of all phases and realms of existence, then; that it, the soul, may not cause disruption in the realm of beauty, harmony, strength of divinity in its companionships with that Creative Force.   805-4

In entering, under the astrological influences we find the Moon and the Sun—as well as planetary sojourns—affecting the physical as well as the mental and soul being.
These are one when viewed or considered in this material plane, yet—when analyzed . . . may well be compared to a formula that may act upon the physical attributes of a body. Alone there may be an influence, an activity, but combined

there may be wielded a greater influence upon all phases of the experience of the entity ...

As it has been often presented by one school of thought, the dwellers upon the Moon (the satellite of the earth) preceded the abilities for matter ... And this entity was among those that so dwelt, and is influenced by two sojourns there.

Hence there have ever been in the experience of the entity periods that are governed by the influence of not only the satellite's drawing upon the earth and the elements of same but of the mental, in such a manner as to make for physical as well as mental and material changes in the affairs of the entity; when the mental being of the entity allows the influence to dominate rather than dominating the influence.

Also as a sojourner in the environ elemental as well as material, the Sun's activity on the mental has wielded and does wield a powerful influence in the affairs, the activities, the thoughts of the entity. As may be illustrated:

On dark days with little sunshine there is an appreciable manifestation of fear and dread. And especially does this occur when the Moon by its position is on the opposite side of the orb or earth.

As to this influence also, if the entity uses the will in reference to such influences in a spiritual sense, much alteration arises.

Naturally, the question would be: How, when, in what manner, may an entity use such influence as to make for a betterment of those that tend to bring an air or a feeling of oppression upon the mental being?

Realizing, then, that there is an influence from without self of a nature that self may be in accord with or in opposition to; for all entities realize they in themselves are both positive and negative influences, and that the first cause—or the spirit— must of necessity within itself be likewise, yet more positive than negative, for it attracts with attraction and repels with rebellion of that same activity of which every entity is a part.

Hence the realizing of self's dependence upon that influence is that which makes for the change in the experience of the entity, in becoming conscious—through the mental-spiritual forces in self—of the willingness to be led rather than leading or demanding other than, "Thy will be done in me ..."

... This entity ... is swayed more by those two greater lights in the experience, both as to hereditary and environmental from the astrological viewpoint than most individuals. Why? Because of that influence which has just been given! 264-31

Again an excerpt emphasizes that the Sun is a positive, the Moon a negative or receptive influence. We ourselves are made up of these two influences; and so is spirit, but there is more of positive than of negative in it. We must, therefore, become willing to be led by spirit.

Fixed Stars

The readings ascribe an influence to fixed stars or those which remain in the same position in the sky.

> Just as those experiences upon the doorways to the greater consciousness of a soul. For here, too, hath the entity had those experiences upon the fixed stars, as upon Capricornus, as upon the influences of that great entrance into the holy of holies.
> 774-5

The few allusions to fixed stars which the author has found in the readings are given below.

Pleiades and Orion

> ... the entity comes under the influence of Mercury, Jupiter, and ... Mars, with the Pleiades and ... Orion in the benevolent influence ...
> ... one of a brilliant mind—easy to learn, yet too easily at times led in the wrong direction. Hence the warning as would be given to those training or directing, that the proper influences are thrown about the entity during the next five years; especially as regarding that training in the entity's relation with those of the spiritual nature—for with those tendencies as are seen in Mars' influence, this will be extraordinarily necessary ...
> One that—with the benevolent influences in Jupiter, and with the mental faculties that are above the normal—will, if guided correctly, go far in those fields of endeavor in which the entity may engage from the material standpoint, bringing much monies, and much of this world's goods ... if guided aright. If allowed to run with that element that would bring the improper association, this would be turned into—as bad. Being then an extremist, being then one that the temper, when aroused, *boils,* as it were, within the entity. Do not break the will, but *guide* and *direct* the entity ...
> 5454-3

The nature of the effect of the Pleiades and Orion is not quite clear.

There is another reference to the Pleiades and Orion, even more difficult to interpret.

> In entering, we find the entity coming under the influence of Jupiter, Venus, Mercury, and of Ox-ides—or the relative force of Pleiades, in that of Orion, with the effect in the Ox-Orion—Y—e—s—unusual!
> 2886-1

The third reference is to the Pleiades alone.

... With the condition in that age, we find both retarding and developing periods in the entity's forces, for with those influences felt at that period from Pleiades, the entity found those diversions and those conditions that were extreme in many ways. 2698-1

Sirius, the Dog Star

In the influences of likes and dislikes in the entity, here we find these become very decided all of a sudden—and as much of a sudden they change. This is a characterization of those whose influences are under Neptune or Cancer, with the days in that period, in that *sphere* in which the entity finds expression, or entering in . . . near the dog days. Then, as to animals and their relationships—these are held too close . . . All *force* and all *power* is of one source, as is life—but the *associations* of each are individual, and should be classified so *by* the entity in its *study* of the relationships of animal matter, celestial matter, material matter. In *spirit* one, but all flesh is not of one flesh—as some are given a cosmic influence only and others the ability to become one with the creative energy itself, in its *cleansing* of itself to be one in its relationships. 1910-1

Apparently the influence of Sirius (positioned in Cancer) has resulted in the person's over-attachment to animals. He needs to hold them in the proper perspective. Although the spirit in animals and man is the same, man is a co-creator with God and an animal is not. According to the reading, this person should recognize the difference.

The sudden changes mentioned as characterizing the Sirius influence are also emphasized in another excerpt. However, such adversities can be used as stepping-stones.

. . . astrological associations . . . would appear adverse in their first appearance, coming much under the influence of the Dog Star and Vulcan. These make for that influence as has been of sudden changes in the social affairs, the relationships as respecting those of kinship, and those changes as respecting physical or business relations; yet these *adversities* may be used . . . as stepping-stones for soul's development, as well as a mental and material change in the experience of the entity. 1727-1

The Great Bear

. . . those [accidents] that have to do with the afflictions of the body come under [unto?] those with the constellation of the Twins, or of Gemini, and that of the Great Bear. They will have to do with those of the digestion as afflicted by Septimus in those that come at two cycles especially in this entity . . .

487-1

The nature of the afflictions from the Great Bear is not spelled out.

A Word of Advice

The readings stress the importance of astrological study and explain how knowledge gained from it can be put to use. However, they also bring out clearly that it is up to the individual to utilize or overcome planetary influences by will. The following selection points this up.

In reading 826-15, an inquiry had been made as to the advisability of the individual's moving to another locality because of astrological aspects. In the answer a move was advised but for a different reason. The questioner was roundly taken to task for considering planetary influences to be of such importance. He was told that this consideration would give them power over him. Instead, he should subdue them.

But, it should be remembered by the body that astrological aspects in the ruling of various spheres in *any* land are merely inclinations or tendencies. Being aware of same, do not give such influences power by giving credit to them so often, or by acting against same. Rather just adjust self, self's hopes, self's desires. For, it has been given from the beginning: *subdue* the earth and its influence; indicating that to be subdued by tendencies is to become subject to those laws rather than to a creative influence in a material, mental and spiritual understanding, controlling through the abilities of self alone.

826-15

As reading 2794-3 so aptly puts it, "Do ye rule them [the stars, planets, Sun and Moon] or they rule thee?"

THE SUN

Now that we have reviewed the astrological influences of the heavenly bodies, we will take up some additional effects of that one most important to us in materiality—the sun.

The relationship between the earth and the sun is beautifully described in a passage on the creation of the earth.

First that of a mass, about which there arose the mist, and then the rising of same with light breaking *over* that as it *settled* itself, as a companion of those in the universe, as it began its *natural* (or now natural) rotations, with the varied effects *upon* the various portions of same, as it slowly—and is slowly—receding or gathering closer to the sun, from which it receives its impetus for the awakening of the elements that give life itself, by radiation of like elements from that which it receives from the sun.   364-6

The importance of the sun is reiterated.

. . . the sun is the source of life in materiality in the earth . . .   805-4

A most interesting sidelight can be found in a comment on Edgar Cayce's activities when he had incarnated as the High Priest in Egypt around 10,500 B.C. (It would seem from the second paragraph of this that Ra Ta—later known as Ra in reading 294-151—was idealized into Ra, the Egyptian God of the Sun.)

But the entrance into the Ra Ta experience, when there was the journeying from materiality—or the being translated in materiality as Ra Ta—was from the infinity forces, or from the sun; with those influences that draw upon the planet itself, the earth and all those about same.

Is it any wonder that in the ignorance of the earth the

activities of that entity were turned into the influence called the sun worshippers? This was because of the abilities of its [the sun's] influences in the experiences of each individual, and the effect upon those things of the earth in nature itself; because of the atmosphere, the forces as they take form from the vapors created even by same; and the very natures or influences upon vegetation!

The very natures or influences from the elemental forces themselves were drawn in [into] those activities of the elements within the earth, that could give off their vibrations because of the influences that attracted or drew away from one another.

This was produced by that which had come into the experiences in materiality, or into being, as the very nature of water with the sun's rays; or the ruler of thy own little solar system, thy own little nature in the form ye may see in the earth!   5755-1

Some Intangible Effects of the Sun on Man

After this evaluation of the effects of the sun in general, it is time to go into particular aspects of its role. The astrological ones have been considered. We have already noted:

The strongest force used in the destiny of man is the Sun first, then the closer planets to the earth, or those that are coming to ascension at the birth of the individual . . . 3744-3

We have examined the influence emanating from the sun in the various signs of the zodiac, particularly as respecting parts of the body. In addition the readings tell us that the sun affects one of the centers, the brain.

Thus, astrologically, in the solar system of which the earth is a part, other environs are manifestations of the influence that controls centers in the human body—as the brain, the sun—sex, the moon—as the centers through which activity manifests in the five senses of the body, and the centers that manifest same . . .   2608-1

Both the sun and the moon help us rule the emotions.

In the sunshine, much; for the moon and the sun are the ruling of the emotions . . .   1401-1

The Effects of Man on the Sun

It is now well to examine the effects we may have on the sun. In the reading which follows, this is made very plain.

Mrs. Cayce: You will give at this time a discourse on what are known as sun spots, explaining the cause of these phenomena and their effect on the earth and its inhabitants.

Mr. Cayce: In giving that as . . . would be . . . helpful information in the experience of individuals gathered here, many conditions and phases of man's experience in the earth are to be considered.

When the heavens and the earth came into being, this meant the universe as the inhabitants of the earth know same; yet there are many suns in the universe—those even about which our sun, our earth, revolve; and all are moving toward some place—yet space and time appear to be incomplete.

Then time and space are but one. Yet the sun, that is the center of this particular solar system, is the center; and, as has been indicated and known of old, it is that about which the earth and its companion planets circulate, or evolve [revolve?].

The beginnings of the understanding of these, and their influences upon the lives of individuals, were either thought out, evolved or interpreted by those of old, without the means of observing same as considered today necessary in order to understand.

Astronomy is considered a science and astrology as foolishness. Who is correct? One holds that because of the position of the earth, the sun, the planets, they are balanced one with another in some manner, some form; yet that they have nothing to do with man's life or the expanse of life, or the emotions of the physical being in the earth.

Then, why and how do the effects of the sun *so* influence other life in the earth and not affect *man's* life, man's emotions?

As the sun has been set as the rule of this solar system, does it not appear to be reasonable that it *has* an effect upon the inhabitants of the earth, as well as upon plant and mineral life in the earth?

Then, if not, why, how did the ancients worship the sun *as* the representative of a continuous benevolent and beneficent influence upon the life of the individual?

Thus as we find given, the sun and the moon and the stars were made also—this being the attempt of the writer to convey to the individual the realization that there *is* an influence in their activity! For, remember, they—the sun, the moon, the planets—have their marching orders from the divine, and they move in same.

Man alone is given that birthright of free will. He alone may defy his God!

How many of you have questioned that in thine own heart, and know that thy disobedience in the earth reflects unto the heavenly hosts and thus influences that activity of God's command! For *you*—as souls and sons and daughters of God— *defy* the living God!

As the sun is made to shed light and heat upon God's children in the earth, it is then of that composition of which man is made, or of that termed the earth; yet, as ye have seen and know, there is solid matter, there is liquid, there is vapor. All are one in their various stages of consciousness or of activity for what? Man—*godly man!* Yet when these become as in defiance to that light which was commanded to march, to show forth the Lord's glory, His beauty, His mercy, His hope—yea, His patience—do ye wonder then that there become reflected upon even the face of the sun those turmoils and strifes that have been and that are the sin of man?

Whence comest this?

All that was made was made to show to the sons, the souls, that God *is* mindful of His children.

How do they affect man? How does a cross word affect thee? How does anger, jealousy, hate, animosity, affect thee *as* a son of God? If thou art the father of same, oft ye cherish same. If thou art the recipient of same from others, thy brethren, how does it affect thee? Much as that confusion which is caused upon the earth by that which appears as a sun spot. The disruption of communications of all natures between men is what? Remember the story, the allegory if ye choose to call it such, of the tower of Babel.

Yea, ye say ye trust God, and yet want to show Him how to do it!

These become, then, as the influences that would show man as to his littleness in even entertaining hate, injustice, or that which would make a lie.

Be honest with thyself, as ye would ask even the ruler of thine earth—the sun—to harken to the voice of that which created it and to give its light *irrespective* of how ye act! For, as given, the sun shineth upon the just and the unjust alike, yet it is oft reflected in what happens to thee in thy journey through same.

The more ye become aware of thy relationships to the universe and those influences that control same, the greater thy ability to help, to aid—the greater thy ability to rely upon the God-force within; but *still* greater thy *responsibility* to thy fellow men. For, as ye do it unto the least, ye do it unto thy Maker—even as to the sun which reflects those turmoils that arise with thee; even as the earthquake, even as wars and hates, even as the influences in thy life day by day.

Then, what are the sun spots? A natural consequence of that turmoil which the sons of God in the earth reflect upon same.

Thus they oft bring confusion to those who become aware of same.

Let not your hearts be troubled; ye believe in God. Then just act like it—to others.

He has given thee a mind, a body; an earth, a land in which to dwell. He has set the sun, the moon, the planets, the stars about thee to remind thee, even as the psalmist gave, "Day unto day uttereth speech, night unto night sheweth knowledge."

These ye know, these ye have comprehended; but do ye take thought of same?

Know that thy mind—thy *mind*—is the builder! As what does thy soul appear? A spot, a blot upon the sun? or as that which giveth light unto those who sit in darkness, to those who cry aloud for hope?

Hast thou created hope in thy association with thy fellow men?

Ye fear and cringe when ye find that the spots upon thy sun cause confusion of any nature.

How *must* thy Savior feel, look, appear, when ye deny Him day by day; when ye treat thy fellow man as though he were as dross and trash before thee?

We are through.   5757-1

According to this reading the turmoil of man is reflected by the sun and turned into manifestations for which man is actually responsible himself.

The effects of solar outbursts or solar storms are of some magnitude. There is a vivid description in an article in *The National Geographic*[2] as to what happened after a solar outburst on November 12, 1960. Six hours later an enormous cloud, made up of hydrogen gas, a cloud ten million miles in width, trailing halfway back the ninety-three million miles to the sun, struck the earth! It was going at a speed of four thousand miles a second.

Although the collision was neither heard nor seen, the energy it dissipated in the earth's high atmosphere was greater than that of the most destructive hurricane and covered the entire globe. A chain of violent disturbances was set in motion—a tremendous electrical magnetic storm.

The needles of compasses wavered back and forth. Long-distance radio communication was at a standstill. Teletype messages became garbled. Communication was lost between airplane pilots and their control stations and between the U.S. Coast Guard and its weather ships in the North Atlantic.

Northern lights flared out at night, regardless of overcast and clouds. Electric lights in the farmhouses of northern areas wavered as though in a thunderstorm; yet the air above seemed clear.

These conditions persisted for more than a week.

The same article alerts us to the fact that man in space would be vulnerable to the particles erupting from a solar storm since with their tremendous energy they can damage or destroy human cells.

---

[2]Herbert Friedman, "The Sun," *National Geographic,* November, 1965, pg. 717.

The flares on the surface of the sun causing these magnetic storms have seemed to run in eleven-year cycles. However, when one such cycle was apparently near minimum activity point in August, 1972, flares occurred nonetheless, which, according to a UPI dispatch[3], were among the most intense that the National Oceanic and Atmospheric Administration had ever observed.

How are we to control these solar storms, which impinge on our lives today? The reading just quoted shows clearly that they are man-made. There is a very interesting point brought out in the same *National Geographic*[4] article! It seems that the reason for the tremendous production of energy by the sun lies in its size. Actually, pound-wise, it is less productive of heat than the human body with normal metabolism. The sun's output of radiant energy, divided by its mass, gives a daily yield of two calories per pound, whereas the average human body puts out ten calories per pound daily.

Is it possible that the human body radiates not only heat but also other forms of energy of considerable magnitude in proportion to its mass? Could these energies be strong enough in the aggregate to trigger a chain reaction on the sun?

Regardless of how man creates solar turmoils, there is only one way to eliminate them. By godly living.

The Sun as a Physical Basis for Human Life

Now let us turn again to the first three excerpts cited in this section ("The Sun"). There is a flat statement made that "the sun is the source of life in materiality in the earth . . ." (805-4) How can this be?

The conclusions of the late Dr. M. Bircher-Benner, well-known Swiss nutritionist, in his book *Food Science for All and a New Sunlight Theory of Nutrition* seem to supply an answer and are certainly worthy of examination. We shall now briefly go over them.[5]

In accordance with the law of the conservation of energy, no energy can appear in life without being there first, nor can it disappear without going somewhere else. For this reason the energy values of the food we eat are of great importance.

Where does the energy in our food come from? The solar

---

[3]"Sun Storms Rake Earth, Blackout Possible," *Virginian-Pilot*, Norfolk, Va., August 6, 1972, pg. A15.
[4]Friedman, pg. 721.
[5]M. Bircher-Benner, M.D., *Food Science for All and a New Sunlight Theory of Nutrition*, translated and edited by Arnold Eiloart, B.Sc., Ph.D., The C.W. Daniel Co., London, 1939, pp. 56, 59-61, 66 and 110.

energy reaching the earth is absorbed by the leaves of plants. In the plant it joins the water, minerals and nitrogen compounds which the roots have sucked up from the ground and also carbonic acid, a gas which man breathes out as a waste product and which has been gathered by the plant from the air. The sun's energy is transferred into a new energy, and the plant grows, builds up its patterned structure, blooms and fruits. The energy becomes fixed in a state of rest and is then potential energy. In other words, chemical vital energy is produced by plants from solar energy.

Man eats the plants and then utilizes the chemical vital energy. Therefore, he is utilizing energy that had a point of departure from the sun.

How about animals? Herbivorous ones eat plants. How about carnivorous animals and meat-eating humans? The meat they consume is still utilizing plant energies. The energy systems that supply life to man and animals, therefore, chiefly originate in plants, according to Dr. Bircher-Benner. He notes one exception so far known. Man and animals absorb and utilize some direct sunlight themselves.

An interesting question now arises. As the food energy undergoes different processes, such as fermentation, decay, salting or the response to the heat of baking, roasting or boiling or to the digestive processes of man or animal, or the dying changes in the slaughtered animal, what happens to the energy level? Dr. Bircher-Benner tells us that such processes bring about a lowering of the energy level. In other words, there is less nutritive value. This leads to his statement that fruits, nuts and raw salads have the greatest nutritive value for human beings, bread and cooked vegetables intermediate, and meat and meat products the lowest. In fact, he states that plant-food units furnish everything our physical organisms need and in the right proportion.

Let us see how this nutritionist's ideas fit in with the Edgar Cayce readings.

Dr. Bircher-Benner's contention that life energy originates with the sun is certainly confirmed by the statement that the sun is the source of life in materiality. The readings repeatedly emphasize the importance of eating plenty of green vegetables, especially raw ones. They also stress that these should be fresh, not kept for any length of time.

[Eat] More of the vegetables that are *raw* . . . This would include lettuce, turnips, cabbage and all of those that may be used as such [salad]. Tomatoes, if they are *ripened on the vine* . . .   135-1

All foods yellow in their nature, that are naturally yellow, carry B-1 ... Also it is found in orange juice, citrus fruit juices, the juice and pulp of grapefruit and the like, and in *all* cereals, and in bread; and especially the *green* leaves of lettuce—not so much in the beautiful white pieces. The green pieces are usually thrown away, and the hearts of lettuce kept that aren't worth very much as food for individuals. Hence lettuce of the leafy variety is really better for the body ...   257-236

... when the spinach, lettuce or celery is selected, use the green portion rather than that which has been bleached. These portions have from twenty to forty percent more of the vitamins necessary for the sustaining of the better health, than those portions that are bleached by being covered or being forced into such a state.   920-13

Q-3. Should I take Dermetic's Vegetable Tablets?
A-3. Not necessary with one meal of raw fresh vegetables. For, although compounds are well, these in their natural state are better. Lettuce, celery, onions, tomatoes, peppers, carrots, spinach, mustard—*any* of these are much preferable *green,* fresh, than prepared in a preservative of any kind.
Q-4. What about fresh vegetable juices?
A-4. These are all very good.   1158-1

Note that in 1158-1 the term "green" is applied to vegetables such as onions, tomatoes and carrots, not primarily green in color, but freshly gathered.

Q-3. It is difficult for me to arrange one daily meal of salad only; therefore, might I supplement my diet by tablets recommended by Dr. Black, taking one tablet daily ...
A-3. These may be taken if there is a lack of those activities from the raw salad; but they do not, *will* not, supply the energies as well or as efficaciously for the *body* as if there were the efforts made to have at least one meal each day altogether of raw vegetables, or two meals carrying a raw salad as a portion of same—each day.   1158-18

More of the vitamins are obtained in tomatoes [vine ripened] than in any other *one* growing vegetable!   900-386

Q-7. Should plenty of lettuce be eaten?
A-7. Plenty of lettuce should always be eaten by most *every* body; for this supplies an effluvium in the blood stream that is a destructive force to *most* of those influences that attack the blood stream. It's a purifier.   404-6

[The raw fresh vegetables] ... would consist of tomatoes, lettuce, celery, spinach, carrots, beet tops, mustard, onions or

84

the like (not cucumbers) that make for purifying of the *humor* in the lymph blood as this is absorbed by the lacteal ducts as it is digested. 840-1

... often use the raw vegetables which are prepared with gelatin ... Those which grow more above the ground than those which grow below the ground. Do include ... carrots with that portion especially close to the top. It may appear the harder and the less desirable, but it carries the vital energies, stimulating the optic reactions between kidneys and the optics. 3051-6

The juices from these [vegetables] are to be prepared fresh each day. Do not attempt to keep them from one day to the next—it would be injurious rather than helpful ... 462-13

... in the vegetable kingdom ... plants used for medicinal purposes, the fresher, the more active, the better! 457-14

... vegetables will build gray matter faster than will meat or sweets! 900-386

Fruits and nuts (more properly seeds), the other plant-food units valued by Dr. Bircher-Benner, were also emphasized by the readings as important to nutrition. Cereal grains, of course, belong in this same category of seed.

Mornings—citrus fruit juices; orange juice and lemon juice combined, pineapple and pineapple juice, figs; or the dried figs stewed, or the cereals that have more of the whole wheat with raisins in same—though do not use citrus fruit *and* cereal at the same meal. Whole wheat bread or cracked wheat bread toasted, with a little butter. Ovaltine or Sanka coffee or milk. 3823-2

Mornings—citrus fruit juices *or* cereals, but not both at the same meal. At other meals there may be taken, or included with the others at times, dried fruits or figs, combined with dates and raisins—these chopped very well together. 275-45

We would have citrus fruit juices, fresh—not those that are canned ... 1187-9

... not a great deal of melons of any kind, though cantaloupes may be taken, if grown in the neighborhood where the body resides, if shipped don't eat it. The fruits that may be taken: plums, pears and apples. Do not take raw apples, but roast apples aplenty. 5097-1

. . . as the finishing, or dessert . . . with fruits—as peaches, apricots, fresh pineapple, or the like.   275-24

Use in the fruit salad such as bananas, papaya, guava, grapes; *all* characters of fruit *except* apples. Apples should only be eaten when cooked; preferably roasted . . .   935-1

The use of raw apples in a cleansing diet was brought out, however. Grape juice was also recommended for this.

And know, if ye would take each day, through thy experience, two almonds, ye will never have skin blemishes, ye will never be tempted even in body toward cancer nor towards those things that make blemishes in the body-forces themselves.   1206-13

Dr. Bircher-Benner's ideas—that nutritive value originates in solar energy and that the energy level is lowered by decay and other processes—seem to be confirmed by the Edgar Cayce readings.

His contention that food from plants is higher in potential energy than that from animal products seems to be sustained by the following excerpt:

Let the diet be only vegetable forces. Do not lower the plane of development by animal vibrations.   1010-1

Then why did the readings advise various individuals to eat certain kinds of meat? The sleeping seer took people where he found them. For a body accustomed to meat products from an early age, the transition to an all-vegetable diet could well prove disastrous. Edgar Cayce advised what seemed best then and there. Consider the following example:

Q-15. Should the body abstain from meats for its best spiritual development?
A-15. Meats of certain characters are necessary in the body-*building* forces in *this* system [second emphasis author's], and should not be wholly abstained from in the present. Spiritualize those influences, those activities, rather than abstaining.   295-10

In time, we as a race, may return our physical bodies to the higher level they once knew. One reference suggests that in a very early Egyptian civilization long before the time of Ra Ta, solar rays were used directly to supply much bodily energy.

What is now the Sahara was a fertile land, a city that was builded in the edge of the land, a city of those that worshipped the sun—for its rays were used for supplying from the elements that which is required in the present to be grown through a season; or the abilities to use both those of introgression and retrogression—and mostly retrograded, as we are in the present.   5748-6

"Introgression" would seem to refer to the direct assimilation of sunlight, "retrogression" to ingestion of the same energy as it is being used up by plants or animals. Because our bodies have retrograded, we cannot assimilate as much of the pure energy as formerly and we chiefly use the diminished energy.

How great should our exposure to the sun be today? It should be largely limited to the early morning and late afternoon. There are other precautions to be observed, also.

Let there not be too much activity in the middle of the day, or of the sunshine. The early morning and the late afternoons are the preferable times. For the sun during the period between eleven or eleven-thirty and two o'clock carries too *great* a quantity of the actinic rays that make for destructive forces to the superficial circulation . . .   934-2

. . . We would take the sun-bath, but take that that adds to the body; *do not* tan the body *too* much! That that gives the full activity to the capillaries, or to the exterior portions of the system, but too much sun is worse than too little; for light is penetrating of itself—see?   275-20

Q-1. What is the cause of the injury to the eyes?
A-1. Too strong a light when very young, in sun light.
                                                        5126-1

Keep [the child] in the open oft but never with the sun shining directly on the face or eyes. These should ever be shaded. Never during the period from 11:00 to 2:00. Then the body should not be in the sun, but the early periods and late periods are very well. It is the absorption of the ultraviolet which gives strength and vitality to the nerves and muscular forces, which comes from the effect of the rays of the sun from [upon?] the activities of the body. It is not so well that there be too much of the tan from the sun on the body. This forms on body to protect the body from same. Thus not so much of the tan but sufficient for the healthy activity of the body.   3172-2

. . . keep the body in the sunshine; not so that there is injury to the body, but sufficient that all of the respiratory system and the capillary circulation is affected by the rays of the sun. At least some portion each day when same may be had. This will keep an even balance of the vitamins through the system.
                                                        299-2

It would be well to continue to rest from the electrical forces in the present through those periods that the activities are in the open, for if there are the activities in the sun it is much better that the ultraviolet rays be absorbed in that manner than to have mechanical applications or other measures. These are natural sources of supply for energies, for the radiation that comes from the sun is nearer to that of physical life.   1861-16

Well that the head be kept bare, in sunshine as much as possible. This will assist, of course, in nature's activity in rebuilding in the system.   195-34

In this particular body we find that in certain climates the sun and the sun's rays would be most beneficial and in others most harmful—because of the actinic value of the rays in those vicinities of a high altitude.   3224-1

Q-3. [For a dentist] Is artificial or daylight best for my work in the mouth?
A-3. Daylight, of course, is preferable, but with the present lighting system, there can be a light artificially produced that will be as restful.   3211-3

Briefly, the Edgar Cayce readings seem to tell us to be out in the sunshine frequently, early and late, but not to sunbathe between 11 a.m. and 2 p.m. (Standard Time). Also, in high altitudes the effects of the sun may be harmful. Particularly one should not expose eyes or face to direct radiation of the sun. The head, however, should be kept bare as much as possible for greatest benefit. The tan, so highly valued, is actually a means of defense, undertaken by the body. Only a light tan should be acquired. Whenever possible, substitute sunshine for treatments from an ultraviolet ray machine as the radiation from the sun is "nearer to that of physical life." (1861-16) Also, when possible, do close work in daylight instead of under artificial lighting.

Although the foregoing evaluation, gathered from the Edgar Cayce readings, as to the role of the sun in sustaining human life may surprise some persons, there is one scientist alive today who is making every effort to acquaint his confreres with the value of natural sunlight. Dr. John N. Ott was a pioneer in time-lapse photography. This led him by circuitous ways into examining the effects of full sunlight on, first, plants and, later, people. The Environmental Health and Light Research Institute in Sarasota, Florida, has been set up under his direction to forward scientific research on the effects of light—especially full spectrum sunlight—on plant, animal and human life with respect to its reproduction, growth, disease and health.

Recently, Dr. Ott has helped to develop special lenses to be used in eyeglasses, which will let the natural spectrum of sunlight through so it can all be utilized by the body. These lenses can be ground to prescription needs. For use in bright sunlight, they can be tinted grey in such a fashion that the light comes through them uniformly. For those who do not want prescription glasses, the same lenses, unground but tinted grey, can be used in regular sunglass frames to help offset solar glare. Dr. Ott, however, does not believe in looking directly at a bright sun. His viewpoint seems to parallel that of the readings with regard to the value of natural sunlight entering the body and also the need for precautions to ward off possible injury to the eyes coming from their direct exposure to the sun.

Dr. Ott has also helped develop a full spectrum fluorescent tube for lighting fixtures. Under its illumination the indoor worker should be able to absorb more of the rays so vital to his health, according to Dr. Ott.

A number of scientific studies based on Dr. Ott's premise of the value of full spectrum sunlight are now under way at different institutions or laboratories. The results will be scientifically evaluated.

Dr. Ott's experiences and thinking on the subject are interestingly and clearly told in his two books, *My Ivory Cellar*[6] and *Health and Light*.[7]

Uses of the Sun as a Tool

Since the energy of the sun is so powerful, the question immediately arises: How far have we progressed in harnessing it? Indirectly quite a bit. We take advantage of its stored energy in fossilized fuel—that is, natural gas, coal, oil, etc. We also use energy the sun constantly generates, transformed into wind and water power. After all, radiation of the sun moves the atmosphere and is responsible for climate and weather. Evaporation, caused by the sun's beams, results in rainfall, streams and rivers.[8]

We use solar rays even more directly, however. Silicon cells have been developed for producing an electric current by the application of sunlight. These cells power electronic equipment

---

[6]John Ott, *My Ivory Cellar, The Story of Time-Lapse Photography,* Twentieth-Century Press, Inc., Chicago, Ill., 1958.
[7]John N. Ott, *Health and Light,* The Devin-Adair Company, Old Greenwich, Conn., 1973.
[8]Friedman, pg. 717.

in spacecraft. Solar water heaters are in use in Florida and California. A 6' x 8' black pan, filled with a network of water pipes and mounted on the roof, serves to absorb enough solar energy to service an eighty-gallon hot water tank, sufficient to care for average home need.[9] Solar collectors may also heat water for swimming pools.

The well-known solar furnace at Mont Louis, France, was built under the direction of physical chemist Felix Trombe, a research director for that country's National Center for Scientific Research. It is used by metallurgists for processing experimental heat-resistant materials and for purifying alloys and is considered capable of melting any substance. This furnace contains several thousand flexible glass mirrors, which form a thirty-four-foot parabolic bowl and focus the sun's rays into a crucible, in which the temperature may rise as high as 6,300° F.[10]

Dr. Charles Greeley Abbot, a pioneer in astrophysical research, as of January 14, 1973, was completing final refinements for a solar furnace to convert solar energy directly into electricity. He had already obtained two patents for the basic design. If his latest patent is perfected and the furnace works, it should operate without polluting the air, at a cost comparable to that of coal or oil power.[11]

The greatest potential use of solar energy has been left for final consideration. To see this in proper perspective it is best to examine the Edgar Cayce readings on the subject of the firestone perfected in Atlantis.

...the entity was in the land now known as...the Atlantean... When those facets were prepared for the motivative forces from the rays of the sun to be effective upon the activities of those ships and the electrical forces then, these turned upon the elements of the earth caused the first upheavals. 1297-1

It appears that the energizing sunlight was originally used for a means of communication between the finite and the infinite. From being a constructive force, it eventually was turned into a destructive one.

Q-1. Going back to the Atlantean incarnation—what was the Tuaoi stone? Of what shape or form was it?
A-1. It was in the form of a six-sided figure, in which the light

[9]"Sunpower May Be Solution to Future Energy Crisis," *Henderson (N.C.) Daily Dispatch,* December 20, 1971.
[10]Friedman, pg. 740.
[11]Barnard Law Collier, "Inventor Races Time at Age 100," *Parade,* January 14, 1973.

appeared as the means of communication between infinity and the finite; or the means whereby there were the communications with those forces from the outside. Later this came to mean that from which the energies radiated, as of the center from which there were the radial activities guiding the various forms of transition or travel through those periods of activity of the Atlanteans.

It was set as a crystal, though in quite a different form from that used there. Do not confuse these two, then, for there were many generations of difference. It was in those periods when there was the directing of aeroplanes, or means of travel; though these in that time would travel in the air, or on the water, or under the water, just the same. Yet the force from which these were directed was in this central power station, or Tuaoi stone; which was as the beam upon which it acted.

In the beginning it was the source from which there was the spiritual and mental contact.

Understand, these are the following of laws—if there would be the understanding or comprehension of these. For, as has been given, the basis, the beginning of law carries all the way through. And that which comes or begins first is conceived in spirit, grows in the mental, manifests in the material; as was this central force in the Atlantean experience. First it was the means and source or manner by which the powers that be made the centralization for making known to the children of men, and children of God, the directing forces or powers. Man eventually turned this into that channel for destructive forces—and it is growing towards this in the present.

2072-10

There is an excellent description of the firestone, and there are references as to how its energy was used in transportation and surgery.

Q-1. Give an account of the electrical and mechanical knowledge of the entity as Asal-Sine in Atlantis.
A-1. Yes, we have the entity's activities during that experience. As indicated, the entity was associated with those that dealt with the mechanical appliances and their application during the experience. And, as we find, it was a period when there was much that has not even been thought of as yet in the present experiences.

About the firestone that was in the experience did the activities of the entity then make those applications that dealt with both the constructive and destructive forces in the period.

It would be well that there be given something of a description of this, that it may be better understood by the entity in the present, as to how both constructive and destructive forces were generated by the activity of this stone.

In the center of a building, that today would be said to have been lined with non-conductive metals, or non-conductive stone—something akin to asbestos, with the combined forces of bakerite [bakelite?] or other non-conductors that are now being manufactured in England under a name that is known well to many of those that deal in such things.

The building above the stone was oval, or a dome wherein there could be or was the rolling back, so that the activity of the stone was received from the sun's rays, or from the stars; the concentrating of the energies that emanate from bodies that are on fire themselves—with the elements that are found and that are not found in the earth's atmosphere. The concentration through the prisms or glass, as would be called in the present, was in such a manner that it acted upon the instruments that were connected with the various modes of travel, through induction methods—that made much the character of control as the remote control through radio vibrations or directions would be in the present day; though the manner of the force that was impelled from the stone acted upon the motivating forces in the crafts themselves.

There was the preparation so that when the dome was rolled back there might be little or no hindrance in the application direct to the various crafts that were to be impelled through space, whether in the radius of the visioning of the one eye, as it might be called, or whether directed under water or under other elements or through other elements.

The preparation of this stone was in the hands only of the initiates at the time, and the entity was among those that directed the influences of the radiation that arose in the form of the rays that were invisible to the eye but that acted upon the stones themselves as set in the motivating forces—whether the aircraft that were lifted by the gases in the period or whether guiding the more pleasure vehicles that might pass along close to the earth, or what would be termed the crafts on the water or under the water.

These, then, were impelled by the concentrating of the rays from the stone that was centered in the middle of the power station, or power house (that would be termed in the present).

In the active forces of these the entity brought destructive forces, by the setting up—in various portions of the land—the character that was to act as producing the powers in the various forms of the people's activities in the cities, the towns, the countries surrounding same. These, not intentionally, were *tuned* too high—and brought the second period of destructive forces to the peoples in the land, and broke up the land into the isles that later became the periods when the further destructive forces were brought in the land.

Through the same form of fire the bodies of individuals were regenerated, by the burning—through the application of the rays from the stone, the influences that brought destructive forces to an animal organism. Hence the body rejuvenated itself often, and remained in that land until the eventual destruction, joining with the peoples that made for the breaking up of the land—or joining with Baalilal at the final destruction of the land. In this the entity lost. At first, it was not the intention nor desire for destructive forces. Later it was for the ascension of power itself.

As to describing the manner of construction of the stone, we find it was a large cylindrical glass (as would be termed today), cut with facets in such a manner that the capstone on top of same made for the centralizing of the power or force that concentrated between the end of the cylinder and the capstone itself.

As indicated [see 996-12], the records of the manners of construction of same are in three places in the earth, as it stands today: In the sunken portions of Atlantis, or Poseidia, where a portion of the temples may yet be discovered, under the slime of ages of sea water—near what is known as Bimini, off the coast of Florida. And in the temple records that were in Egypt, where the entity later acted in cooperation with others in preserving the records that came from the land where these had been kept. Also the records that were carried to what is now Yucatan in America, where these stones (that they know so little about) are now—during the last few months—*being* uncovered.

Q-2. Is it for this entity to again learn the use of these stones?

A-2. When there have come those individuals who will purify themselves in the manner necessary for the gaining of the knowledge and the entering into the chambers where these may be found; yes—if the body will purify itself. In '38 it should come about, should the entity—or others may—be raised.

In Yucatan there is the emblem of same. Let's clarify this, for it may be the more easily found—for they will be brought to this America, these United States. A portion is to be carried, as we find, to the Pennsylvania State Museum. A portion is to be carried to the Washington preservations of such findings, or to Chicago.

The stones that are set in the front of the temple, between the service temple and the outer court temple—or the priest activity, for later there arose (which may give a better idea of what is meant) the activities of the Hebrews from this—in the altar that stood before the door of the tabernacle. This altar or stone, then, in Yucatan, stands between the activities of the priest (for, of course, this is degenerated from the original use and purpose, but is the nearest and closest one to being found) . . .

Q-6. How many facets did the crystals previously referred to have?

A-6. Would be better were these taken from that pattern of same that will be eventually put in the museum in Pennsylvania. For, as given, do not confuse self in the attempt to use something without having prepared self to know what to do with same—and bring, unintentionally as before, destructive forces in the experience of self and those about self. Not that this should not be sought. Not that information may not be asked for, but be sure that the records are read—and those that have been given may *only* be read by those who have cleansed themselves, or purified themselves!   440-5

The force engendered by the firestone was also used for remote photography, even through barriers, and for the overcoming of gravity.

Before that we find the entity was in the Atlantean land when there were the preparations of those things that had pertained to the ability for the application of appliances to the various elements known as electrical forces in the present day; as to the manners and ways in which the various crafts carried individuals from place to place, and what may be known in the present as the photographing from a distance, or the fields of activity that showed the ability for reading inscriptions through walls—even at distances, or for the preparations of the elevations in the various activities where there was the overcoming of (termed today) the forces of nature or gravity itself; and the preparations through the crystal, the mighty, the terrible crystal that made for the active principles in these, were a portion of the activity of the entity in that experience.   519-1

Apparently the stones were of the crystalline substances we find in the earth today.

The name then, as we would term in the present, was Deui (pronounced Dar, or D-R); and the entity was active in the recording of the messages, the directing of those forces that came with the use of the light that formed the rays upon which the influence from without was crystallized into what would become as the sound from the outer realm to the static or individual realm.

These were not only the rays from the sun, set by the facets of the stones as crystallized from the heat from within the elements of the earth itself, but were as the combination of these.

For it was these gases, these influences that were used for what we call today the conveniences as for light, heat, motivative forces; or radial activity, electrical combinations; the motivative forces of steam, gas and the like—for the conveniences.

Then this entity, Deui, was among those who attempted to make such influences a part of the experience of those who were—as indicated—the producers of that used for food, clothing; for the *machines* as it were for the producing of these—as we would call them today; rather than the machines used for the sources of the correlating or centralizing or crystallizing of the activity in their very forms.

The use of these influences by the Sons of Belial brought, then, the first of the upheavals; or the turning of the etheric rays' influence *from* the Sun—as used by the Sons of the Law of One—into the facet for the activities of same—produced what we would call a volcanic upheaval; and the separating of the land into *several* islands—five in number.   877-26

The stones were used as prisms.

. . . those mighty upheavals from the destructive forces used for the people from the prisms' activities . . .   820-1

It would seem that the energy was guided directly into pits and that eventually it connected with internal earth forces, thereby causing destruction.

When there were those destructive forces brought through the creating of the high influences of the radial activity from the rays of the sun, that were turned upon the crystals into the pits that made for the connections with the internal influences of the earth.   263-4

The energy was stored, to be used not only for transportation but also for voice transmission and television.

. . . in Poseidia the entity dwelt among those where there was the storage, as it were, of the *motivative* forces in nature from the great crystals that so condensed the lights, the forms, the activities, as to guide not only the ship upon the bosom of the sea but in the air and in many of those now known conveniences for man as in the transmission of the body, as in the transmission of the voice, as in the recording of those activities in what is soon to become a practical thing in so creating the vibrations as to make for television—as it is termed in the present.   813-1

The eventual misuse of the energy from the crystals and the resulting destruction of an entire civilization are both events much emphasized in the readings—not only in the foregoing excerpts but also in various life readings.

Today's scientists have been progressing toward rediscovery of this use of the sun's rays to energize prisms. Just how much progress has been made is brought out in a most excellent and detailed study entitled "The Tuaoi Stone, an Enigma," *The A.R.E. Journal*, January, 1974. The author, Dr. John H. Sutton of the National Aeronautics and Space Administration, has been involved with applications of low energy plasmas. As part of his doctorate work at American University, he developed an electron gun which may be the fastest in the world today. He is especially interested in gravity and in this study goes into related theories which seem to fit in admirably with the Cayce readings. Dr. Sutton thinks that the readings on the firestone may describe a laser-fusion reactor-GWG (gravity wave generator) combination and that today's science may be quite capable of developing it.

For further details we refer the reader to this article.

In light of the warning contained in the excerpt from 2072-10 (cited previously) that there was a "growing towards" turning "directing forces" into "destructive" ones, it seems extremely urgent that science should reexamine its goals and put bounds to the uses of new discoveries. Without such safeguards, redevelopment of the firestone could prove as disastrous to our civilization as its original development did to that of Atlantis. But if this potent energy is contained and directed, it may eventually fulfill its original purpose "as the means of communication between infinity and the finite." (2072-10)

The future is up to us.

THE MOON

Increase on Earth

The astrological effects of the moon have been considered previously. There are, however, other effects, all of which seem to spring from a common cause. The moon rules growth and increase on earth.

The moon in its effect gives that of the great increase in the physical.   288-1

Moon's forces being earth's spheres.   221-2

Man can utilize these lunar forces in various ways.

Lunar Agriculture

Planting by the moon is a practice that has persisted during the period of recorded history. The readings tell us that it originated when Ra Ta, the Priest, was in the Nubian land during his exile from Egypt. He became conscious of various natural forces, including those of the moon, and showed his followers how to make use of them in ways such as planting according to moon phases to achieve an abundant and fruitful yield.

Hence in the Nubian land there were first begun the reckoning of those periods when the sun has its influence upon human life and let's remember that it is in this period when the *present race* has been called into being—and the *influence* is reckoned from all experiences of Ra Ta, as the effect upon the body physical, the body mental, the body spiritual, or soul body; and these are the reckonings and the effects that were reckoned with, and about, and of, and concerning, in their various phases and effects. These all were set, not by Ra Ta—but *expressed* in the *development* of Ra Ta, that these *do* affect—by the forces as set upon all—not only the inhabitant of a given sphere or planet, but the effect all has upon every form of expression in that sphere of the Creative Energies in action in that given sphere, and this particular sphere—or earth—was the *reckoning* in that period. Hence arose what some termed those idiosyncrasies of planting in the moon, or in the phases of the moon, or of the tides and their effect, or of the calling of an animal in certain phases of the moon or seasons of the year, or of the combining of elements in the mineral kingdom, vegetable kingdom, animal kingdom, in various periods, were *first* . . . given . . . first *conscious* of—by Ra Ta, in his first giving to the peoples of the Nubian land.   294-150

When Ra Ta returned to Egypt, the knowledge he had gained in exile was made available to the Egyptian people, so it is reasonable to assume that planting by phases of the moon was adopted then in that country.

There is reference to this practice in the "Inca or Peruvian or Ecuador land" when many Atlanteans were migrating to it. Since communication existed between Egypt and Atlantis, possibly the concept was passed along by these Atlanteans.

. . . in the . . . Inca or Peruvian or Ecuador land, during those periods when the people from On [?] and Og were making . . . so many changes—by the disturbing forces which arose from individuals who came into the land from the Atlantean land, as well as those who were to journey for the establishing of activities in what is now the Yucatan land . . .

. . . the entity advanced far because of its abilities in judgment as drawn from nature, as well as from the signs of the heavens and those activities that same bear upon the influencing of man—as well as the seasons and the crops and the like, that were a part of the dependence of each people during those periods.   1895-1

What is this system of lunar agriculture?

An article in March, 1965, *Organic Gardening and Farming*[12] summarizes the general principles. The practice calls for planting those crops which bear above ground, such as leafy vegetables, while the moon is going from new to full and planting root vegetables, such as carrots (the better part of which mature below ground), while the moon is going from full

---

[12]M.C. Goldman, "Should We Plant by the Moon?" *Organic Gardening and Farming,* March, 1965, pp. 58-60.

to new. According to this article, other factors such as planetary position, zodiacal sign, latitude and sea level are taken into consideration, also.

According to the *1974 Llewellyn's Moon Sign Book*[13], the zodiacal sign in which the moon is found is of the greatest importance. Some signs, the reader is told, are barren and dry, others productive and moist, very fruitful and moist, barren and moist, semi-fruitful and moist, productive though dry. It is of interest to note that the geocentric system is used in this book in calculating the moon's signs, whereas a number of almanacs and calendars use the heliocentric one. In an Edgar Cayce excerpt previously cited the geocentric one was specified. This book also advises times for cultivating, fertilizing, harvesting, irrigating, pruning, transplanting, etc., according to the natural timing of the moon.

Briefly, it would seem that with the increase of light from the moon, vegetation above ground is stimulated. (Perhaps the pull of the moon results in the formation of tender leaves and shoots filled with moisture.) When this light is waning, vegetation stores what energy (or possibly fluid) it possesses in its roots. (This would reflect the effect of the moon on water.) If the zodiacal signs *do* vary, that is, have a barren, moist or other influence, they also should be taken into account.

The phrase "calling of an animal in certain phases of the moon or seasons of the year" (294-150) is obscure to this author. Possibly it refers to breeding animals at the increase of the moon.

The Moon's Effects on Man

The moon affects the bodies of men, also, and the processes going on in them.

One excerpt advises against tonsillectomy (quite a blood-letting affair) on the increase of the moon. Another indicates that a short time before a new moon is best for this operation.

Very soon—but not on the increase of the moon—we would have the tonsils taken care of. 2963-2

Q-1. When would be the best time to have the tonsils removed?
A-1. Whenever it is most convenient—a little time before there is the new moon. 189-8

[13]Carl Weschcke, "Gardening by the Moon," *1974 Llewellyn's Moon Sign Book and Daily Planetary Guide,* Llewellyn Publications, St. Paul, Minn., 1973, pp. 290-300.

From these references we might infer that the bleeding would be greater at the time the moon is increasing; so, to avoid excessive loss of blood, the operation should be performed at the conclusion of the moon's wane, when bleeding could be checked.

Certain medical men today have found this condition concerning bleeding to be true. In an article, entitled "The Moon and You," which appeared in *This Week Magazine* during 1968[14], the author tells of the experience of Dr. Edson Andrews of Florida. After his nurse called his attention to the fact that there was more bleeding at the time of the full moon, he checked the records and discovered that during this time more patients had to be returned to the operating room following surgery. A later study of a thousand cases revealed to Dr. Andrews that 82% of the bleeding crises occurred between the "third and first" phases of the moon. Nearly all attacks of bleeding ulcers came when the moon was full. This physician reported his findings as "conclusive."

According to this article yet another doctor had reported that hemorrhages occurred chiefly at the full moon.

Scientific proof supports these conclusions. In a paper presented by James B. Beal of the World Institute, there is reference to a summary made by Rolf Schaffranke of information on the basic causes of the overall beneficial effects of biological DC field application. This summary calls attention to an experiment carried out by George Bose in 1745 in which it was demonstrated that increase in the viscosity-index of blood and lymph fluid in humans and animals corresponds to the earth's natural E-field. For this reason to avoid complications with bleeding, operations should be avoided during full moon and the third quarter. This is when the earth's positive potential gradient reaches its maximum and there is an increase in metabolic processes and O_2 consumption.[15]

If, because of malalignments of the spinal column, any of these fluids becomes blocked and the surrounding area swollen, the effects can be considerable. Add lunar pull, and the

---

[14]Norman Carlisle, "The Moon and You," *This Week Magazine,* November 17, 1968, pg. 12.

[15]James B. Beal, *Electrostatic Fields, Electromagnetic Fields, and Ions—Mind/Body/Environment Interrelationships,* presented at the Symposium and Workshop on "The Effects of Low-Frequency Magnetic and Electric Fields on Biological Communication Processes" and the 6th annual meeting of the Neuroelectric Society, Vol. 6, February 18-24, 1973, Snowmass-at-Aspen, Colo. (Publisher) The Neuroelectric Society, 8700 West Wisconsin Ave., Milwaukee, WI 53226, reference 15, pg. 5.

situation could get out of hand as the next group of excerpts implies.

The first reference contains an account of what happens in such a case.

In the improvements that have come to the body, *more* have come in the last six to seven days than we have had to this time. The changes . . . are *especially* the relief in the pressure in the lumbar or pelvic regions. Also those coordinations through the active forces in the 9th and 10th dorsal region. We would, then, *keep* that as we have given for the better improvement of the body. Ready for questions.

Q-1. *Would a life reading be a help?*

A-1. Not at present. It's the physical forces that we must combat at the present. That physical conditions exist that are accentuated by influences in the entity's experience is apparent, as does also the moon influence most (This would be very interesting to the physician in charge to watch the changes in the moon and watch the effect it has upon the body). Now, when we have the new moon we will find that for the first two days, as it were, following same, a *wild, hilarious* reaction of the stronger; as the *wane* begins, then we will find the changes will come about, as will of a bettered condition. These are merely *influences, not* those that may not be overcome by the activities as may be changed in a physical organism; for with pressure in the lumbar and sacral region, as has been first indicated, there is that activity to those forces as operate to and through the pineal gland to the upper portion of the body, which corresponds to those forces as are spoken of, even in that of the [Book of] Revelation. Be very good for the doctor here to read The Revelation and understand it! especially in reference to this body! These forces as applied to this are the activities as are seen in the sympathetic nerve system, and *advance* in their activities as the force of same impel through the sympathetic and the cerebrospinal plexus from the 9th dorsal to the brain itself—at top, see? Hence in the changes as are being brought about in the system through the activity of the change, there is seen less pressure is on the solar plexus center. Hence there is less *incoordination through* the pineal *from* the effect of the sympathetic system.

2501-6

This excerpt seems to imply that if the sympathetic nerve system is in better adjustment, lunar effects will be less. A further implication would be that osteopathic adjustments relieve pressures.

Another reading for the same person ties in manipulations, an electrically driven vibrator and the sympathetic nerve system, and specifically states that the sympathetic system and lunar conditions are connected.

> ... following this manipulation, the vibratory forces of the electrically driven vibrator used, and preferably the sponge applicator should be used . . . this . . . makes that quick vibratory motion as becomes active especially with the sympathetic system, and . . . this has much to do with the changes, or the lunar conditions, see?   2501-7

The sympathetic nerve system is one about which not so much is known—in contrast to the cerebrospinal one, whose effect is generally considered to be paramount. In *Music, Its Secret Influence Throughout the Ages,* a volume transcribed by Cyril Scott, a well-known English composer, there is a discussion of artists (creative persons, including musicians) and their problems. It is brought out that the creative person is generally considered different from the average man. The author tells us that this is because most artists function in the sympathetic system, rather than in the cerebrospinal and are swayed more by emotions than by the mind.[16]

This statement ties in with Edgar Cayce reference 1401-1, previously cited, that the sun and moon rule emotions, and also with our last reference, connecting lunar influence and the sympathetic system.

One conclusion might be that most creative persons, under the influence of the sympathetic nerve system, are more sensitive to emotions and also to lunar conditions than average individuals and that other persons with special pressures or situations which affect the sympathetic system markedly, are also highly subject to lunar influence.

On the basis of this hypothesis let us examine more Edgar Cayce excerpts.

The first two concern epilepsy.

> Also begin with periodical applications of the castor oil packs—that is, begin preferably about the twenty-eighth of each month—though each month it must change according to the phases of the moon. In this month it would be about the twenty-eighth, but in next month it would be about the twenty-fourth, and so on—according to the phases of the moon ... Do these an hour each day for three days, about every twenty-eighth day—or according to the phases of the moon.   2286-1

> This unbalanced condition (in lacteal duct area) produces those periods when there is, as it were, a *monthly*—or a moon's activity within the experiences of the entity, from its sojourn in that environment, which brings an urge by its latent

---

[16]Cyril Scott, *Music, Its Secret Influence Throughout the Ages,* Rider & Co., London, Revised Edition, 1958, pg. 145.

manifestation—and finds its material expression in those activities which we have designated as a period of mishap, an accident, a slip of that which is just a little beyond the normal.
2155-5

For a person whose reflexes had been affected by a birth injury, treatment was advised on lunar timing. In this case it would seem that the massages were designed to improve the reflexes and, therefore, were to be administered at the time of the new moon so that the increase could be utilized (possibly in fluid flow).

These conditions, then, should be handled by a good orthopedic *osteopath;* one in sympathy with the applications that may be supplied through suggestion as well as through the information here; who may aid a great deal not only in bringing sooner corrections but in the manner in which the recovery will be made by the body, and the speed with which it will be accomplished.

As corrections are thus made in the upper cervicals, extending even to the upper dorsal areas and those areas about the right base of the brain, and to the left side of the frontal bone of the brain, it will aid materially. These should not be given too often, but there should be regular intervals of attending to these for several days in succession. During such periods use not merely the corrective measures for the structural portions, but do so with oils—that are partially the anointing oils, the sacred oils—in this combination; adding these in the order named . . .

These if combined in their correct proportions will aid in alleviating any strain in the muscle and tendon forces, and also aid at the base of the brain, by assisting the nerves to be normal in their reflexes—internally as well as externally—and thus gaining control of the locomotory centers (and these will come first in upper portion of body), and the reflexes to the auditory centers; as speech, hearing, vision. For, all are partially hindered in the present—some more than others.

The oil massages should be along the upper portion of the spine, base of the brain, and the frontal portion on left side especially. These should be given only when the adjustments osteopathically (or massages, not so much adjustments) are made; about three days in sucession, at those periods when the moon changes—or the new moon, see? That is when the osteopath should give these massages, you see, about once a month for three days straight running—and it should come near the change of the moon.
3375-1

Another person, with impaired sensory organs, was advised to have osteopathic adjustments at the first quarter of the moon.

The osteopathic adjustments should be taken periodically; say three to four treatments right along together each month. And for this body, if they are taken at the first quarter of the moon, it would be preferable. There should be long periods of these treatments—that is, periodically have these over a long period of time.

Q-1. What causes and what could relieve occasional pain in back of neck?

A-1. This is from vocational conditions, holding the neck in one position for such long periods. The adjustments osteopathically, if taken regularly, should aid this particularly. These treatments should not be just to the area indicated but they should be general treatments with specific reference to those areas mentioned.

Q-2. What is wrong with my eyesight?

A-2. There's nothing wrong with the eyesight. This is a general condition from impairment to the activity of the organs of the sensory system. For these have been slowed by these pressures indicated. See, these are part of the nerves that supply association with the central circulation of nerve and blood supply to all the organs of the sensory system. Not only then does it affect the eyes and ears at times, but also the speech or the vocal cords. But these corrections should change all of these. It will take a long period, but the body can be materially aided.   3211-3

"Lack of glandular activity" indicated glandular therapy for another person. It was to be given:

At those periods when there is the new moon (and not before)—the day of the new moon, you see . . .   2207-1

It was to be continued "for 10 days" and followed by juices, which would be given until the day before the next new moon. On the day of the next new moon the treatment would be started over again.

In this case, as in the preceding one, the increase of the moon was to be utilized.

A person with tendencies toward insanity was definitely bracketed as being greatly affected by the moon. Treatments during the increase of the moon were advised.

. . . conditions in the present do not appear to be greatly improved from some of the periods through which the body has been passing. These are the conditions that . . . are inclined to come and go, *governed* considerably by the amount of anxiety that is aroused in the surroundings for the body at periods when there is the change in the moon.

These are not then purely mental aberrations but physical also.

We find that the castor oil packs over the abdomen and right side would be well occasionally for the lack of eliminations ...

The oil rubs have not been given as *consistently* as has been indicated.

When possible we would keep the vibrations of the Appliance as suggested.

We find that the suggestive treatments will be more quieting to the body if they are continued in the present, especially during those periods when it is the *increase* of the moon and the full activity, or during the light of the moon period.

The tendencies for violent reactions to manipulations—do not *over*force, of course; but these are necessary if there will be the better conditions brought for the body.   1553-7

According to the *This Week Magazine* article previously cited[17], researchers today have recorded other lunar effects besides that of the stimulation of bleeding. Criminologists have studied police records of cities in Europe and the United States, which showed more crimes of passion at the time of the full moon. A New York City Bureau of Fire Investigation study brought out the fact that there was a "100% increase in arson cases" then, with unbalanced persons responsible for a great deal of the increase. Dr. Leonard Ravitz of Duke University, placing electrodes against the temples and chests of students and patients at a VA hospital, was able to make daily recordings of the voltage measurements of their body electricity. Hundreds of readings showed that there was a considerable change in the voltage in all subjects every 14 to 17 days, the changes coinciding exactly with the new and full moon. In some subjects the measurements jumped at full moon, fell at new. These were reversed in other subjects. (Could the thought brought out by Cyril Scott about creative people account for the difference?) All the persons felt better when their voltage was low.

The various facts related in this article, as given above, seem to fit in very well with the information given by the readings on lunar influence.

One other physical effect might be considered. We have previously learned that the sun rules the brain and the moon rules sex (2608-1), also that the head should be kept bare in sunshine as much as possible to assist in rebuilding the bodily system (195-34). It would seem that the sunshine probably stimulates the brain. Could it be that exposure to moonlight would stimulate sex? Perhaps lovers have chosen moonlight rendezvous from some subliminal knowledge!

Is there a physical basis for the moon's effect on human

---

[17]Carlisle, *ibid.*

thinking? It is clearly brought out in the following reference that the initial increase of the moon stimulates groups' formation and organization. Perhaps the individuals' brains are affected at that time by a flow of liquids in the tissues, just enough to trigger clear thinking and feelings of friendliness. Later, more fluid with resulting pressures might make the persons think poorly and become quarrelsome.

As for those associations and the action of groups respecting formation of banks, these . . . are coming together much in the way as has been outlined. As for forces or conditions set in motion that would bring about the meeting, the association of minds in the general way and manner to complete associations, here . . . by the beginning of the new moon (again we turn to another element having its forces and its effect upon the conditions in the affairs of men), in . . . the coming January, will be seen during that period those conditions wherein the perfection or the perfecting of the organization may be made complete, see?   900-357

The Moon's Possible Effects on Discarnates

A final instance of lunar influence poses some tantalizing issues. A reading was given in 1937 for a diver, anxious to make underwater motion pictures around the wreck of the *Lusitania*, a large vessel torpedoed during World War I off the South Irish coast. In this reading the point was made that the souls of many of the drowned were still "earthbound" in the wreck and that at certain times they could help the divers with their work because the moon's influence on the waters would be greater then. These times would be the harvest moons of August, May or June.

Q-3. What is the best time to dive as to month, day and hour for best visibility and photographic work?
A-3. As for the hour, as has been indicated. As for the time, the harvest moon of August or May or June.
A-5. . . . And there is combined with these [details of wreck] much that should be taken into consideration by those working upon same; as may be indicated by the periods as are given for visibility, work, activity.
As the moon's influence upon the waters is greater at those periods indicated, and especially in these portions of the sea, these individuals—the souls of those whose bodies are here confined—work with same; for their release to many is just as important as on the day torpedoed.
Q-7. Can the divers expect sympathy or antagonism from the souls of those who lost their lives when the ship sank?

A-7. Sympathy and help, as has been indicated. For the many hundreds are anxious, and would aid and would direct.

1395-1

Apparently the lunar influence at these times of full moon, acting on the waters, would increase the ability of those passed on to communicate (in intangible ways?) with living men.

In conclusion, the general information on lunar influence given in the readings reinforces the statement that the moon gives great increase in the physical. Processes—vegetable, animal and human—are stimulated during the increase of the moon, particularly those involving fluid flow. At the time of full moon, the fluid in a human may have accumulated to the point that it may create pressures in various parts of the body, including the brain. In the period immediately ensuing, surgical operations may trigger excessive bleeding. The time least subject to lunar influence would appear to be that at the end of the moon's wane, just prior to the new moon.

By timing activities in accordance with the phases of the moon we may help ourselves.

WATER

Now that we have considered the effects of the sun, moon and other heavenly bodies on human beings, it is time to move in closer to the earth. There are varied influences in, on and around the earth with which persons deal constantly. Most of us do not think of these as influences at all because they are adjacent to us and capable of being modified by us. Their effects, however, are often profound and we often misuse them because of lack of knowledge of their nature—to the detriment of ourselves and others.

For this reason it is well to inquire as to what the Edgar Cayce readings have to say about certain of these forces. The ones to be considered in this book are water, electricity, color and sound. Since they are taken up in great detail by the readings, it would appear they are of considerable importance.

The study of water is best approached from a spiritual viewpoint. This will lead to an understanding of those physical effects to be explored later.

The readings refer to water as "the mother . . . of all material experiences." (1554-6)

When the earth was created, a mist enveloped it. Then over the waters rose "the sound of the coming together of the sons of God."

First that of a mass, about which there arose the mist, and then the rising of same with light breaking *over* that as it *settled* itself . . . as it began its *natural* (or now natural) rotations . . .   **364-6**

. . . when the forces of the universe came together, when there was upon the waters the sound of the coming together of the sons of God, when the morning stars sang together, and over the face of the waters there was the voice of the glory of the coming of the plane for man's indwelling.   341-1

Water constitutes three-fourths of the universe and by the same token three-fourths of the human body.

Q-16. Why do all my big experiences begin near the water or on the water?
A-16. Is not water the mother, the life of all material experiences? Is it not a natural law? Is it not as He, the great teacher gave? that ye are born of spirit and of water? Hence all become a part of the creation as related to *manifestation.*
For ... which, to be sure, is the symbol of man's experience—the firmament above the firmament, and these were separated and came into what ye know as materiality. Hence *water*—the most flexible, the most solid; the most destructive yet the most necessary; three-fourths of the universe; three-fourths of the human body; three-fourths of all that is—contained in water.
Hence all expression as manifested in a three-dimensional world arises from same. For, it is three-fourths of the whole.
                                                                                      1554-6

Water is, also, a stage of consciousness or activity.

... there is solid matter, there is liquid, there is vapor. All are one in their various stages of consciousness or of activity for what? Man—*godly man!*   5757-1

All life forms out of water.

... we find we pass then into the water sign, or the mystic forces, of that source in earth's force from which man determines that all forms of life *form,* or predominate, from the water, or the mother of all natural forces in this nature ...
                                                                                      311-2

... the fish representing the water from which all were drawn out ...   5748-2

For as the spirit is the beginning, water combined of elements is the mother of creation.   2533-8

... pure water, the mother of creation, for this is the beginning through which all matter which takes material form one day, some day, somewhere has passed. Hence the earth and man and matter all are three-quarters or more water, H_2O. These are well, and that is a beautiful book: "H_2O."   5148-2

. . . water is the mother of materiality. From spirit the activity of mind upon matter brings into being elements, as in evolution, that become manifested in materiality . . . 4047-2

. . . there are those things that make for harmony in their relationships as one to another, as do the turmoils of the mother-water that brings forth in its activity about the earth those tiny creatures that in their beginnings make for the establishing of that which is the foundation of much of those in materiality. Hence the red, the deep red coral, upon thine flesh, will bring quietness in those turmoils that have arisen within the inner self . . . 694-2

The readings emphasize the spiritual nature of water.

As is known of all, water is a necessary element in the material forces for the sustaining of life in the material plane; hence this element often is called the mother of creation. *How* does water, then, supply that which nourishes in the material plane? Being made up of elements in itself that are the essence of that which may truly be called spiritual . . . it gives that association and connection between the spiritual forces acting in the material elements of the earth, or material forces; hence in entering in the kingdom of the Father is knowing and following and *being* those elements that supply the needs of that which builds in the material plane towards the continuity of the spiritual forces manifest in the earth. 262-28

The spiritual nature of water may be found in man in creative forces.

Q-5. Has the entity any psychic ability or powers and if so, in what way may this be developed and used, primarily for the welfare of others?
A-5. These are latent in each and every individual . . . The mystic as calls to the entity in and through the Neptune forces, as has been seen as regarding waters and of the universal forces—as is relating to water, as the creative force; for . . . out of these all force or form, or matter, begins *its* development, and in this relation the entity has his share—and it may *be* developed by application, not by just thinking—but by applying. To think is to act, to some; to others it is only an interesting pastime. *Application* is a different condition. 256-2

One reading tells of an entity manifest in the beginning of the earth plane, through the waters above and on the earth then. As a result the individual had been "saved" often spiritually, mentally and financially because of a great amount of water.

One saved spiritually, mentally and financially often through a great amount of waters, for it was from the beginning, and will be so unto the end of time, as time is reckoned from the earth plane, for this entity ... was first manifest in the earth plane through the waters as were on the earth, and above the earth. Hence through these elements and forces is the spiritual, mental and financial ... manifest in the earth plane.   294-8

Water as the mother of creation is also the mother of materiality. One person was warned not to let association with water result in too great an emphasis on the material.

We find also the urge in Neptune to be associated with those things, people, places having to do with water. Water is the mother of materiality. Don't let materiality and material things, then, be put first and foremost in thy experience.
                                                                                    4046-1

Since water is tied in with the creative forces, proximity to it stimulates these forces.

Hence the entity is innately and naturally a leader; one of artistic temperament. Hence the entity is greatly influenced at times by water as a *creative* force, and should thus be close to large bodies of water—oft in meditation by deep, running water or spring or rills; and should pass over waters for the finishing of his preparation, or for the obtaining of the centralizing or localizing of the abilities in the finishing of its preparation for the activities of its choice.   1815-1

Hence ... the entity should live within the sight of water at all periods. For as water is the basis of expression of creative influences or forces in matter in the earth, it becomes as an expression in the experience of the entity for harmonious experiences.   1895-1

Q-6. Why is there such a feeling of exhilaration when near the ocean?
A-6. The general nature condition from creative forces and energies.   480-45

From what does the spiritual nature of water stem? The readings point out that it is composed of two gases out of the air or from the divine itself.

... as indicated, from the basic principle; first: "H_2O," two elements not of material gases, but of air, of the divine itself, combined to form what ye call water.   5148-2

Water and the Human Body

Any influence of the extent pictured in the preceding excerpts would surely have not only a spiritual but also a very material effect. How can man use water in regard to the betterment of the human body? The readings have a great deal to say about this. The need for purity in water is stressed.

... keep the body—physically, mentally—*clean,* in that those of pure water give life, vital forces, both internally and externally.   5613-1

The entity's transition came at the age in years . . . of a hundred and seventy and eight (178). For those things in the diets that were as a portion of the entity's activities, clean living as to the relationships of the soil, of the air, of the sun, of the water . . . were those tenets that were presented by the entity during that sojourn [early Persian at time of Zend and Zoroaster] . . .   826-4

These references indicate that by pure water the body can be kept clean. Other readings suggest cleansing techniques, and still others deal with the quantity and kind of water a person should ingest daily.

Cleansing Techniques

Cleansing techniques will be considered first. It is interesting to note that in the Persian culture of which [826] was a part (see above), hydrotherapy was one of the healing arts.

Before that the entity was in the Arabian or Persian land, in the "city in the hills and the plains"; when there were those activities in which there was the application of the healing arts of the various groups. It was when there were those particular groups that by injury, or by old age, or by mental derangements were given particular attention . . .
. . . there were those activities in which the healing of self made for the building of those places for the care of these, and especially the water cures that were prepared.
Thus, as would be called in the present, the plumber, the heater—having to do with those things today called hydrotherapy, were portions of the entity's activity there.
In the application of the healing arts, this phase of electrotherapy and hydrotherapy for the entity will have more effect than quarts or gallons of medicine or other means of application for self. For, the entity sold self on those things accomplished there.   289-9

The need for hydrotherapy arises from lack of proper elimination in the system. Again and again the readings emphasize that with proper assimilation and elimination the body can keep itself resuscitated. The following excerpt points out that with these two processes nearer normal, human beings might live as long as they choose.

These [disturbances] . . . have to do with the assimilations and the eliminations of the body. There should be a warning to *all* bodies as to such conditions; for would the assimilations and the eliminations be kept nearer *normal* in the human family, the days might be extended to whatever period as was so desired; for the system is *builded* by the assimilations of that it takes within, and is able to bring resuscitation so long as the eliminations do not hinder.   311-4

The forms of hydrotherapy advised in the readings include colonic irrigations (stressed most often), cabinet sweats, needle baths or showers, thorough massages and hydrotherapy baths. Advice concerning the various procedures follows. From the references we learn that keeping the colon clean is extremely important as fecal cakes may collect in it. Congestion here causes a toxic condition, which makes pressures on the sympathetic nerve centers and on the cerebrospinal system. Migraine headaches and bursitis are only two of the ailments that may result.

. . . purify the body with plain water—through hydrotherapy applications, yes. These should include colonic irrigations, cabinet sweats, and thorough massages.   3174-1

Q-7. How often should the hydrotherapy be given?
A-7. Dependent upon the general conditions. Whenever there is a sluggishness, the feeling of heaviness, oversleepiness, the tendency for an achy, draggy feeling, then have the treatments. This does not mean that merely because there is the daily activity of the alimentary canal there is no need for flushing the system. But whenever there is the feeling of sluggishness, have the treatments. It'll pick the body up. For there is a need for such treatments when the condition of the body becomes drugged because of absorption of poison through alimentary canal or colon, sluggishness of liver or kidneys, and there is the lack of coordination with the cerebrospinal and sympathetic blood supply and nerves. For the hydrotherapy and massage are preventive as well as curative measures. For the cleansing of the system allows the body forces themselves to function normally and thus eliminate poisons, congestions and conditions that would become acute through the body.   257-254

Here we find some complications—the effects of or the beginning of migraine headaches. Most of these, as in this case, begin from congestions in the colon. These cause toxic conditions to make pressures on the sympathetic nerve centers and on the cerebrospinal system. And these pressures cause the violent headaches and almost irrational activities at times.

These . . . should respond to colonic irrigations. But first, we would x-ray the colon, and we will find areas in the ascending colon and a portion of the transverse colon where there are fecal forces that are as cakes.

There will be required several full colonic irrigations, using salt and soda as purifiers for the colon; and . . . these conditions will be released. The first cleansing solution should have two level teaspoonfuls of salt and one level teaspoonful of soda to the gallon of water, body temperature. Also in the rinse water, body temperature, have at least two tablespoonfuls of Glyco-Thymoline to the quart and a half of water.   3400-2

. . . there are the acute conditions of neuritis; and a combination of disturbances arising from pressures in the colon. Though the disturbance is in the bursa of the arm and shoulder, the source of this arises from a colon distress . . . [Immediate measures next advised.] Then, when these have acted, *do* have a good colonic. This will remove the pressure and alleviate the distresses.   340-47

Q-5. [Is there trouble with the] Prostate gland?
A-5. These are rather pressures from the lack of peristaltic movement in the lower portions of the colon. Take a colonic irrigation occasionally, or have one administered, scientifically. One colonic irrigation will be worth about 4 to 6 enemas.   3570-1

For a woman rapidly losing her hair—after other specific advice:

Have the full evacuation of alimentary canal at least once a day and do at least once a month purify the colon by the use of high enemas. These may be taken by self, provided the colon tube is used. Use about a half gallon of water, putting at least a heaping teaspoonful of salt and a heaping teaspoonful of soda in same, dissolved thoroughly. Have the water body temperature and have the thermometer at least ninety above. (Thermometerize the water.)

Do these, be very careful with the general eliminations.
                4086-1

. . . Use a soft tube for the colon tube, one that opens on the side rather than on the end.   533-6

. . . Give a colonic irrigation, using the high tube; not just an ordinary tube, but a colon tube, see? For this must empty the colon, so that there will be a reaction of the peristaltic movement.   1312-5

. . . have a good hydrotherapist give a thorough, but gentle, colon cleansing; this possibly a week or two weeks apart. In the first waters, use salt and soda, in the proportions of a heaping teaspoonful of table salt and a level teaspoonful of baking soda [both] dissolved thoroughly to each half gallon of water. In the last water use Glyco-Thymoline as an intestinal antiseptic to purify the system, in the proportions of a tablespoonful to the quart of water.   1745-4

Q-2. Have the colonics been sufficient and frequent enough to clear up all mucous?
A-2. We would not imply such if these had been correctly given. Do have them sufficient to remove the mucous, which causes the disturbance. This should be observed in the periods of giving colonic irrigation.   3480-2

. . . The body should consider as to the sources and causes for the neuritic and neurotic conditions that exist through the body. This is what might ordinarily be called a condition wherein the general taxation has run down the battery for the body; that is, the toxic forces in the body have become excessive. Thus there are pains in the arms, or shoulders at times, in the back, through the lower limbs and through the abdominal area. All of these come and go, dependent upon how well and how thoroughly the eliminations are in the body, and as to whether in the diet the body keeps the general physical forces alkaline or allows the greater portion to become acid. Then we have those reflexes that cause some disturbance with the heart, with the kidneys and with the liver. These all arise from toxic forces that affect naturally (for, as the body battery is) heart, liver, lungs and kidneys. These must coordinate. When they do not, some portion of it is going to revert.
These for this body would be the better:
Take at least once each week a general hydrotherapy treatment. This should include a cabinet sweat followed by a thorough rubdown.
About every twenty days have a high colonic irrigation, until there is no reaction of mucous in the stool at all.
After the sweat bath there should be the needle baths or showers followed by the massages.
These will aid the body in bringing back near to normal resistances.
In the diet beware of too much starches or too much combinations of proteins with starches.
Keep the eliminations better with the use of minerals for this body rather than vegetable laxatives. Owing to the batteries

as it were—liver, kidneys and heart—being run down.

These will add to the system—or being more acid, as in a battery, then the water will create more activity in the system. Just as the creating of energies in locomotion in any machinery where such is needed.

In the general activities, these should not be excessive, but the massages with hydrotherapy will be the better for the body.   3255-1

As we find for this body, the hydrotherapy bath would be well; which would be to lie in a great quantity or a tub of water for a long period—this being kept a little above the temperature of the body; then followed by a thorough massage by a masseuse. This would be better than adjustments *or* deep treatments, though it will be found that with the massage along the spine, with the body prone upon the face, these would—with the knuckle on either side of the spinal column—tend to make many a segment come nearer to normalcy, by being so treated *after* having been thoroughly relaxed for twenty to thirty minutes *in* the warm or hot water, see?
                                                                    635-9

Daily—when preparing the body for bed of evening—bathe thoroughly, especially along the spine, with quite warm water; not to blister nor to overheat it, but so as to open the pores of the body-forces along the ganglia of the cerebrospinal system that takes up from that assimilated through the body the life forces themselves.

[Directions for packs and massage follow.]   2994-1

Q-8. Do you advise the use of colonics or Epsom Salts baths for the body?
A-8. When these are necessary, yes. For everyone, everybody, should take an internal bath occasionally, as well as an external one. They would be better off if they would!
                                                                    440-2

There are disturbances, physical, as well as confusions, mental . . .

Physically, the strengthening of the organs of the sensory system are the more necessary. There are certain centers along the spine where there is greater coordination between the central nervous system and the sympathetic and those of the organs of sensory forces. So . . . first, we would, through hydrotherapy, thoroughly purify the body forces. Three to six, then, thorough fume baths; then thorough massages, including colonic baths . . . Thus we will purify the body by removing a great deal of dross that is preventing better conditions. [Directions followed for massages, oil rubs and diet as well as advice for the mental attitude.]

117

Q-1. Will the exercises I know now develop normal eyesight if practiced daily?

A-1. Depending upon whether the system is purified, the attitude is correct, and the diet bettered. It should help.

5401-1

. . . choose three days out of some week in each month, not just three days in a month, but three days in some definite week each month—either the first, the second, the third, or the fourth week of each month—and have the general hydrotherapy treatments, including massage, lights, and all the treatments that are in that nature of beautifying, and keeping the whole of the body-forces young.

3420-1

Clear the body as you do the mind of those things that have hindered. The things that hinder physically are the poor eliminations. Set up better eliminations in the body. This is why osteopathy and hydrotherapy come nearer to being the basis of all needed treatments for physical disabilities.

2524-5

With reference to the foregoing statement concerning osteopathy and hydrotherapy we should remember that today some practitioners of chiropractic use techniques similar to those of the osteopaths of Edgar Cayce's time and some osteopaths now combine other treatment with manipulative therapy. The term "osteopathy" in the statement above might, therefore, be considered in a generic way to include both osteopathy and chiropractic when, *but only when,* the techniques used are similar to the osteopathic techniques with which Edgar Cayce was familiar.

A final reference to hydrotherapy makes clear that it should not be carried to an extreme. Too frequent colonics can result in difficulties involving the lymphatic system.

Q-8. Do you find the eliminations with colonics have been helpful?

A-8. At times the eliminations through colonics are helpful; at other times these can be overdone, so that there is taken from the system the necessary energies and influences that cause the normal activity or assimilation through the alimentary canal. For . . . the food values should be digested and assimilated before entering into the larger intestine or colon itself; for digestion or assimilation takes place throughout the system. The lacteal ducts take from that assimilated for stimulation through the blood supply, turning same there into those forces that enter directly; but throughout the jejunum there is the absorption of those things,

118

and when there is the strain made on the lymph circulation through those portions of the colon that produces irritation there, it is like keeping scratching on a sore that doesn't heal properly.   440-18

Drinking Water

Amount

The Edgar Cayce readings advise ingestion of a quantity of water sufficient to keep the reactions of the stomach normal and to eliminate drosses in the system. In particular, plenty of water should be drunk before and after meals. The stomach is a storehouse for food values needed for proper digestion, and if the food has been acted on first by pure water, the reactions are more normal. In addition, it is advisable to take one-half to three-fourths of a glass of warm (not tepid and not unduly hot) water on first arising in the morning to "clarify the system of poisons."

In the general condition, there should be more water taken in the system, in more consistent manner, that the system, especially in the hepatics and kidneys, may function more nominally [normally?], thus producing the correct manner for eliminations of drosses in system, for . . . there are many channels of elimination from system. For this reason, each channel should be kept in that equilibrium, or in that balance wherein the condition is not brought to an accentuated condition in any *one* of the eliminating functioning conditions; not overtaxing lungs, not overtaxing the kidneys, not overtaxing the liver, not overtaxing the respiratory system, but all kept in that equal manner, see?
The lack of this water in system creates, then, the excess of those eliminations, that should nominally [normally?] be cleansed through alimentary canal and through the kidneys, back to the capillary circulation; finding at times, through congestion and weakened condition; either through strain mentally or physically to portions of the system, the producing of ill effects.   257-11

Well to drink *always plenty* of water, before meals and after meals—for . . . when any food value *enters* the stomach *immediately* the stomach becomes a storehouse, or a medicine chest that may create all the elements necessary for proper digestion within the system. If this *first* is acted upon by aqua pura, the reactions are more near normal. Well, then, each morning upon first arising, to take a half to three-quarters of a glass of *warm* water; not so hot that it is objectionable, not so tepid that it makes for sickening—but this will clarify the system of poisons . . . Occasionally a pinch of salt should be added to this draught of water.   311-4

119

For some persons the amount of water needed daily was six to eight tumblers full.

Q-10. *How much water should the body drink daily?*
A-10. Six to eight tumblers or glasses full.   1131-2

Q-12. *How much water should I drink daily?*
A-12. From six to eight tumblers full.   574-1

Kind

Just what minerals "pure water" should carry it is difficult to determine since different individuals need different minerals and these varying needs are considered in the readings. The several references which follow seem to indicate that an ideal water might be of the freestone variety and contain a medium amount of lime, also silica, lithia, magnesia, soda, iron, sulphur, and iodine.

. . . Be careful of the water as is taken in system. Let that be pure. Not too much lime, not too little, but carrying much silica, lithia, magnesia and soda. That is nearer *pure* waters.

3762-1

. . . the water that is used for this body should carry the elements necessary to give the correct incentives to the system. They should be in their makeup, magnesia, iron, sulphur, lithium, silicious, such as we would find in the spring here, see.   4439-1

Q-5. . . . *is there any specific water he has been drinking he should avoid?*
A-5. Be sure that the water is of the freestone and tends towards that at chalybeate and lithia.   853-1

Q-6. *Is the water I drink harmful to me? Is it pure or impure?*
A-6. There is no such thing as an absolutely *pure* water! In this particular environ [Powellsville, Bertie County, N.C.], and for this particular body, if there were added a teaspoonful of *lime* to each five gallons of water it would be much better.

677-1

The water to be used should not be the well water, as has been used, because it caused too much calcium.   5421-2

Q-2. *Is the drinking water being used at present harmful to this body?*
A-2. Better were there more of the properties of the carbohydrates with that of lithia, than so much of the lime.

1100-5

120

... the lack of iodine is one of the things that has caused disturbance in the system [thyroid condition], or from improper water supply, which first started these conditions.
4600-1

If drinking water does not contain the needed minerals or contains too great a quantity of some, damage may result to the individual, such as constipation, cystitis, kidney affection, thyroid trouble (see last reference, 4600-1), fevers and breaking down of tissues.

... there has been for some times back an accumulation in the drosses of the system, produced ... principally from the water, or the character in some waters that have been taken ...
4996-1

Now . . . with the changes in altitude, in activity and environment, and especially with the character of the water change, there are those reactions that might be expected; especially with those activities of the eliminating system as related to the activity of the ducts and glands of the eliminating system . . .
391-4

[For a person with cystitis]. . .irritants to the portions of the body—principally by the character of the water that has been taken into the system at times—see?
3972-1

Q-10. What is the condition of the kidneys?
A-10. That's why plenty of water should be given, that no sediments are formed from conditions as have existed through these portions of the body. Well to drink plenty of water that carries—not heavily lithia, but lithia—with much of the lime and of sulphur.
5453-9

One that would be warned as respecting stomach or digestive troubles, and especially of fevers. Hence this warning taken: Ever be mindful physically of the character of water taken as drink . . .
Q-2. . . . what should this body drink—what kind of water?
A-2. Pure water. None contaminated with any element.
345-1

...beware rather of temperature or fevers for the body in the present year . . . Be sure the water taken is pure.
5680-1

In the general physical forces there should be kept that which, in its proper analysis, would make for the continued resuscitation of vitality and vital forces without *any* destructive forces being builded in the system.

These, as we find, are usually—and as in this case—either of the nature in which an unbalancing is created by the eliminations of the system, or there is builded too much of some portions or characteristics of development in that as is assimilated, as to make for an unbalancing.

The greater condition to be warned of in this body is that of something of a combination of these, as would tend to make for those of the typhus [thymus?] glands, that as would produce temperature of the nature as to become destructive in the system.

This . . . that warning as should be had by the body, that the body should take those precautions as to prevent the system from *losing* its balance, as to become susceptible to such conditions; and *ever* should the body be very mindful of the character of the *water,* especially, as is taken.   853-1

[For a person needing treatment] stimulating to assimilations and to keep down those tendencies of tissues breaking in portions of the body . . . much of this arose from some times back in the activity of certain types of water, as well as a repression to the nervous system when it began.
1295-1

The character of water, the elements constituting it, those things soluble in it and those acting as irritants to the mucous membranes of the mouth, throat and digestive tract had been matters of interest to one person as a Navy man in a preceding life. Consideration of diets had gone along with these. Apparently the impetus for the interests had arisen in an incarnation at the time of the entrance of the Children of Israel into the Promised Land. For forty years they had had little to eat besides manna and quail. Now a variation in diet would cause new conditions in their mouths. So this man attempted to study the conditions and became the first dentist for the people settling around Shiloh.

In this connection an important point is brought out, that in different places the vibrations, the minds of people, their teeth, the products of the land, all vary. It is for this reason that those in one place require different dental treatment from those in another.

Another point is also worth examination. This man had ministered on a medical or physical level in a previous life in ancient Egypt. His interest and application had persisted through several lives. Still a dentist, he was continuing his study and ministrations. Because of his past experience, dentistry was a field in which he might excel.

Before that—the greater period of activity of the entity in the earth—the entity was among the sons of Eleazer and of the

122

priesthood; among those born in the wilderness and one taken when journeying over Jordan . . .

The entity was active when setting up the settlings of the land, in the care for the mouths of individuals who for forty years had tasted little other than manna or the flesh of quail. But with the variations in the diets, this became a study of the entity. And it may be said that among the children of Israel the entity was the first dentist, as would be called today, or one caring for the welfare of the peoples when they settled around Shiloh.

Hence . . . an interest in diets, an interest in the spiritual things as manifested in the appearance just before the present sojourn as Dejahn—in those activities when there was the service in the Navy, or pertaining to water crafts.

The entity in that period was also interested in the character of water, the elements constituting same, those things soluble in water and those acting as an irritant or restrainer, or those causing through radiation those conditions in soft tissue of mouth, gums, throat or digestive tract.

Then in the name Ersebus [?], the entity excelled; not only in the administrations to the people in his abilities to care for his own group, but as a teacher, as an instructor.

Thus may the entity in the present contribute to that which may be a helpful influence or towards that which may aid others to be cared for in their own particular sphere of activity.

For, as will be indicated, those in Connecticut or New York would not require the same care of their teeth as those in Ohio or in Tennessee or Georgia. And those in other portions of the land would require other characters of treatment. As in the teeth, so in the mind, the vibrations, the products of the land are different. Those so oft described, with which the land flowed, to which the entity went, are too seldom a part of the diet of those that would be healed of those tendencies in their youth—milk and honey.

Before that the entity was in the Egyptian land when there were those establishings of the tenets or truths as might be drawn from the activities in the Temple of Sacrifice.

The entity was among those that ministered in those services or activities.

Thus in the field of medical or physical applications for the benefit of the material and mental conditions in the experiences of individuals, the entity may excel.   3211-2

Purification

The purity or contamination of water is a matter of concern to those drinking it. In a state of nature with free movement, water purifies itself within twenty feet. This fact was taken into account in the water system set up in Poseida, a city of ancient Atlantis.

Q-1. Describe briefly one of the large cities of Atlantis at the height of its commercial and material prosperity, giving name and location.

A-1. This we find in that as called Poseida, or the city that was built upon the hill that overlooked the waters of Parfa [?], and in the vicinity also of the egress and entrance to the waters from which, through which, many of the people passed in their association with, or connection with, those of the outside walls or countries. This we find not an altogether walled city, but a portion of same built so that the waters of these rivers became as the pools about which both sacrifice and sport, and those necessities for the cleansing of body, home and all, were obtained, and these . . . were brought by large ducts or canals into these portions for the preservation, and yet kept constantly in motion so that it purified itself in its course; for . . . water in motion over stone or those various forces in the natural forces purifies itself in twenty feet of space.

364-12

Today no such municipal water system is yet in operation. How can water that is not in motion be purified? For one person faced with a questionable source, the readings advised thorough boiling as a method. Slaked lime was to be added, and after boiling the water was to be strained and cooled.

. . . if it were practical, the having of water shipped in would be the better for drinking water.

But for all intents and purposes, that would prevent any disorders, if the lake water were boiled (of which there is plenty) with slack [slaked] lime in same, it would be all right for drinking. To every two gallons put about half a teaspoonful of slack lime, but *boil* thoroughly; then let it settle and strain; and then keep it cool, see?

1224-9

For entire populations such a form of purification is not likely to be undertaken. What effect, if any, did the purification processes used in Edgar Cayce's day have on the health of those drinking this water? It appears that once, at least, authorities made an error, which was corrected only after illness in the population.

In February, 1942, a 55-year-old woman, who was teaching English at a college in South Carolina, asked Edgar Cayce what was causing acute illness in herself and others. Fifty people in the college alone had been stricken the week before. She was told that the purifiers in the water supply were responsible. They had affected some persons more than others.

As we find, there are the effects of some acute conditions that have arisen with the body.

These were produced from those properties in water to purify same. Owing to the chemical reaction, this was not wholly effective universally upon the populace.

To all [who] tended towards anemia of any form, as this body, the conditions became more involved than in others.

To be sure, all anemia is not of the same form. With this body it produced an upsetting of the assimilating system, because of its tendency to dry the alimentary canal—or, in the attempt to meet the needs of the conditions, the using up of the quantity of lymph circulation.

Hence this drying, tingling sensation through portions of the body; nausea, weakness, headaches, and the concurrent conditions as would arise from same . . . [Treatment advised]

Corrections have been made in the water, and unless there are mishaps again in the adding of the properties to water, it should not reoccur.   2067-9

It is apparent that a thorough study should be made of any water purifiers before they are added to a public water supply. Their effect on those under par should be the prime consideration.

Question of Fluoridation

Since Edgar Cayce's time the question has arisen of the advisability of fluoridating the public water supply of a whole community on the assumption that the addition of fluorine (in the form of a fluoride) will retard or prevent cavities in the second set of teeth, which generally appear in children between the ages of 6 and 14.

The dentist from whose readings sections have already been given, queried Edgar Cayce about the advisability of adding fluorine to drinking water. The answer is significant.

Note that the fluorine should be associated with free limestone. In other words, there should be calcium along with the fluorine. Also, too much fluorine will affect the body in ways other than tooth formation. Care should be exercised in adding fluorine where there is iron, sulphur or magnesium. Minerals in the water vary with different localities. The entire situation needs to be considered on an individual basis to ascertain whether the addition of fluorine would be beneficial or detrimental. In some cases the addition of even a small quantity would be very detrimental.

In summation, the reading states that the way to avoid decay in children's teeth is to maintain a proper balance in their diet and to see that they clean their teeth.

Mrs. Cayce: You will have before you the research field in dentistry pertaining to chemical preparations and patents, and dental abnormalities. You will answer the questions submitted by Dr. [3211] dentist, present in this room, as I ask them:

Mr. Cayce: Yes. If this information is to be obtained for individual use, it may be given from one approach, if it is to be for universal use, it is another approach. If it will be indicated as to which of these the entity wishes to subscribe, then we may give information as to the activities for individual application or that as may apply for the universal knowledge as may be indicated regarding dentistry or care of the teeth.

Q-1. Regarding the universal approach: Is it true, as it is thought, that the intake of certain form and percentage of fluorine in drinking water causes mottled enamel of the teeth?

A-1. This, to be sure, is true; but this is also untrue unless there is considered the other properties with which such is associated in drinking water.

If there are certain percents of fluorine with free limestone, we will find it is beneficial. If there are certain percents with indications of magnesium, sulphur and the like, we will have one motley, another decaying at the gum.

Q-2. Does too much fluorine cause decay of teeth, and where is the border line?

A-2. Read what has just been indicated. It depends upon the combinations, more than it does upon the quantity of fluorine itself. But, to be sure, too much fluorine in the water would not make so much in the teeth as it would in other elements or activities which may be reflected in teeth; not as the cause of same but producing a disturbance that may contribute to the condition.

But where there is iron or sulphur or magnesium, be careful.

To perfectly understand it would be preferable to understand these:

There are areas within the United States—such as in some portions of Texas, portions in Arizona, others in Wyoming—where the teeth are seldom ever decayed. Study the water there, the quantity of fluorine there, the lack of iron or sulphur or the proportions of sulphur; that is in the regular water.

There are many sections, of course, where fluorine added to the water, with many other chemicals would be most beneficial. There are others where, even a small quantity added would be very detrimental.

Hence it cannot be said positively that this or that quantity should be added save in a certain degree of other chemicals being combined with same in the drinking water.

But there are some places where you have few or none. For, here we will find a great quantity of either iron or sulphur, while in some places in the West—as in the central portion of Texas in certain vicinities, you won't find any decay. Certain cases in the northwestern portion of Arizona, or close within some parts of Cheyenne, Wyoming, will not be found to show decay—if the water that is used is from the normal source of

126

supply. But where there have been contributions from other supplies of water, there will be found variations in the supply of magesium [magnesium?] and other chemicals—as from the flowing over, or arsenic and such—these cause destruction to the teeth.

Q-3. What is the best manner of protecting teeth against decay?

A-3. Keeping the best physical health of the body and protecting it from iron or iron products that may become a part of the body-physical in one manner or another. These are needed, but when their proportions are varied the teeth do not show the proper relationships—when you lose that quantity of iron needed.

Q-4. Could the diet give the required amount of fluorine for prevention of decay?

A-4. It could aid but depending upon the water and other conditions there's no definite [answer].

Q-5. What other factors are there that control and have an effect on mottled enamel and decay of teeth?

A-5. The general health of the body and the chemical processes that are a part of the digestive system, the process of digestion, the chemical processes through same, and the blood stream. These, of course, are the processes within the body itself.

Q-6. How can this condition be prevented in children's teeth?

A-6. By keeping a proper balance in the diet and in the protection from the ordinary causes—which are the lack of cleanliness.   3211-1

After still another question from the dentist, the point was again made that before fluoridation of any water supply, it should be tested for conditions or minerals or elements in it. That these should be evaluated carefully before any action should be taken on fluoridation is an unstated but evident conclusion.

Q-13. Should drinking water in certain localities be prepared with a percentage of fluorine for prevention of decay and for preventing mottled enamel in teeth? If so, how and where?

A-13. This would have to be tested in the various districts themselves, much as has been indicated. There's scarcely an individual place in Ohio that it wouldn't be helpful, for it will get rid of and add to that condition to cause a better activity in the thyroid glands; while, for general use, in such a district as Illinois (say in the extreme northern portion) it would be harmful. These would necessarily require testing, according to the quantities of other conditions or minerals or elements in the water.   3211-1

Even the matter of fluoridated toothpaste was taken up. Another question elicited the response that it was best not even to use fluorine in a dentifrice (a tooth paste, powder or wash) because of variations (of minerals in the water supply, as previously noted).

Q-8. What chemical preparation, or should any form of fluorine be best for desensitizing the necks of teeth that are so sensitive, and how applied?
A-8. This would have to be applied locally if it is to be used. This is not best to be used in a dentifrice because of quite a variation that is found in the various districts where the processes in a dentifrice have their effect upon various conditions.   3211-1

Beneficent and Healing Water
There are at least three passages in the readings referring to beneficent or healing water.

A spring in Pickaway County, Ohio, was evaluated as being of potential help to many persons but not all. A general analysis of its properties followed. The conditions that might be helped by it were constipation, especially of nervous or dyspeptic digestion; and difficulties stemming from liver and kidneys, though not kidney difficulties associated with the pelvis. Moreover, a hot bath in this water would help alleviate skin diseases, especially eruptions from suppressed elimination which the capillary circulation had been unable to handle completely.

Gladys Davis: Now, you have before you the water in the spring located on the Finkle Farm, nine miles east of Circleville, Ohio, Pickaway County. A sample of the water from this spring is in this room. You will give us the analysis of this water, telling us if it has any beneficial value to the ailments of the human body. If so, what ailments, and how should it be used?
Mr. Cayce: Now, we find, as to the value of this water for the benefit of the human ills, that there are many that this would be beneficial to. There are conditions in the physical body that this would be detrimental to.

We find this is the analysis, and this is the condition that this water as a body would be beneficial to, and how:

First, we find this a light water in the respect that there are many minerals that will be found in solution in this water. The principal that will be beneficial is the light form of iodine and iron, and magnesia and soda in composition, or being by heat there would be left the basis of salt, of soda, of bicarbonate of soda, of sulphate of soda, of sulphite of soda, and these in composition with lithia give . . . the lightness in gravity of the water, for we find this comes through the bed of soda and salt in its rise to the surface, and portions of this are from old salt petrolia [petrous?] beds carrying these properties. Many of these are slight, but in action on the system we find many of these in correct solutions for the benefit of ills of the body. Specifically, in this character of cases would be the benefit as should be derived in using the water, though few would be the benefits derived in using the water alone, for nearly all derangements, save mental forces, come from some center being so separated by pressure that another functioning position in body becomes either deranged by lack of nutriment received or by over stimulus and producing too much of another character,[18] but these conditions especially; constipation, especially, that in the character of nerve digestion, or that of dyspeptic digestion. Conditions that have to do with the liver and with the kidneys proper. [For] those that have to do with the kidneys that are affected by conditions in pelvic troubles it would be detrimental. Those that come from the lack of elimination beneficial, and should be used in conjunction with other conditions applied to the body. Should be taken in quantities and without the interference of other waters. Heated it becomes an excellent bath for all skin diseases, especially that produced by eruptions caused from suppressed elimination or poisons eliminated through capillary circulation.   1447-1

Healing water once used by the Indians in the vicinity of Talladega, Ala., was discussed in several readings. The person requesting these had in another life been a medicine man and chief, Tecum Tec or The Rock, who had arranged for this water to be run through cedar conduits to a primitive hospital or "tepees of rest." It was only among "those peoples" (those *particular* Indian tribes?) that such facilities could be found. The water was helpful in warding off old age, infections, digestive disturbances and fevers.

The medicine man had buried gold and jewels committed to his care there by the well-pump and the springhouse. [707] was told that if he went to the area of the old Indian camp and meditated, he might have some recall of his activities as the chief and even find the site of the buried treasure. There is nothing attached to the readings to indicate that he ever did identify the spot. However, directions for its general location could be the guide to a rediscovery of this source of healing water.

---

[18]Note how this reference to malalignment of vertebrae as being one of the chief causes of illness ties in with the statement previously given (2524-5) at the end of the section on "Cleansing Techniques," that osteopathy, designed to correct malalignment of vertebrae, and hydrotherapy are the two best methods of treating the body for general disabilities.

In the excerpts which follow, the degree of advancement of these Indians and the nature of their alliance with the whites is evident.

The medicine man had incarnated in this lifetime as the great-grandson of the white man with whom, as an Indian, he had made a pact.

Before this we find the entity was in the land of the present nativity, about those portions of the land joining nigh unto the last birth place, in and about what is now known as Talladega.

Thou wert among the natives of the land that made for the first of the associations with thine white brethren that came into that portion of the land, thine own peoples in whose name thou hast come into the earth again. For with thine own present great grandfather in the flesh didst *thou* then, as the medicine man of those people, make the first pact of brotherhood; for there the great camp of those people of that land was made—what is now about those little streams, thou in thine strength did set what was to those people—and as may be found intact in many places at present—the first of the conduits for the waters of that particular land, that brought *healings* to many that were afflicted with those things that made for the warding off of what is known as *age* in the present. And, as Tecum Tec, or The Rock—as was called by those above thee in the other lands, and those with whom thou did associate, thou did bring much of strength; for thy abilities to call forth the understanding of the happy hunting grounds, the rest places for those that made for the activities in bringing the greater of the understandings in seeking out. And, my son, that thou didst bury in the form of the gold, the jewels that were committed to thy care, is *still* buried there by the old well-pump, by the old springhouse . . .   707-1

Q-5. State exact location of conduit, placed by me in another incarnation, near Talladega, Ala., through which healing waters flowed.

A-5. In the site where thy peoples were, the red men, the sons of La[?] and those peoples from the temple in Poseidia. There we find, as indicated, the medicine man, the mystic, the sage, the teacher, made for his people a resting place, through those periods after the hunting seasons in the north toward the mighty falls and the rock that's made salt, through those darkened bloody grounds where there were those mighty people, they gathered again to listen to the words of the teacher. The entity then builded the cedar conduits where there might be carried the sustenance to those places, or tents, or tepees of rest; where only among those peoples there was found even a semblance of a hospital or a place of care or rest set aside. Hence by the stream that carries the waters that are yet helpful to those who have received the infectious forces from contaminated waters, the disturbances of a digestive system, the fevers and such. Most of this is faded, filled in; yet the camping site to the south and west of that known as Talladega may be easily pointed out by any. There upon the banks of that stream now most hidden may there be found same. Then, when the entity, the body in the present seeks *self,* in self, to know of self upon the same grounds, there may come those that walked with Him, in self, with self, to know not only where the possessions of the entity may be found, that were to stand as an understanding of brotherly love between his own blood later as he entered again, not only those places where peace was declared, where there are the jewels, gold and the like buried, but those emblems of peace to those peoples in that day. Seek in self to find. There may be pointers through these sources, but there must be the real finding by self.   707-2

Hence as has been given and intimated for the entity, it would be well—for not only the material satisfaction but for the mental satisfaction—that the entity attempt at least to locate same; by being in that portion of the land during certain seasons, as has been given. For then there are the natural forces, or nature's forces that would work together with the desire of the entity in making the proper, definite location or site of same.

Then, to give something of the background, these to be sure now represent an activity in a period when the landscape or the material environ was in that period when the entity now called [707]—was in that experience.

It was near what is now Talladega, Alabama; to the west, and a little south, there is what is known as the old Indian camp of this entity's people.

It was from that camp that all of those peoples of the Cherokees as well as the other tribes held or had headquarters. From there were given out the various distributions of not only the hunting lands but the farming lands for the associated tribes.

The entity then, when there was in those periods the coming of the white man, with Levitt[?], Boone and others into the territory, eventually made an exchange for the privileges of trades or barter of the use of those lands. And when the entity with the Indians or his own peoples journeyed from the land, the entity received the exchange that was given and made a cache of same, that there might be at the period of the gathering of *all* the warriors, all the various tribes as were represented, an equal and proper division of same. It was then in 1769 to 1789-90-98.

Hence as has been given, the entity made for a development during that particular period in the very concept of the idea of dealings with not only its own peoples but all those who were contacted.

Those friendships meant much not only to the Whites but to

131

those of its own native peoples.

Now: In making the location in the present, it would be well first that the entity go to those grounds themselves—see—alone! In the evening and early morning, go about the grounds; for they are still marked, not only by the clearings and the various mounds where varied activities were carried on in a main camp of the entity's people, but the entity then will be able in its meditation, in its seeking—not digging, but seeking within self—to find much returning to self of the experience.

To be sure, the stream of water is now very small, compared to what it was during those particular periods. These interpretations, to be sure, then, become somewhat harder to make; but there will be found that ledge over the stream nigh unto where there was the conduit of cedar; not visible to the eye in the present, that was arranged by the entity as a means of sanitation as well as a means for a supply of water in another conduit (these were of cedar, but they are still a part of this).

And when this is found, this will point the way to where the entity may locate the treasure.

To be sure, this is not to be just go and picked up; it will require much of self's own meditation in same, and then there may be the aids given as progress is made.

When there is the locating, then first there must be a returning to the conditions as exist in the present. The lands are under the supervision of companies that have been organized for not only the farming and the mineral rights but both are taken into consideration. The owners then are to be considered, after there is determined where search is to be made. The owners are to be then reckoned with, that there may be in all, in every way, no questions of any legal phases to arise.

Begin by first going then to those environs, those surroundings; and these then may be gradually *realized, experienced*—the happenings of the entity in the experience at that period!

The amount is sufficient for the entity to give due considerations for its location, to say nothing of the satisfaction of the proof of many phases of human experience that are now only partially conceived of.

Ready for questions.

Q-1. *Approximately how far southwest of Talladega, Ala., is the site?*

A-1. The inquiry would be made as to the old Indian camping ground. This is approximately a mile and a half to two miles. But the inquiry would be made as to the location, and the best one to inquire from is the Postmaster at Talladega!

Q-2. *By what landmarks now visible may I recognize the location?*

A-2. As has been indicated, there are still the mounds, there are still many of the indications of an old camp ground; and the

132

stream that is about a hundred yards from the main body. Along the line of the conduit is the manner—where the way is to be sought. But the first activity is for the entity to get, as the best words would be, the "feel" of it, the experience of it, by quiet, meditation about the grounds. Not attempting to reason by what may be materially seen in the beginning, but to get what would be called a "daydream," an introspection of self, seeing self in the role of the Chief Medicine Man and the Chief of the Tribe, or what would be called today the last word in all of those five, yea ten tribes who made that their headquarters. And the "feel" of this, as it comes over the entity.

Do not reason from purely material. Take time; two, three, four days. And then begin to make marks, and we may aid.

707-5

The readings suggest that one source of healing water used in remote antiquity be restored to service today. This is the well at Bimini in the Bahamas, which was in use during the time of the Atlantean civilization. The surrounding waters also have regenerating power because of the life in them.

Q-5. Could the well in Bimini be promoted and reconstructed?
A-5. There has been much given through this source ... as to how that particular portion of what was the Atlantean period might be developed ... For it could be established as a center for two particular purposes; a regeneration for those with certain types of individual ailments (not only from the well, or water from same, but from the surrounding waters—because of the life in same), and a center for archaeological research. And as such activities are *begun,* there will be found much more gold in the lands under the sea than there is in the world circulation today!

587-4

It would seem that once these two projects are started, gold will be found to finance their continuance.

The Sea

The sea is a body of water of such magnitude that we seldom consider any possible interaction between it and humankind. Two references in the readings, however, indicate that we affect it, and then, of course, it affects us. The first tells how our use of its activities leads to changes in its composition.

Q-5. Is the salt in the ocean water the same as in our blood?
A-5. Not necessarily. At times it is. It is the nearest composition. But as the blood in a body constantly changes, as

133

hot and cold, as the various diets, so does the saltiness or the position of same in the ocean change according to its turmoil or the use of the activities about same, see?   658-15

The second reference points out that the combination of density of population and solar conditions may institute changes in the sea and its currents. These, in turn, affect the weather.

Mrs. Cayce: You will have in this room a printed report of Long Range Weather Forecast, dated January 15, 1926, by Herbert Janvrin Browne. You will answer the questions as I ask them relative to statements made in this report and the solar theory upon which this report is based.

Mr. Cayce: Yes, we have the report as printed here. There are many conditions given in same that are rather of the speculative nature than from sound reasoning. There may be expected many conditions to arise that will remind the people (who think) of conditions which have existed from period to period, age to age, and these in this report have been attempted to be related with the solar phases—the combinations rather of conditions in the land and in the sea. Rather we would say that the emphasis be placed in the condition of density of population, combined with the solar conditions to bring about certain changes in the sea and the currents therein, than the sun's radiation on account of sun spots.   195-29

An explanation clarifies the situation. Heat is radiated off from the earth. This naturally varies according to the amount generated by mankind in its combustion of different materials. A dense population would throw off more heat. This heat becomes correlated with "reflection in the earth's atmosphere," or solar heat. The combination returns to earth, changing ocean currents. Some of these carry their warmth to certain shores while others are carrying cold to different ones.

Q-1. . . . [Are] Herbert Janvrin Browne's theories correct—whereby weather is forecasted several years in advance by measuring solar radiation and its action on the ocean currents?
A-1. Were these varied accounts considered of that information intimated here, these would be *not* correct. For this may be established as a theory: That thrown off will be returned. As the heat or cold in the various parts of the earth is radiated off, and correlated with reflection in the earth's atmosphere, this in its action changes the currents or streams

in the ocean; and the waters bring or carry the heat in a manner to the various shores, or bring cold or carry cold to the various shores. 195-29

This interaction of radiation and water is only another illustration of the beautifully complex operation of universal law.

FORCE FROM THE SUN

Before undertaking a study of electricity, color and sound and of how they affect us, it is best to understand their origin. This is found in the sun, according to Edgar Cayce excerpts.

A reading about this solar force is, therefore, included. It was given for a realtor and manufacturer of auto accessories, who was interested in developing a motor and also wanted comments on an article he was preparing concerning positive and negative force. The answers to his questions show that force emerges from the sun and is drawn toward earth and that magnetism, electricity, light, color, heat, sound and, lastly, matter are developed in its flow.

Although the information is highly technical, a study of it shows it deals with basic principles in keeping with the other principles discussed so far.

For greater clarity the author has interpolated her own conclusion on each answer after its occurrence.

Mrs. Cayce: You will have before you the body and enquiring mind of [195], of ... Street ... Ohio, and the article Positive and Negative Force that I hold in my hand. You will answer the questions I may ask concerning statements made in the context, as I read them, and make suggestions for the bettering of the article.

Mr. Cayce: Yes, we have the body, the enquiring mind, [195], and the article as written by this body as regards Positive and Negative Force. In making suggestions for the better presentation of such data in such an article, this should be kept in mind—that these may be made either in answer *to* that written or in keeping *with* that written; or, to put in *different* words, may be answered in a positive or a negative manner, even as the article; or it may be given as in keeping with, and presenting in, a different angle.

Ready for questions.

Q-1. "The positive may be considered as the active forces in their activity and the negative as those tending to keep the balance." Please expand on this and give better explanation of Positive and Negative force.

A-1. This is as *good* an explanation as may be given, other than illustrating same; for it *is* a positive or a *plain statement* as to the conditions as regarding relativity of force; for *positive* is the active and negative is passive, as illustrated by the article in its various phases. The statement we would *not* expand upon in *this* instance, for it (the statement) must react with the individual development of each individual who takes the time to become positive *or* negative to the statement, and as one responds to same the activity of the statement may be seen.

Conclusion. Positive forces are active in their activity while negative ones tend to keep the balance.

Q-2. *"Consider Gravity—This applies right here, there and everywhere. This too may be considered a negative force, for it tends to balance the positive forces. Gravitational forces are vibratory forces and might be defined as the centralization of vibratory forces ready to change into power by non-activity."* Is gravity a negative force? How could this be better explained here?

A-2. Gravity in this *sense*—as explained in that, in the activity that becomes passive in its force—gravity becomes the negative force, see? even as is illustrated. Better illustration may be had in that of the Radio-active Appliance, as to how one becomes positive, the other negative, dependent upon which way the cycle begins by the change in the active force by which one is applied to a body in the first place, see?

Conclusion. Gravity is a negative force because it is a passive one. Force goes through a cycle, and whether it is positive or negative at any one time depends on the position in the cycle. Gravity happens to be in the receiving or passive position.

Q-3. *"With the assumption that their radial forces are thrown off this planet at or near Cancer and Capricorn, then it were possible when the vibrations of sun's rays [are] at a certain deflection on passing through these emanating radial vibrations to set up a partial vacuum, thereby causing winds."* Is this correct?

A-3. This correct.

Conclusion. Radial forces are thrown off from earth at or near Cancer and Capricorn. When the sun's rays at a certain deflection pass through these radial forces from earth, a partial vacuum may be set up, which causes winds.

138

Q-4. "*The one substance vibrates in different dynamic degrees, and sound, heat, light, electricity, are the effections of the one substance by specific degrees of the One Energy, and there is no difference between anything such as electricity and, say iron, save in rate of effection.*" *Is this correctly stated?*

A-4. Correctly stated.

Conclusion. There is only one substance, and there is only one basic Energy. The Energy acts upon the substance at different strengths, thus causing the substance to vibrate at different dynamic degrees. The rate of vibration determines the form the substance assumes—that is, sound, heat, light, electricity, etc. The difference between such things as electricity and iron arises from the difference in stimulation by the One Energy.

Q-5. "*The heart in the human body may be compared to the sun of a solar system. Then by analogy the sun is the center of forces of the solar system. Similarly to the blood flowing from the heart through the arterial system, Force emerges from the sun drawn to the opposite polarity of the planets and in this outgoing flow it would be possible to develop magnetism, electricity, light, color, heat, sound, and lastly matter, in the order of lessening dynamic degrees of vibration. Matter then would be the offspring of energy and not the parent, as is often thought.*" *Is this correctly stated?*

A-5. Correctly stated, and just what happens in the human organism.

Conclusion. The sun of a solar system is related to the system in the same way that the heart is related to the human body. The sun is the center of force of the solar system as the heart is the center of force of the body. Force emerges from the sun as blood flows from the heart. The force of the sun is drawn to the opposite polarity of the planets just as blood is drawn through the arterial system. (If the sun is largely positive in its activity, the planets, including earth, would appear to be largely negative.) There are doubtless negative forces in the body, pulling the blood along. As the solar force is drawn toward the planets, it is possible to develop magnetism, electricity, light, color, heat, sound and, lastly, matter in this descending order of dynamic degree. Matter is, therefore, the offspring of energy, not the parent, as often incorrectly concluded.

Q-6. "*It is more than probable that at the sun's surface there are many higher degrees of vibrations than are known or understood on this planet.*" *Is this correct?*

A-6. Correct.

139

Conclusion. There are many higher degrees of vibration at the sun's surface than are known or understood by man.

Q-7. *"When this force, decreasing in vibrations to light and light waves, enter[s] spectroscope, they [it] will emerge as colors. Evidence of flames and metals on fire on sun and stars is in all probability due to etheric vibrations being broken into color by formation of natural spectroscope at the sun or satellite under observation."* Is this correct?
A-7. This correct.

Conclusion. When solar force, decreasing in degree of vibration, finally turns into light waves, it shows up as colors in a spectroscope. What man takes to be flames and metals on fire on the surface of the sun and stars, are actually etheric vibrations broken into colors by a natural process, similar to that utilized in a spectroscope.

Q-8. *"As given above these radial emanations are negative forces."* Are radial forces negative forces?
A-8. Not always are radial forces negative forces. Only when they become passive, or of being acted upon as gravitation, do they become negative forces—while they are emanating from the positive; else they would not be drawn to the earth's force, in *its* emanation with the positive rays—and they are positive rays. From the sun's emanation does it produce the heat, see? This is seen in a *better* application, in that the deflection from—and the direct rays *of*—the sun's emanation *to* the earth, *through* the various stages of its activity, brings summer, or the heat wave, or the moving *of* the various forms; for these—acting [acted?] *upon*—become negative, and then are *positive* in their action, though at times these, to be sure, become negative in their action; for each has its radial activity and is throwing *off,* as well as drawing *to.* Hence the various positions or conditions as is seen in sun, through the activity of the various forms of gas or metal, or those various conditions that seem to cause the various eruptions as apparent within the sun itself. It receives as well as throws off, is positive as well as negative—see? and only until it becomes in such a force that it is altogether negative, as the gravitation that holds in place—for when each are lost in their relative position, these then are thrown off, as was the moon from the earth, or as is [were] the various satellites of the various planets, as *well* as the various effects out in space.

Conclusion. Radial forces (those radiating from a body such as the sun) can be positive or negative. When they become passive and are acted upon they become negative. This is what happens in gravitation. The force of gravity is then drawn to the earth by the earth's positive rays. Other portions of solar force become negative and then positive in their action, bringing heat. The deflection of the sun's emanation to the earth and the sun's direct rays reaching the earth determine how great this heat will be. The seasons are, therefore, dependent on the earth's varying position in its passage round the sun. However, both earth and sun possess negative and positive forces. The sun receives as well as gives. Note reference to this in the reading on sunspot activity (see "The Effects of Man on the Sun"). The turmoils, wars and hates of man reflect onto the sun and are received there and thrown back to earth as solar outbursts. The magnitude of the effect on our weather has been taken up in detail.

The relationship between the sun and the planets, including earth, is obviously a complex one, involving positive and negative forces from both, which interact and maintain an equilibrium or balance. It is only when a mass becomes completely negative in force, as in gravitation, which holds objects in place, that the relative position is changed and the mass is thrown off by the planet with which it was balanced, as the moon was by earth and as the satellites of the various planets have been by those planets and as other masses have been similarly thrown off in outer space by the planets holding them.

Q-9. "*Therefore, there could be in the solar system a dynamic reservoir or solar storage battery that would correspond to the lungs of a human system.*" *Is there a solar power reservoir corresponding to lungs of a human system?*
A-9. Solar power corresponding.

Conclusion. There is a solar storage battery or power reservoir corresponding to the lungs of the human system, which makes the foregoing situation possible.

Q-10. "*Ether may be defined as the combination of a higher plane, leading us to metaphysics, to where every consideration of the atom finally leads one.*" *Is this statement concerning ether correct? Will you please give a better definition?*
A-10. There's no *better* definition! This is correct—for, same as the statement of positive and negative forces as relating to gravitation, they act upon the individual's *development,* or individual's application of thought as applied *to* metaphysical condition or position as is occupied from within itself. Hence, as is seen, there are (this may be an illustration for this same condition) certain *characters* of disease that accentuate mental forces, or the metaphysical activity of a human body.

There are others that so *dull* the senses as that they become one-sided, or only passive not positive; yet a *normal*, perfectly well and normal mind may be so active as to be considered by others in its activity as of being unbalanced, but only is it considered *peculiar*.

Conclusion. Ether is the combination of a higher plane, leading one to metaphysics. Positive and negative forces act upon individual development or an individual's application of thought as applied to the metaphysical condition or position within him. Certain kinds of disease accentuate mental forces or the metaphysical activity of a human body. Others dull the senses so that this activity becomes passive. However, a perfectly normal, balanced mind that is very active may be considered unbalanced and peculiar by other persons.

Q-11. "A mechanical device might be constructed where a vacuum even excluding ether could be drawn and maintained, developing thereby a levitating force; this similar to that force which exerts pressure upward when air is pumped into a steel barrel while submerged below surface of a medium such as water. This levitating force will be utilized in many ways, particularly in so-called heavier-than-air ships, with the result that air navigation will be possible without the use of wings or gas." Is this correct?

A-11. This correct when the elements must be made so condensed in their form as to prevent the ether in its finer sense from being, or escaping through the various elements that are ordinarily used for creating of such vacuums. [195] will understand that! You don't get it, but [195] will! That is, the container—you can get it here—a container in which a vacuum may be made must be of such a *condensed* element as to prevent ether from going through the atomic forces of the element itself, as is seen in that of an electric bulb—this is *not* a vacuum, only a portion! To the finite mind this is *considered* as such, but were the same character—or these same conditions produced in a *different* way—*then* these may be made to *become* an element that would act in that way and manner, see? As is seen at present, helium becomes the greater usage in containers that may be made; yet these *themselves* (this is working from the opposite side, see?)— but were those gases, or those metals used that the supply of helium itself becomes the container *for* the vacuum *itself*, see? This condensed, see? into a metal form, *then* the vacuum may be made that would lift without being lifted, see?

Conclusion. A levitating force might be developed with a mechanical device in which a perfect vacuum could be drawn and maintained. However, the container would have to be made of elements so condensed that they would prevent the

142

ether from escaping through these elements. This would result in a vacuum that would facilitate levitation.

Q-12. "Pressure of metals on earth could possibly be accounted for by the breaking up of solar rays through formation of . . . [natural] spectroscopes during formation era of the planet earth." Is this correct?
A-12. This is a very good expression of that. Very good, and very well stated—that it may be possible, for it *is* very well stated.

Conclusion. The breaking up of solar rays through formation of natural spectroscopes, as the planet earth was formed, may account in some measure for the properties of metals here on earth.

Q-13. Give suggestion as to how to improve on the article and how to better explain positive and negative aspects of force.
A-13. This as is given is *very well* presented, and with the various comments as will come *from* such presentation, these will develop for the body mind that necessary. Begin with that as is expressed here.

Conclusion. The facts previously presented are an excellent basis for further study by the human mind.

Q-14. With motor as now laid out, embodying new leverages and gears with same pitch, will this work as designed?
A-14. When balanced properly, it will work.

Conclusion. The motor on which [195] was working needed to be properly balanced.

Q-15. What argument would be most conclusive to prove that sun is not hot at surface?
A-15. The breaking up of the rays, just as has been described, in that it takes *back* as well as gives off, being both positive and negative.

Conclusion. Since the sun takes back rays as well as gives them off, it is not hot at the surface.

Q-16. What could be given as cause for appearance of corona of sun?
A-16. Just as has been explained, in that the forces as are thrown off by the various activities of the forces in all—that is, the planets, the stars, and those about it that are thrown off

from same in their active principle, as draws to and throws off at the same time—these may be seen as the forces which produce or cause the various effects as seen.

Conclusion. The appearance of the corona of the sun is due to its positive and negative forces, which draw to and throw off forces coming from the planets. Similar effects occur with regard to the planets, stars and satellites. The active principle is both positive and negative at the same time.

Q-17. *What could be given as cause for appearance of solar flames and metal coloring in these so-called solar flames?*
A-17. This is as has been given.
We are through for the present.   **195-70**

Conclusion. The situation just mentioned accounts for the appearance of "solar flames" and metal coloring in them.

Electricity

Proceeding on the basis established in the last section that electricity is one of the first manifestations of solar force, we can easily understand why it is so potent and needs to be handled so carefully. In fact, the average individual who comes into contact with it probably has no idea of its possibilities. For this reason the Edgar Cayce excerpts directly following are especially valuable both as warning and guide.

Electricity and the Human Body

The readings suggest various electrically energized devices to be used in healing but always specify limited application.
The following excerpts illustrate this point with regard to violet ray, ultraviolet ray, infrared, diathermy, sinusoidal forces and hand applicator. The first reference, also, contains a general warning.

Violet Ray and Ultraviolet Ray

At times the electrical forces [violet ray hand machine] have been used too much. As should be interpreted by the body, or those who may use such measures, there are—to be sure—in the minds of individuals, and in the experience of entities, varied theories as to what takes place with the application of electrical forces of varied natures.
Life in its manifestation is vibration. Electricity is vibration. But vibration that is creative is one thing. Vibration that is destructive is another. Yet they may be from the same source.

144

As in electrical forces in the form or nature prepared even for use in the body.

We would be more careful with these, and use according to those directions that have been given; not too long. Some use the theory that if it is good for a little, more would be better. Usually, more is worse—in most anything. The best is that individual or soul-entity that keeps well balanced, never the extremist—but all things to all men. For the first law is, "The Lord thy God is *one* Lord." And so does it apply in the body forces.

It would be well to continue to rest from the electrical forces in the present, through those periods that the activities are in the open, for if there are the activities in the sun it is much better that the ultraviolet rays be absorbed in that manner than to have mechanical applications or other measures. These are natural sources of supply for energies, for the radiation that comes from the sun is nearer to that of physical life.

Thus these applications may be continued when there is less of the physical activity in the open, when they are needed to prevent the resultant forces from confinement.   1861-16

Well were there taken, at least once a week, . . . medicated ash to *produce* oxygen, *as* it is carried in the system. When this is taken, over the sacral and lower limbs apply the ultraviolet ray. Apply same to the sacral region and the back portion of limbs, so that along the nerve impulses *to* the limbs the whole of the ray is carried. Let this be at least thirty-eight inches from the body in the beginning, and not given over two and one-half minutes in the beginning, see?   130-1

And every third day apply the rays of the ultraviolet light to the head—first one side (head and neck and shoulders), then the other—at least thirty-six inches from the body, and begin with not more than one minute exposure. Do not increase until there is shown reaction from the manipulation and from the eliminations.   470-7

For the same individual 13 days later:

. . . occasionally—once a month—the application of the ultraviolet ray should be given head, neck and shoulders, until there is perfect coordination through the activity of the auditory system, or a perfect accord established between the auditory forces and that of the cerebrospinal system, as affecting with that of the sympathetic nerve system.   470-8

Q-12. Where and under what conditions should ultraviolet ray be used in dentistry, and how?

A-12. Ultraviolet rays should be used in dentistry when there are indications of any form of Riggs's disease. It should then be used about half a minute on the back of the neck, and the jaw. And you'll have it! 3211-2

Infrared

Q-2. *Would the violet ray be of benefit to me?*
A-2. The ultraviolet would be more helpful for this body. But these should not be too severe, too long. And use the quartz light for this body rather than the mere heat light, but the penetrating. Or the infrared would still be better for this body, for then it would act more upon the deeper tissues and attune the activity of the circulation to the conditions of the body.

This should be, of course, not too long but sufficient that there is a warming as it were to the internal forces of the system itself.

Q-3. *How often, where and how applied?*
A-3. The natural application is to the spine, especially in the areas from the central cervical to the lower lumbar; and applied once a week should be sufficient, and for a period of twenty minutes *after* the light and lamp has heated. And it should be at least thirty-six to thirty-eight inches from the body.

Q-4. *Does this refer to the infrared light?*
A-4. To be sure, to the infrared. 470-17

Diathermy

[These disturbances] may be gradually corrected if there will be sufficient of the osteopathic adjustments to cause a more perfect circulation, and if there will be used the low vibrations of static electricity or the heat treatment that may be had with certain types of electrical treatments—as the short wave, though it will require long periods . . .

Use the Radio-active Appliance [description later] to coordinate vibrations in the body-forces themselves. Apply this for an hour each day over a long period of time.

Also we would use the short wave electrical treatment for fifteen to twenty minutes twice in one week, three times the next week, over a long period of time. 3211-3

. . . we would apply the low heat of the diathermy in the area of the sixth dorsal and over the gall duct center—about three minutes in the beginning, gradually increasing. But keep this at a very low voltage. 3556-1

Sinusoidal Forces
. . . sinusoidal forces . . . *low* form of the vibratory forces.
5-1

. . . vibrations from the sinusoidal reaction, as will make for the *secondary*—not the high, not the low vibration, but of the secondary vibration. 53-1

146

Also we would add to those, those of the sinusoidal ray, especially as related to the liver and the spleen ... Not giving the vibration longer than three minutes each treatment.

98-1

In the matter of the application of the reverse coil, or the sinusoidal ray, these are to act with the muscular forces as coordinate with central nerve system, and the *locomotaries* of the lower limbs; placing, then, one anode at or about the first portion of the sacral or last dorsal, the other at the 4th and 5th dorsal center, see? This should be given, beginning with only one and a half minutes. Increase, as the contraction, or the activities of the system are stimulated. These should not be given more than once each week, at least for the next thirty days.

99-2

Were those vibrations of the reverse coil, or those in the sinusoidal, added to the liver vibrations ... these would be beneficial, but would be rather *severe* unless the body rested most of the time the treatments were given!

5613-1

Hand Applicator

The character of the electrical forces ... would be of the *low* form but of the *high frequency* and these should be about once a week applied while the general manipulation and the full hydrotherapy treatments would be about twice a week ...

Q-1. Is the sinusoidal the electrical treatment referred to?

A-1. No; it is rather ... the low current of the high frequency machine—it's applied with the hands!

1706-1

Wet Cell Appliance

In addition to recommending the use of electrical appliances already devised, the readings give directions for constructing two others, generally identified as the Wet Cell Appliance and the Radio-active Appliance or Impedance Device. These two devices appear to contain very basic electrical circuits which, from outward appearances, would have very limited effect on the human body. However, the readings indicate that there are therapeutic vibratory effects of a nature beyond the scope of present-day electrical theory. The two devices are discussed in a booklet *Two Electrical Appliances Described in the Edgar Cayce Readings,* Edgar Evans Cayce, A.R.E. Press, 1965. This publication is available to A.R.E. members.

The Wet Cell Appliance produces within itself a measurable D.C. potential of 0 to 1½ volts. When its two electrodes are connected to the body, it causes a small current to flow, the amount of this determined by the body's resistance. Solutions of elements placed in the circuit presumably introduce modulations of extremely small amplitudes and of frequencies which are dependent upon the natural rates of vibration of these elements. These modulations, however, have not been measured nor has their existence been proved. Solutions such as gold chloride are suggested in the readings for use in the circuit with the Wet Cell.

Radio-active Appliance or Impedance Device

The Radio-active Appliance is a device which completes an electrical circuit through parts of the body. The body itself supplies minute voltages. (The existence of such voltages has been proved, and their characteristics are actually analyzed by electrocardiograms.) The two electrodes of the device are attached to designated parts of the body, usually the extremities. The circuit includes specified elements and a temperature variation. It is speculated that the current flowing through the circuit is modulated at frequencies which are dependent upon the elements involved, but such modulations have not been measured, nor has their existence been verified.

The following reference clarifies somewhat the nature of the Radio-active Appliance or Impedance Device.

In the manner of applying those vibrations of the Radio-active Appliance, this . . . is *builded* in this manner:

That of life vibratory force in electrical vibration is of the *lowest* electrical vibration, that that builds for active forces or principles with that that is of the highest known vibration in a human body. Now the active forces of these are built from the elements that make for an electrical activity in those as make for the variations in the temperature of elements, and in their application to the high vibration produce—by that being built up with the elements in which, or about which, this is held in its active forces, and produces then to the body that of an impelling force as may be seen by the test—after the first or second application—that there is a scarcely perceptible, but gradually increasing change in the pulsations for the body, which makes for—or is—that of a vibratory force or rate as impels first to the nerve plexus, especially to the sympathetic nerve system, of which and through which the activities of same are the most perceptible to the senses and to the active principle forces of reaction from impulse, or the senses of the body, and with the vibration of gold itself will add to the system. Patience, persistence, consistence—as will the activities of those that apply same, apply that that aids in creative forces becoming active through the elements in the material world, that makes for the active principles of life in its spiritual essence and force. **2155-1**

148

In other words, our bodies contain forces of the lowest electrical vibration. This same type of electricity is evident when there is a change in the temperature of elements. If such an electrical force is used as a carrier for an element which has a vibration needed by the body and this is added to the body, it will respond. The improvement resulting can be proved in due time by the reactions of the sympathetic nerve system. With patience, persistence and consistency on the part of the person receiving the treatment and the person giving it, results will be apparent. The spiritual will have manifested in materiality.

Low Amplitude
The importance of low amplitude in applications to the body is stressed in the next two references.

Making application of same in the study of electro-therapeutics as related to the activities of the body.

He should remember, in making a study, while life is an electrical energy, there are vibrations of the nature in the system. All disorders as set themselves up in a body, by correlating of their individual vibrations, create a specific disturbance. Not *all* of galvanic nor all of *any one* type of electrical vibrations then are set up in the varied disturbances, but *all* types are indicated. And there are those that are constructive to certain vibrations, there are those that are destructive. There are those vibrations that will enable organs to be aroused to an activity. There are those that would destroy the activity of organs, whether these are in accord with the general system or to that balance to which the body is best adapted in itself.

These then should be studied, and know that *constructive* are the *lowest* forms, destructive the higher forms.

In this study may the entity *find* not only the application of the inclinations and tendencies but a field of service. 1249-1

Q-2. *Is the blood radiation treatment I am now using beneficial to me?*
A-2. Insofar as that which is taken as elements is for body and blood building, for it to combine with, very good. But this, too, may be overdone. Better to use the lower vibrations in which life itself finds or takes up urges as of emotion, as of life energy expending itself and the like . . .

Q-4. *What other vibrations in the low form do you refer to?*
A-4. It has been given again and again; those that are the lowest form of electrical forces that move as energies from the etheronic forces—or of the lowest form of static, or the electrical creative forces. The Radio-active Appliance, to the extremities. 681-2

Is the electrical current introduced into human bodies by today's technology as limited in application as the readings advise? In a recent book *The Medicine Men,* Leonard Tushnet, M.D., refers to a statement by Dr. Carl W. Walter, Chairman of the Safe Environment Committee, Peter Bent Brigham Hospital in Boston, which says that the number of undiagnosed accidental electrocutions of patients in hospitals each year is unknown, that an insurance actuary has estimated it at twelve hundred (1200) but that Dr. Walter is inclined to believe five thousand (5,000) would be more accurate. Dr. Walter states that these unrecognized electrocutions are usually considered cardiac arrest and that they occur while efforts are being made at resuscitation and while electric monitors, pacemakers and other appliances are being used.[19]

Are we, perhaps, being careless in our procedures for passing electric current through the human body?

The Use of Electricity in Metallurgy

References to electricity in the readings are not limited to the field of its direct application to the human body. Among the various readings mentioning it one series stands out as suggesting a possible breakthrough for metallurgists. The most pertinent excerpts of this series now follow in the hope that they will be of real use to present-day scientists. Such a breakthrough could institute many changes in the conditions of man's living.

[470] was told he had been an Atlantean who had migrated to Peru and there worked with electricity in the preparation of metals in a way unknown today. These metals had proved very useful. The man's questions elicited much helpful information as to how the art could be revived. There is, however, no record that he ever attempted to revitalize it.

Idea as conceived by [470] for introducing into a molten mass of iron the vibratory rates of other minerals through electrical current so as to produce a steel with the same elasticity and tensile strength but 50% lighter than produced at present. You will tell us whether this process can be worked out and give advice as to just how to proceed in the first preparation for experimentation . . .
Mr. Cayce: Yes.
In considering conditions of this kind, as we have given, the body has those abilities within same of making not only the

---

[19]Leonard Tushnet, M.D., *The Medicine Men,* Warner Paperback Library, New York, 1972, pp. 59-60.

150

experimentations but plans that may develop those applications of electrical forces to metals, in ways and manners such that there may be made many changes in the activity of metals, chemicals, and other products of these in varied combinations.

That various forms of the activities of electrical influence upon metals have often been used is a common knowledge. The use at the various stages of same has been and is the variation that we find may make for a product that will be of a lighter nature, yet of a tensile strength for greater activity or usage of same in many fields; that is, of the steel itself.

While many another product presents itself, this for the beginning—though among those of the more necessity for the experimentations to be carried to a varied degree—would be the manner for its preparation:

First, as has been indicated, in the separating of the ore from slags and impurities (which is necessary for its usage), for a great period an ordinary ore of one form or stage has passed through a state of preparation by the heating to such an intensity that, with the addition of the chlorate, the manganese and the carbon, it has brought forth—by its natural settlements, or natural sediments being removed—a state, or gained such a state (the ore) as to turn to metal.

In these manners, then, the preparations would be made. When the combinations are made for the various types of the metals, that are later to be reheated and other properties added—or the variations made in the heat and its working for the production of that temperament wherein it is termed steel; in the *first* add the current in such measures—not as high as it is in the present, so as to destroy or to break the atomic forces, but—that the direct currents are passed through same in its stages of development. Thus the solution or the problem of its forming into the metal will produce a much different tensile strength, and turn much of that in the varied qualities of ores in the various sections of the producing fields to quite a different usage.

Hence the *idea* may be said to be partially correct. Or, if it is carried to its application in the *beginning* of the operations, then the idea is correct.

Q-1. Is the arc-resistance type of furnace suitable for this process?

A-1. The arc; so long as it is made of the *direct* current—or of that frequency that is the direct.

Q-2. In what state should the mineral be from which the vibratory rate is to be introduced; that is, solid or liquid?

A-2. As indicated or given, when the *heating* process of the ore is in its original state—or when it is *begun*, then the vibratory rate should be applied.

Many processes. And much that has become as the usage, of course, in the various forms of the producing organizations, has arisen from the manner in which these have been handled.

Remember, there is a variation in the ore that would be had from Minnesota and Michigan and Pennsylvania and Alabama or Colorado. Yet all of these—the lowest (as some of those, of course, where the larger deposits are indicated) may be turned into the finest, by this electrical force being sent through same in its *formative* stages.

For here:

Begin at the first, not only of the chemical but of the atomic chemical reaction upon its influence.

The very ore itself is classified by that number of the positive and the negative forces or influences that *form* the unit about which the vibration makes it an ore in the first premise, see?

Then, the very activity of electric energy upon same *turns* same into an energy that becomes different; yet partaking of the very influence or elements that *make* for the metal-bearing ore to become more of the affinity to that it will produce in its clarification, or when it has been purified, see?

Hence we set, then, the first premise: Not in the molten fluid, you see, but in the beginning—before and as it becomes the molten fluid.

Thus we will produce, by the very force, that quality force of the character of current passed through same, as to how high the purification does become.

Hence it requires, then, that it be set up in such a way and manner that the various experiments with the ore itself may be had; to know the number of the electronic forces or ions or ohms that make up for the force that passes through same in its formative state.

Q-3. What minerals should be used?

A-3. *First,* we begin with that making for its first separation. The minerals, or the greater portions of those that are added, are the amounts of carbon, the amounts of the manganese—that separates afterward. This should be a secondary consideration. Let's *begin* the process in its formative state. Then we may find how this has added (this passing of the current through same) that will seem so easy once it is shown or perfected, in comparison to all that which has been necessary heretofore to produce a lighter steel and of greater tensile strength—or greater flexibility, lasting.

Begin, then, at the beginning.

Q-4. Should more than one mineral be used at a time? If so, in what order should they be used; that is, one mineral to an anode and a different mineral to each anode of the furnace, if they are to be used at the same time. If at different times, how?

A-4. This is getting the cart rather before the horse. These would come later, to be sure, but the first passing of the current to make for a different variation from that which has been indicated begins when the ore, the iron ore, is being reduced to the metal state, see?

In the beginning, then, for the preparation of the first ore, there is only the addition of the lime, the carbon—these with a very small quantity of the manganese (that is, mixed *with* the ores—as these are); then the course of the current through same.

Begin with these; then we may aid.   470-13

We find the entity there [in the Peruvian land] made use of the metal known as iron, or the combinations of iron and copper—which have long since been removed from use in the present; or copper so tempered by the use of same with a little of the iron, or in its formation in such a way and manner as to be hardened to the abilities for same to be used much in the way that many of those combinations have been found in the Egyptian, the Peruvian and portions of the Chaldean lands— and *more* will be found in the Indo-China city yet to be uncovered.

All of these arose from the applications of same that were a part of the activity of the entity then, now called [470].

In the activities the application of these was in a little different order, of course, from that in the present. For the characters of the dynamo or the generators for same were used in a way and manner in which there was the transformation of the direct to the activities for using same much in the same manner (the entity will understand, in the study of same) in which gases are now used as a means for propelling force or influence to act as a pump for the transformation of casing-head gas to gasoline, and the *refuse* used to produce or make the power for the machine producing same.

That is, from the direct current passing through the activity of the fusing of metals and the transmutation that forms from same, and the active forces as turned into that in which it makes for the clearing of the refuse forces of the ore in such a manner that the very fuse itself becomes the source of an alternating current to which there is added then a stepped-up activity in which the direct current then becomes the source of the energy to produce this fusing of the metals or ores.

                    470-22

It appears reasonable to infer that the materials used in such a processing of metals may introduce modulations upon a unidirectional flow of current ("direct current") which may be passed through them during purification and fusing processes. It is surmised that such modulations are dependent upon the nature of the materials through which the current passes. These modulations may be responsible for the improved nature of the metal.

When subsequently [470] reincarnated in Ra Ta's Egypt, he employed a similar process with metals to develop cutting instruments or electrical knives that could be and were used in the bloodless surgery of the period. The knives induced coagulation.

153

Again we find in the activities of same the entity made a soon return to the Egyptian land, when the entity made preparations for a part of the armor, or part of the defense; as the armor bearer or the protector for the activities of the King.

All of these activities then became a part of the use of electrical forces for metals and their activity upon same to be used as carbonizing them, or directing them in manners in which they became as magnetic forces for the applications to portions of the body for transmuting or changing the *effect* of activities upon the physical energies and forces of the body; able to use same as re-ionizing or re-generating the bodily forces themselves.

For as the very forces of the bodily functionings are electrical in their activity, the very action of assimilation and distribution of assimilated forces is in the physical body an active force of the very *low* yet very high *vibratory* forces themselves.

Hence there the entity made application in those directions; and these act upon the influences or forces or metals, or active principles within the human forces themselves.

For within the human body—living, not dead—*living* human forces—we find every element, every gas, every mineral, every influence that is outside of the organism itself. For indeed it is one with the whole. For it is not only a portion of, and equal to, and able to overcome or meet every influence within, but there is not the ability in the third dimensional force or influence to even imagine anything that isn't a part of the activity of a physical *living* organism!

Hence the use of these was a portion of the entity's experience, when there was the preparation for the cleansing and the transmuting of the bodies in the preparations for the new race.

Just so the entity in itself, in study, in listening to the influences within, conceives of and sees these changes that are possible. Why not? He helped to make them in those experiences, through those activities!

Ready for questions.

Q-1. Please give the name of a book or books which will explain the ionic theory.

A-1. As just indicated, those from which there may be gained another concept of gas and its activity. Through those same channels or sources may we find the greater theories, and the active forces, of electronics upon metals, or the ionics, or the activities of iron with the influences or forces themselves.

Or, a study with one who has prepared much with the Tennessee Coal and Iron; the engineerings there, and the findings there; in the study as to the application of the various elements necessary—for then there will be found channels through which there may be gained the insight into the study of same.

154

But the real *findings* may come within, see? within self!

Q-2. Where should I seek information on electrical currents, direct and alternating?

A-2. As we find, any of those who have studied with or in the General Electric, or those who have studied the combinations of same with or through the same channels as indicated—about the activities of same upon iron.

Of course, the partner with the entity [in a former life]—who is now called Ford [Henry Ford]—will be the one through whom and to whom these will become the most interesting, and where there may be channels through which much may come; as in the mines in portions of Kentucky where there is the coal activity and portions of iron and manganese—which is a portion, or the fusion of same in the use of these—all become a part of the activity. These will be the channels and the sources and the places through which much of this will eventually come, if the entity is active in *making* a further study of these—and the application to the use of metals and irons especially.

. . . For the father then [in the Egyptian land] . . . was a close companion with the entity . . . in those activities where there was the transmuting of the bodily energies through electrical forces. For the father . . . was then what would be called today a doctor!

. . . in those periods when the entity, Ajax, came into the Egyptian land . . . the entity now called [470] made the application or use of the abilities in engineering, and the building of machines for the application of these to the bodies of individuals—where there were appurtenances to be left off, where there was blood to be changed, or where the vibratory forces were to be set so as to remove those influences or possessions; and where there were those activities in which with the combination of sodas the bodily forces were enabled to reproduce in a manner as cross to that to which it had been set in its natural forces.   470-22

. . . then [in Egypt] the entity being in the name Asphar.

Being interested in every form of activity that might bring better conditions for individuals or groups, the entity was interested in those tales or experiences told by Ax-Tell [or Ajax]; and sought demonstrations and experimentations with those influences which had been a part of the experience of the Atlanteans that brought about destructive influences.

With the return of the Priest to better establish a coordinant, united force or effort on the part of those of the King's household as well as those who had led in the various rebellions among the natives, as well as the rebellion in Ibex of the King's household—there came periods of a great deal of mental disturbance to many.

But during that period a great deal of the time of Asphar and Ajax-ol was devoted to the use of the electrical forces maintained from the use of static forces, as called today. And in their attempts to demonstrate or use these influences for a helpfulness rather than as they had been used upon nature or individuals, or those activities of a destructive nature, these were turned to minerals. Thus the conditions in which there were the abilities for the fusion of copper and brass with the alloy that comes from gold impregnated with arsenic, with the casting of electrical forces through same. This brought those abilities of sharpening or using such metals as these for cutting instruments.

Also there were those activities and abilities of the entity to use the electrical devices as prepared through those periods of their investigation, for operative measures; wherein the electrical knife was in such a shape, with the use of the metals, as to be used as the means for bloodless surgery, as would be termed today—by the very staying forces used which formed coagulating forces in bodies where larger arteries or veins were to be entered or cut.

Then, such were the greater activities of the entity through those influences which had to do especially with the Temple of Sacrifice . . .

In making practical application of those forces in the present, then, it will necessarily be through experimentation, of passing the powerful currents of electrical forces through the ores, the metals and those combinations of same in which there may be seen the uses of metals in forms as indicated, that were *only* used through the experience and the experimentation of the entity as helpful forces during the reconstruction period in Egypt.

The entity then grew to be one who prompted the greater development along those lines, yet sought in a manner to preserve to self the purely technical manner in which those operations were cast. Thus much of that ability was lost after that period, and after the passing of those who labored or worked with the entity.

Ready for questions.

Q-1. Considering the work in Egypt with electrical forces, explain just how I should apply those talents now.

A-1. As indicated. In conducting experimentations, by passing a great current through certain compounds or mixtures of metals, that would produce—in smeltering—a different metal.

The combinations of iron, copper, of course impregnated with the various forms, which heretofore and in the present have been unable to be used in the forms of smeltering that are the experience of man today.

Q-2. Describe in detail the construction and purpose of the more important machines used by me then.

A-2. As indicated, the machine in which there was the combining of metals in those periods of fusing or smelting, that combined them in such ways that they might be used in forms not used today.

Especially the use of electrical forces with the character of instruments in operations, as well as the fusion of such metals indicated.

Q-3. What specific experimental work should be done now that would lead to an awakening of that ability manifested in the Egyptian period?

A-3. The combining of the metals in their crude state by the passing of current in the various forms through same, during the period of smelting same, see?

Q-4. Was Ajax, with whom I was closely associated in engineering, the same as Ax-Tell? Please explain the reference to him as Ajax in my reading, and as Ax-Tell in other readings.

A-4. Called Ajax in the Atlantean land, being *of* the Atlanteans, and Ax-Tell in the Egyptian activity. One and the same. Ajax-ol was a different individual, see?

Q-5. How may we work together now to accomplish much that we did in Egypt?

A-5. In interesting those who use or require great quantities of iron, or the varied metals, to experiment in making lighter— and yet strengthening—the usages of such metals. Copper and brass, gold and iron—through the combinations in their crude state—may be made to be much stronger in usage, lighter in the needs for present developments, and not as expensive in the combinations.

Q-6. Will Henry Ford become greatly interested?

A-6. This, to be sure, depends upon the manner in which the interests of this entity are presented to that body. But Henry Ford was one who first interested this entity in these activities, see?

Q-7. In just what manner should he be approached now?

A-7. Through the regular channels. Do not attempt to force the issue.   470-33

Note: although [470] at various times attempted to establish personal contact with Henry Ford, there is no indication he was ever able to do so.

Color

The Role of Color

Color is another manifestation of the force proceeding from the sun. Since it emerges after electricity, we would expect it to be not quite so potent in its effect. It is, however, much more potent than most persons realize. A study of the effects of color and an attempt to ascertain to what colors we individually are attuned can lead to personal color therapy.

Such a study should begin with the question: Of what does color consist?

157

Colors are naturally the spiritualization of tone or sound.
288-38

... the entity gets the *color*, rather than what is ordinarily called the tonal vibration, see? though, of course, the tonal vibration is that which *produces* color. For, of course, color and tone are just different rates of vibration.   2779-1

Why are persons so influenced by color? We have already learned that in Egypt at a very early date bodies were able to absorb directly a great deal of energy from the sun and that it was only after they had retrograded that the energy derived from plants and animals had to be utilized more. These same purer bodies were able to vibrate with not only light but also color, tone, activity. Now they are encased in much more hardened matter. At the time of Ra Ta certain chants, odors, activities were used in specific ways to arouse these earlier vibrations. A person in such a high level of consciousness could then be a channel of healing for others. The same is true today.

In the activities then, there were first the songs, the music, as we have indicated that *ye* sing ... which makes for the losing of even the association of the body with that save the *vibrations* of which the body was then composed; yea now is, though encased in a much more hardened matter, as to materiality; which made for the vibrating of same with light, that *becomes* color, that becomes tone, that becomes activity.
Seek then *in* tone, all of you ... that ye may know how the emanations, that are termed as the colors of the body, make for the expression then given.   281-25

"The colors of the body" refer directly to man's aura, the colors in which are indications of his health, development, etc.

All bodies radiate those vibrations with which it, the body, controls itself in mental, in physical, and such radiation is called the aura.   5756-1

Auras are twofold. That which indicates the physical emanations, and that which indicates the spiritual development. These when they are kept more in accord with the experience of individuals make for the greater unification or purpose and ideal.
The aura, then, is the emanation that arises from the very vibratory influences of an individual entity, mentally, spiritually—especially of the spiritual forces.   319-2

For a baby two days old:

158

The aura, to be sure, develops with the *mental* influences of the body. It may be seen, even in the present, to be blue—or the higher shades of blue, to almost white.   314-1

In other words, the aura, which is composed of vibrations surrounding the body, contains colors as part of its makeup. These colors are indications of the person's mental and spiritual development.

The aura of an individual may be perceived by someone who is psychic or highly sensitive. The readings had advice for one such person and an explanation of the significance of some of the colors in auras.

Colors—these become as means in which the entity may, for itself, determine much. But know as to what colors mean. For the entity is not only able and capable to receive the vibrations of individuals about the entity as to their colors but as to their vibrations. And these then make for a sensitiveness that is often disturbing to the entity.

This may be developed or it may be passed over. But those that are as symbols or signs or conditions that may be used constructively, use same; do not abuse same. For that which is good . . . may be used to one's own undoing.

Know that when there is felt, seen or experienced those vibrations of low, leaden or dark reds, these are as dangers; not only for self but self's associations with individuals. This is not always to the entity, neither will it be found to be compatible. For there will be oft, as has been in the experience, those individuals that mentally or materially the entity likes and likes the associations, yet there are resentments.

Then study those influences. And know when such arise in the experience that warnings are ahead, and govern the associations and the activities accordingly.

When there is felt that glow of orange, and the violet hues with the orange, know that these bespeak of sentimentality in the experience and are not always good; yet these in their proper relationships should be a portion of the experiences . . . in which one may know what such vibrations and such colors mean—that the individuals may be trusted.

When these reach those stages as to where there is felt the lighter red, and those that turn to shades of green with the influences that make for shadings into white, then these trust, these hold to; for such individuals, such associations, may bring in the experience of the entity that which will make for spiritual enlightenment, a mental understanding, and the influences that would bring helpful influences in every experience.

Hence the opal that is called the change, with the moonstone, should be stones about the body (or entity) oft. Wear the fire opal as a locket about the neck. This would be well. Not upon

159

the hands nor upon the wrists, but about the neck.

Wear the others, as of the pearl with moonstone or the like, as rings or amulet or anklets; but never those upon the neck or on the ears—rather upon the extremities; for they will make for the bringing out—in the experiences of those the entity meets—of those very colors and vibrations that have been indicated to which the entity is so sensitive . . .

These then may be summed up as put in another manner: To thine own self be true and thou wilt not be false to anyone . . .

For being a "sensitive" and capable of the interpretations of the emotions of others is not easy, yet it must not be abused; else there may come those experiences in which there may arise many misunderstandings—and gossip is never kind! . . .

Know that that which has not its foundation in spiritual way *must* eventually fade . . .

It would be impossible for the entity to go even among a group of a thousand and not all be conscious that the entity had entered. Why?

As the colors, as the vibrations are a portion of the entity, they also radiate from the entity. Hence, many, many, *many* are influenced by the entity . . .

Hence of that one to whom much has been given is much expected.

Hold fast to that which is good. For the way is before thee, and many look to thee—even as in all thine experiences in the earth—for directions.   1406-1

From the foregoing it is evident that low, leaden or dark red vibrations indicate resentment, which may prove dangerous. Orange ones, with or without violet, show sentimentality. Although this is not always desirable, it brings assurance that the person can be trusted. Vibrations of lighter red and green shading into white come from persons who should not only be trusted but also be held close for they may bring with them spiritual enlightenment, mental understanding and helpfulness.

To another person who was developing sensitivity the meaning of the colors she saw in meditation was made clear. They were indications of her own spiritual advancement. Green signifies healing; blue, trust; purple, strength; white, mercy.

Q-6. What is the meaning of the white lightning I have seen?
A-6. That awakening that is coming. More and more as the white light comes to thee, more and more will there be the awakening. For as the lights are in the colors: In the green, healing; in the blue, trust; in the purple, strength; in the white, the light of the throne of mercy itself. Ye may never see these save ye have withheld judgment or shown mercy.   987-4

All of us may not have the benefit of a psychic's perception of the colors surrounding us nor that of personal perception. We are not, therefore, in a position to proceed with personal color application. For such persons, however, there is additional matter in the readings. Individuals were advised as to the color of the material objects to be kept around them. This would help to influence them and, consequently, their auras. By reflecting on which of these references best apply to us, we may be guided into understanding of our own development as indicated by color. Then by utilizing specific suggestions we may help ourselves.

Significance of various colors is noted in the following reading excerpts.

The Significance of Various Colors

Blue

The following excerpts touch on some aspects of the effects of blue.

You will rarely find individuals being intolerant with others with something intrinsically carved being worn; or never very, very mad with blue being worn . . .   578-2

The blue and white giving then the pure, the true self in that prayer and supplication . . .   136-26

Let the raiment be something of blue, *ever,* upon the flesh of the body, whether in the waking or in the sleeping—and especially in the sleeping hours, for it will bring the influences as the music that quiets, through the vibrations that are set off by such . . . as also will the pigments of blue to the body bring the air, the fragrance of love, mercy, truth and justice that is within self.   694-2

Q-10. I desire to have an air of refinement and complete contentment, a place free of all confusion and hurry, a shop where patrons may come and feel completely at ease. What colorings and furnishings will give the best vibrations to others and to myself?

A-10. Light blue and gold. These would make for the *body,* and for that type of policy that would be a part of the entity's experience, the better vibrations . . . For you will find that all of these will change, as there is the better comprehending of the various problems that are to be met in such an undertaking.   2448-3

Again we see *blue* as the color about the entity, or that worn next the body should ever be a portion of the dress. Not that as

161

is of the mode (mauve), but rather that which stood in the Roman experience not for that flaunted in strength but as of power, of a might; yet tempered with mercy and justice. 729-1

Q-12. To what color or colors do I vibrate?
A-12. Blue. And when wearing blue you won't get mad! And make much of these in the underthings, too, close to the body. 594-1

Q-43. What is the best color for health room walls?
A-43. Between green and blue. 165-17

. . . those influences of white and blue, those forces as of truth, love, brotherhood of man and Fatherhood of God . . . 1151-29

Purple and Gold
Purple and gold represent the highest.

Q-6. What would be a good symbol in the form of colors, of our ideal?
A-6. These . . . are *many*—in the *various* phases of expression. Those of purple and of gold present the highest of that as attained in color vibration. 2087-3

Individual Response

On the whole, individuals respond to color on a personal basis. Sometimes the response comes because of associations in past lives.

Q-13. What are my best colors, or does it really make any difference?
A-13. Each body, each activity, each soul-entity vibrates better to this, that or the other color. As with this, certain colors of green and blue are those to which the body vibrates the better.
Q-15. Are we supposed to spiritualize all colors?
A-15. Colors are naturally the spiritualization of tone or sound; they are the natural spiritualizations of same. 288-38

The entity came from the land of Saad or . . . the Indian land. Thus we find that dress, certain colors and tones have much of a "feel" in the experience of the entity. And if the entity will wear white, mauve and shades of purple, it will be as a helpful vibration to the entity. For what is builded from any experience in the earth is as a habit in the present, having that same character of influence upon an individual's ability towards things and conditions; not having power within themselves, but as that which has been builded by the entity. 3395-2

... we will find for the entity, that colors influence the entity a great deal more even than musical forces in its tone—or color in music.

Drabs, or certain greens, have an effect that is almost that to bring *illness* in the physical body; while the purples or violets, or shades of tan, bring an exultant influence that would make for the bringing of building influences in the entity.   428-4

Q-7. What are my colors?
A-7. Those that are of soft tints—blue, green and shades that are delicate. These bring the harmonious things. Or those of great contrast. For the entity to look, if it wants to be overglamorous, black and gold! If it wants to succeed in intriguing others, blue or green! If it wants to appear as it really is within itself, the delicate tints or shades.   2753-2

Q-6. What colors . . . are best for me?
A-6. . . . The colors—mauve and violet. These are the better for the body—they are healing to the body.   3374-1

Keep colors blue and mauve about the entity ever. *Never* anything very red, nor anything that is very pink or pinkish; but blue, pearl, mauve—these very close about the entity.
1775-1

Insist that the body [female, 14 years old] wear blue, gold and yellow close to the body; not by force but because of their varying effect and their beneficial effect.   3806-1

Do not lay aside the rosary! Have about the entity stones that are red; as the bloodstone, the ruby, or everything of that nature—in stone but *not* in hanging or draperies.   1616-1

. . . the entity responds to coral red and . . . arbutus flowers should be about the entity . . . but these are only influences.
963-1

Hence red, as the ruby—or the onyx, or the chalcedony, that may be the color as stones or things of the nature should be about the entity in its closer activity.   1273-1

. . . Wear coral; rose color—not red, not white but rose coral.
2154-1

Q-10. To what colors does the body vibrate?
A-10. For good to those of blue. For bad to those of purple and red.   1131-1

Never wear colors of red, or any pertaining to same. Always wear gray, green, delicate shades—these will not only create a

163

better reaction to thy temperament, but [also] will give a greater assurance in self and from those ye meet day by day.
2522-1

Violet of all shades or tone or vibrations should be kept about the individual for it is of the higher rays that this body is capable of shedding or giving to others. 4286-1

Certain characters of stones and colors are well to have about the entity. Especially plaids, mauves, and certain colors or shades of purple are well; for they bring those vibrations that become in accordance with what may be said to be both the mental and the physical aura of the body—which is in the purple, or the *developments* within the experience of the entity. And these bring the vibrations that are not clashing, or activities that are not of the nature of detrimental influences or forces in the experience. 1532-1

Purple indicates the royalty, white the purity, green the helpfulness or healing forces . . . the purple—the loyalty, the royalty to which the entity has attained, and may attain . . . the white is that of the purity of purpose in the entity being sought . . . 1223-4

As to colors—black and gold should be much about the entity. Not that these natures *are* as the background, but the urges innately for keeping self purged, and keeping the mental attitude as well as the purposes and desires in the way in which these may be kept in the forefront the greater application of the purposes of an individual making material manifestation. 1849-2

A beautiful record—all white, with knowledge . . . 1837-1

Suggestions for colors to be used in the proposed marketing of Ipsab (a substance recommended for gum massage):

Q-7. What color scheme would you suggest for cartons, labels and advertising?
A-7. Considering those that are interested here, let's take it from their own color scheme. Do not use these: yellow, nor black, nor red.
The blue package with the white lettering would, then, make a preferable type . . .
Yellow partakes of those things that are contagious.
Red, of those things warned of or against . . . Black, that which is of death itself. 1800-20

164

Importance of Color

From the foregoing references it is clear that response to color is a personal matter, the effects of which are of real consequence. Their importance is stressed in the following philosophical and comprehensive conclusion.

And it may be found in the experience of the entity, as from those activities in the experience before this, that sounds, music and colors may have much to do with creating the proper vibrations about individuals that are mentally unbalanced, physically deficient or ill in body and mind; and may be used as helpful experiences. Just as the entity has found and may find more and more . . . that [in] the manner of conversation to individuals in making mechanical or mental suggestions for their physical welfare, there is as much in the tone and the gentleness of manner as in the command itself.   1334-1

Colors of Cities

Some general considerations as to color are of more than passing interest.
Response of individuals to different cities may be influenced by color vibration.

And each city has its own color.   1456-1

Colors Associated with Glandular Centers

Particular colors are associated with the seven major glandular centers, though they may have varied meanings for different individuals.

Q-1. Please discuss more fully the relation of colors to the seven major glandular centers. Do the colors vary for each center with different individuals, or may definite colors be associated with each center?
A-1. Both. For to each—remember, to study each of these in the light not only of what has just been given but that as is a practical experience in the material world—as is known, vibration is the essence or the basis of color. As color and vibration then become to the consciousness along the various centers in an individual's experience in meditation made aware, they come to mean definite experiences. Just as anger is red, or as something depressing is blue; yet in their shades, their tones, their activities, to each they begin with the use of same in the experience to mean those various stages. For instance, while red is anger, rosy to most souls means delight and joy—yet to others, as they are formed in their

165

transmission from center to center, come to mean or to express what *manner* of joy; whether that as would arise from a material, a mental or a spiritual experience. Just as may be seen in the common interpretation of white, but with all manner of rays from same begins or comes to mean that above the aura of all in its vibration from the body and from the activity of the mental experience when the various centers are vibrating to color.

Q-2. If so, give color for: (1) Gonads (2) Lyden (3) Solar Plexus (4) Thymus (5) Thyroid (6) Pineal (7) Pituitary.

A-2. These come from the leaden, going on through to the highest—to that as is the halo. To each they become the various forces as active throughout, and will go in the regular order of the prism.   281-30

From these answers we learn that the various centers vibrate to the colors of the prism in this order: gonads, red; lyden, orange; solar plexus, yellow; thymus, green; thyroid, blue; pineal, indigo; pituitary, violet. The leaden shades or tones are the lowest vibrations of each color. Those in the halo are the highest. As the individual develops spiritually, the colors of his aura change from leaden to those of the halo. The various shades come to represent different activities to different persons.

Advice to an artist on the execution of aura charts ties in the meaning of colors with other symbology.

By color certain activities are also symbolized—for instance, black indicates the whole combination of all. For, to material interpretation, white is the absence of color, black is the combination of them all.

The dark blue indicates awakening; purple, healing; white, purity; gold, attaining. All of these and their varied shades indicate the activity; this applying to the stars as well as to the sun or moon.

The sun indicates strength and life, while the moon indicates change—and in one direction indicating the singleness of that activity through an individual experience—the variations being indicated by the variations in the color.

Star—the white, purity; the five-pointed, the whole senses of man indicated as attained to activity—the colors showing the variation; the forms of six, seven or eight pointed indicating the attainments—as do the seven stars in a figure indicate the attaining to the seven particular centers of the body. 5746-1

Color as a Tool

From foregoing references it is evident that the colors of a person's clothing, gems, household furnishings and other equipment are very important. These items should be chosen with great care and an awareness of the effect their colors may have on the individual. Two persons were advised how to help others by choice of color.

. . . take note: In any form, which will be seen from the sojourns in the earth, which has to do with color, as in decoration, as in wall-paper designing, as in wallboard designing, might the entity bring a great deal of joy, or harmony into the experience of those with whom he might work . . .

The auras as compared to the stones these would work in 99 percent of the conditions where these are considered as those things that work with, not against, the colors seen in the auras . . .   5294-1

. . . the entity then [in Egyptian period of Ra Ta] in the household of that king and with the abilities and thought of adding *color* in body, in the paintings of the house, in the pigments that were gathered from the various silts as came from the mountains in the waters, as well as those gathered from the fishes in the sea, did . . . combine these in making many of the colors in that period; and *renowned* in this respect was the name, for the entity was looked upon rather as one with *supernatural* powers in these directions, and in the abilities to gather these together . . . In the present those abilities to *match* colors, to match those things that are necessary for pigment building in the body, for the adding of color in the dress, for the shadings of the colors, in the care for, the attending to those little things of the body that makes same attractive both to self and others; bringing a satisfaction for same . . .   2887-1

Color as a Therapeutic Measure

Color as a therapeutic measure instead of medicine was suggested for one person.

Colors will also find an influence in the entity's activities, especially those of not too severe, but the violet, ultraviolet, shades of green, of mode [mauve?], and pink; though the others may make for a rigor oft in the entity, the delicate shades—or those as may be termed the spiritual—will influence the entity. When illness or the like were to come about, soft music and the lighter shades or tones will quiet where medicine would fail.
773-1

Another person was told that because of response to color, she should not take medicine.

Now, to meet the needs of these conditions, there is the necessity of the body's bringing the closer coordination between the sympathetic, cerebrospinal, and sensory nerve system, and supplying in the building of the forces in the cellular building portions of system that necessary for the stabilizing of the reactory forces between the nerve systems of the body and the purely physical functioning; for the body is high strung ... Brilliant of mind, and brain forces respond to the reaction of sensation of vibration of those forces that build in the system—for ... the body mentally—and the body in its nerve reaction—would respond as quickly to color forces as it would to medicinal properties; so medicine within the system would be destructive, destroying that reaction that is necessary for coordination. But the *vibration* as is *necessary* to coordinate these conditions should be applied, which would be found in using the Radio-active Appliance, with the negative center applied to the umbilicus—and through that anode take those properties ... [Treatment advised.] 4501-1

Use of a combination of color and music was advised in the case of an individual who was no longer normal.

Keep close about the body the colors of purple and lavender, and all things bright; music that is of harmony—as of the Spring Song, the Blue Danube and that character of music, with either the stringed instruments or the organ. These are the vibrations that will set again near normalcy ... mentally and physically, if these influences will be consistently kept about this body.   2712-1

Another person was apprised of an allergy to certain colors.

In the sympathetics we find the body rather supersensitive to certain, or to *various* activities in self, in others, in the relationships to others. These have their effect in a general manner, and more specifically in that of *colors,* do they affect the body, even as *pollen* does many another.   5511-1

Active reflexes to color, stemming from the sympathetic nervous system are somewhat psychopathic in nature.

... the body *sympathetically* is reflexly active to colors, surroundings and conditions, but these are more of a psychopathic nature, through the activity of the sympathetic system.   5468-1

Treatment with Color Through Light

Treatment with pure color was suggested for a number of ill persons. This was to be applied by means of light.

Often the reading called for the application of one color only. It appears that such a specialization was in order for persons with severe difficulties. Sometimes ultraviolet was to be used, sometimes ultraviolet with a green glass interposed between it and the body, sometimes infrared with the same arrangement. The green glass replaced those healing influences taken out of the infrared. Doubtless the same healing forces reinforced the ultraviolet.

Very particular directions were given as to the distance the light should be kept from the person being treated and the length of time the treatment should be carried out. A potent force was being harnessed, and care must be taken against overuse.

The following excerpts serve to bring out these points.

Ordinarily, because of improper application as for diet and such—this condition becomes of such a nature as to be . . . malignant . . . This need not necessarily be true here—if there is the application of that which through radiation, or absorption and radiation, will keep the area tending towards an alkalinity; and then the adding of those vibrations through the radiation from the ultraviolet, with the projection of the green glass between it and the body.

To be sure, these radiations by some are termed to be of such refractory that the value of electrical forces is eliminated. But those coming to such conclusions do not consider that all vibration, color, and color with radiation—that is the aid here—is to set the vibrations in the body for body-forces; and this body is in the developing stage [1½ years] . . . physical, mental and spiritual. This vibration of the ultraviolet is as a "seeking out" in the body. In bodies of a varied vibration, where there are such conditions as here, the ultraviolet without the green light might be helpful. But in most instances where there is needed a change in vibration, the projection of a green light is preferable—because green is the healing vibration. Here, in the character or nature of disturbance where there is the formation of that which is [of] any malignant nature, the green light will be more effective than even that of a more penetrating nature, or even the x-ray—that destroys tissue, but not being enabled to eliminate that destroyed, tends to come back upon itself after certain radiations. Some forms of such might be aided if radium with its extra vibrations were added to that of the destructive nature.

But do not administer here other than the ultraviolet—the mercury light, with the green glass projected between the body and the light. Have the light at least thirty-seven to thirty-eight inches from the body, and the green glass about fourteen inches from the body. Use for only a minute and a half, about twice each week.   3370-1

... tissue in lung, in breast ... of the malignant nature ...

[Suggestions for treatment follow, including taking a certain amount of animated ash twice a day. Then—]

Five minutes after the ash has been taken, apply the ultraviolet light for one-and-a-half to two minutes, at least thirty-eight to forty inches from the body, over the lower cervical and upper dorsal area. Preferably use the quartz light, or mercury quartz light. This is the heavier of such machines.

Should this redden the body too much, then we would use the green light, or glass *between* the body and the ultraviolet, which will prevent so much irritation to the superficial circulation and such strong light—taken twice each day for this period. Or the light may be moved some more distance from the body.

The light taken after the ash will cause the action of the ash of the carbon to clarify through the releasing of oxygen in the blood stream, by being centralized in the portions of the lungs thus affected, and in the tissue adjacent to same.

[Other suggestions follow.]   511-1

The manipulations and the electrical vibrations, which may be given in *any* low form, whether the violet ray, the red ray, or the ultraviolet ray—but a very *low* form of same.   140-27

Q-1. *What light should be used? [To be applied to cerebrospinal system, over a given area.]*

A-1. Any penetrating light. That of the dry heat, or that that acts the quickest with the blood stream, see? for ... this is the effect of light—of whatever nature that may be applied to a body: All bacilli or all germs are afraid, as it were, of light—or light is destructive to all. Some ... accumulate in heat that is not penetrating. Hence the variation in the quartz light, the ultraviolet light, the blue light, the red light—each one taking out that that filters through the system. Hence for this, that one most penetrating without being destructive to the tissue proper.   140-21

During those rest periods after the fume bath and massage, do rest for at least fifteen minutes under the ultraviolet light. But *do* have always the green light projected between the ultraviolet and the body. The ultraviolet should be at least sixty inches from the body, and only the mercury light. The green light should be eight by ten, or ten by twelve, and about fourteen to eighteen inches from the body. These are healing influences of that taken out of the infra ray, see?   3008-1

Begin with the use of the ultraviolet ray (only the mercury light, not the carbon light). But do use the green glass between the light and the body. Give this about every other day, until we get some reaction. Have the ultraviolet at least forty-eight inches (48″) from the body, and the green glass (8x10 or 10x12)

170

at least fourteen inches (14″) from the body. This changes the therapeutic reaction of the radiation produced in body activity, by the color. This should be applied every other day for about twenty minutes . . . if used at these ranges, and with the green glass.

Following this give the body not a stimulating osteopathic adjustment, but a relaxing treatment.   3045-1

Q-3. Am I using the infrared and the ultraviolet correctly and at the proper distance from the body? I am applying these to the back only, or shall I apply them to the front of the body also?

A-3. These are very well, and very well in distance as to all of the applications. Better not to be applied to the front of the body—unless the infrared over the breast bone or plate, see?
1758-2

The following excerpt suggests the use of a total of two colors, to be used alternately on different days.

. . . unbalancing . . . in the blood supply . . . First we would take the animated or carbon ash . . . with the application of the rays; which would preferably be the infrared, rather than the ultraviolet, in the beginning. While the dosage would be taken once each day, the red rays should be applied only three times each week—as Mondays, Wednesdays, Fridays. These . . . altered; that is, the application of the ray altered—that the prism of the *green* light in the red light, or *between* the red light and the body, be used, that there may be a diffusion of those vibrations as would be set up in the system *by* the alteration in the color vibration as it affects the system. This . . . from the beginning, will make for a different effect in the circulation, especially in the external or the capillary and skin disorder will be improved.   5530-1

Other readings advised the application of several colors. It seems these were to be used for persons whose difficulties were not so severe. However, the need for precautions as to the distance between the body and the light and as to the length of time of exposure was stressed here, too. Note that only one color was to be given per day.

And then these, with the lights—those that are colored, or varied so that the effects of these may be through the breaking of the waves of the light as affect the body by exposure, would prove the more beneficial . . .

Each day we would use the light rays—once the infrared. Break this, the infrared, with a green light—this between the infrared and the body.

The next day use the ultraviolet. This also should be broken with the green light.

When using the sun light, or clear light, break with the blue light. This would be projected, of course, to that area between the body and the light source, or light itself.   1758-1

Such vital energy may be aided ... by *varying* the character of the lights for the body. The ultraviolet changed to the infrared, as well as the green and blue. Cobalt blue, and Nile green. Changing these through the prism reflection.   302-9

These [better conditions] may be *best* had by the applications, as have been taken, as are being taken at times, of the massage, of those reactions to the exterior portion—but adding *with* same those of the changeable lights. The ultraviolet, the infrared, those of the Nile green, those of the orange, and so on—in their various orders—dependent upon that condition, whether necessary for the reaction in the liver—as to an excretory or as a secretive functioning, or as to be made positive in its action or to be made negative in its action ...

Q-8. *What causes the burning sensation from chest through throat?*

A-8. This ... is that attempt of the system to adjust itself to that condition existent in spleen, and a portion of the liver at times. The application of the vibrations in the varied lights ... will *equalize* the circulation, relieving this condition in the central nerve system. See that these are applied in the order named. Ultraviolet for the superficial portion of the system. Infrared the second day, or third day—or one may be taken one week, one another. The infrared that [for] the central system, through the soft tissue of bone, wherein accumulation of red blood cells form an active influence with the system. Of the green, that the actuation of the sympathetic with the cerebrospinal nervous system may be generated in their normal order. Of those of the orange, that there may be the separation in the system of those of white and red blood, or of the lymphatics *with* the *emunctory* reaction in the capillary.
                                5439-1

Then, following these conditions, we would give those properties as would nearer centralize the location of distress by the application of those of the varied colored lights in the system, or on the system, that the activity *in* the system would bring better influences in the blood supply; using those as we would find in *this* as the relief: this as the dose ... [Directions follow.] ... Then apply that of the ultraviolet ray, with the infrared, following—and with the green following same. This will produce absorption, will resuscitation take place and the natural drainage from the system, and in ten to fifteen days we would change these applications, will the body respond ...

Q-2. *How often should the lights be used, and for how long?*

A-2. Once each day, beginning with not over two minutes, at least forty inches from the body.

Q-3. Two minutes for each light, or two minutes including all?

A-3. Two minutes for each light. One one day, one the next day, to be sure . . .

Q-5. What is the original cause of the present condition?

A-5. A character of anemia in the system, with a depression in the intestinal system.   5524-1

The Color in Food

The ingestion of food carrying certain color vibrations was touched on in the readings. B-1 can be found in "all foods . . . naturally yellow." (257-236)

The B-1 should be rich in the foods which are taken. We would find this from all foods which are yellow in color, not as greens that would turn yellow, but as the yellow variety of squash, carrots, wax beans, peaches, all these are well.
                                                                      5319-1

. . . do take all those foods, whether in breads or cereals, that are reinforced especially with Vitamin B-1 and iron; these in whatever form that appeals to the body, and in whatever form desired, whether in cooked cereals or the dry preparations, with fruits of any or all characters, but especially those that are yellow in their color. Hence at least three times a week there should be the grated raw carrots . . . also yellow peaches, also squash and such vegetables and fruits.   2800-1

Q-14. In what form should B-1 tablets or capsules be taken?
A-14. If the body does not desire to take them in the food values, take the tablets or capsules! But they are better assimilated with the system if taken in the food values. No synthetic principle is as good as the real thing! It may be used as a substitute, but is a substitute ever as good as the best which nature provides! These vitamins may best be taken through the vegetable forces that are yellow in color; as carrots, squash, yellow corn and yellow corn meal; peaches; oats and the like. If the desire is to supplement these with the tablets, then do so—but it is not the best!   257-224

From a later reading for the same person:

Q-13. Should B-1 be taken at the same time?
A-13. This depends upon whether the foods taken carry sufficient quantity of B-1. B-1 is a vitamin not stored in body, but it is necessary that there be the consumption of such each

day. While A, C, D and G at times attempt to take the place of same, the B-1 activity is much better taken in foods than in the segregated pellets or capsules. When it is impractical for obtaining the foods with sufficient quantities for the daily needs, very well to take B-1. But to overstress same may at times cause the reaction of the *very* distress that is attempting to be aided!

All foods yellow in their nature, that are naturally yellow, carry B-1. Re-enforced flour, and especially whole wheat, corn flakes, most cereals—if re-enforced with same. So, a normal helping of such each day is about a *fifth* of that necessary. Also it is found in orange juice, citrus fruit juices, the juice and the pulp of grapefruit and the like, and in *all* cereals, and in bread; and especially the *green* leaves of lettuce—not so much in the beautiful white pieces. The green pieces are usually thrown away, and the hearts of lettuce kept that aren't worth very much as food for individuals. Hence lettuce of the leafy variety is really better for the body, carrying the greater source of the nicotinic acid.

Q-14. Yellow peaches in the can?

A-14. All good. Yellow corn meal, squash and every food that is naturally yellow in color. Carrots, raw and cooked—all of these.   257-236

The excerpts above make it abundantly clear that "supplements" (in tablet, capsule or whatever form) cannot replace food values completely.

It is possible that in certain circumstances red and a particular kind of yellow might prove poisonous to a body because of a problem of the lymphatic circulation. [45] was advised that continued increase in the quantity of white blood corpuscles might adversely affect the red blood supply since the white blood corpuscles might attack the hemoglobin. Apparently the ingestion of foods that were red or a special type of yellow could stimulate the production of these white blood corpuscles. This person was to be strengthened by being given blood internally.

Much of the condition comes from the throat and teeth, as *well* as the character of the *lymphatic* circulation—or poison absorbing for the body would find that even colors, as *well* as certain characters of foods, become immediately poison in the system . . .

[Suggestions for specific treatment follow.]

. . . the continued increase in the numbers in the white blood may become such as to attack or *destroy* those portions *in* the hemoglobin as are *necessary* for the red blood supply. Hence the conditions *must* be met by *alleviating* that *causing* pus, and *giving* strength *by* assimilation with *blood—internally* taken, we would give it—that the *digestive* forces may alter in the assimilation; for we find the *capillary,* the *lymph, absorb* certain characters—that is, reds to the body [are] poison— certain characters of yellow [are] poison; just as certain plants that the body would contact would be poison to system, see?

45-3

A Plan for an Aurascope

This discussion of color would be incomplete without mention of the aurascope dwelt on at length in the Edgar Cayce readings.

It is apparent that a knowledge of one's aura could be of real use. On the basis of it a person could plan color therapy in areas that needed it, could augment helpful influences and try to avoid harmful ones. A host of possibilities opens up.

[440] felt this so strongly that he asked for help in making an aurascope, which would detect the aura. There is no record filed with the readings at the present time indicating that this project was ever completed. As with the metallurgy directions, these aurascope directions could be used perhaps as a basis for a firm invention. Important portions of the discussion on the aurascope, therefore, follow.

To gain the proper aura from a mechanical manner, prepare an aurascope like this:

Make prisms, or combined prisms—see? Jena* glass for the white one, lapis for the blue one, the blood ruby for the red one, the yellow lapis for the yellow one. Combine these on a spindle, so that each may be turned through an opening that is directed towards a body. With the second turn there will come into vision, for anyone of any psychic ability, the direct aura— physical *and* spiritual—for anyone at whom it is pointed.

In making the diagnosis, it would require the nude body; and those portions of the body affected will show the various tints or forms of depressions, ranging from all colors that are negative in their action to life—which are leaden and various shades of purple, and the orange that turns towards red. These prisms would be set. They would be of these dimensions: From a quarter inch ($\frac{1}{4}''$) on the thin edge to a three-quarter ($\frac{3}{4}''$) on the heavy edge. An inch (1″) wide and two inches (2″) long. Necessarily two sets would be prepared, so that there may be the vision from both eyes—for in few people is vision exactly the same in both eyes; but these would be so set that they would be turned on an axis, an inch to two inches (1″ to 2″) apart, see? so they would turn around, see?

*[*Encyclopedia Britannica* ᶜ 1957: JENA, a university town of Germany . . . seat of the famous Zeiss firm of optical instrument makers]

Q-24. Would the axis be through the center?

A-24. The axis would be that the prisms would be set in a holder on the axis. Of course, do not attempt to bore through the prisms themselves—but these are set in holders, see, in something like the leaves of a willowing [winnowing?] fan.

Q-25. What is the distance from the eyes to the prisms?

A-25. Nine inches (9″).

Q-26. Are any other lenses necessary?

A-26. Naturally the plain glass in the end of the scope, and turned—you see—or set on axis so that the vision comes as one; as when looking through the scope that makes for the projection of flat objects as to give them the perspective value to the whole, see?   440-3

Q-1. First, the aurascope—diagram in [440]'s hand.

A-1. As suggested, the theory of the mechanical device is to determine not only the aura of individuals but to use same in the diagnoses of disorders in various portions of the body.

As is known, the body in action—or a live body—emanates from same the vibrations to which it as a body is vibrating, both physical and spiritual. Just as there is an aura when a string of a musical instrument is vibrated—the tone is produced by the vibration. In the body the tone is given off rather in the higher vibration, or the color. Hence this is a condition that exists with each physical body. In the material things we find that to tone, or to find a tone or the color to the eye, only three colors are necessary to make, for the perfecting of the various shades or tones that may be had in *any* vibration. In any print in nature itself we find these are existent. Hence these set with the absence of color, or with the crystal, in their rotation so that they are turned (by the hand, preferably), being on the same spindle or same manner so that when one turns the other turns also. With these changings of the color there soon sets those vibrations by the beholder, in its active force of beholding or discerning the variations, so that there is set in a practical manner the aura *about* the body. To be sure, as indicated, it will necessitate the developing of the psychic forces. Not that it is not positive, but these may be discerned the more readily by an optometrist—or one that looks for the visions, or one that gets tone or color as an artiste, or one that mixes colors. These may the more easily or more readily find or get the response from such a mechanical instrument for determining the emanations in colors from a living organism.

Ready for questions.

Q-1. Are sides of crystal cut perpendicular to XX axis or perpendicular to a face of crystal?

A-1. To a face of crystal, though the diagram as seen here is not drawn properly at all, see? You have turned the face so that this would necessitate extra mechanical—and you do not get the value of the flat surface of the crystal or the active force of

176

the colors that are emanated through the eyes in this position! Rather would they be turned crosswise, so that the longer side or portion is as the slit in the eye—or as the vision perceives same, see?

Q-2. Does the eye see first through the side at right angle?

A-2. Eye sees through the side, as the *prism* angle, see?

Q-3. I do not see.

A-3. Through the *prism* angle; that is, either the heavy side or the thin side is encased in a holder that brings into view, see, the full side of the prism glass. See?

Q-4. The body does not understand.

A-4. We have the glass, the prism, see? It is set in a holder, in the rotation or in the manner that has been designated, see? the width, see, the length, see? This set then in the holder, in the way as a willowing [winnowing?] fan—as given, see? This, then, on an axis, see—the leaves, you see. These turn as leaves to those portions where the vision or the scope itself of the vision strikes the *side*—as the angle side, see, or prism side of the color.

Q-5. Do these prisms rotate toward the eye?

A-5. Toward the eye.

Q-6. What is the rate of speed?

A-6. This will depend upon the individual, as given. See, there will be periods, as the rotation is carried on, when *no* vision of the color is seen, see? So that the alternate changes of the various colors, as given, makes for the impressions to the optics that reflect back that seen through the vision as set before same.

Q-7. Is the crystal fixed permanently in its fan-shaped holder?

A-7. Fixed permanently, just so that when it comes to that portion of the scope or in the vision it stands at the angle as indicated.

Q-8. What angle should the X Sub-C axis take with the X Sub-S axis?

A-8. As indicated, these would be preferably set by experimentation; for it will be found that minor changes may be necessary, but these are set so that the surface (flat, see) is direct in line for the vision in its observation of the person, individual or body in front of same.

Q-9. Can you give a substitute for the red blood ruby?

A-9. This is the *color!*

Q-10. It can be made of glass?

A-10. It can be made of glass. *All* should be glass, so that the same character of vision—or altered by the color—is met by the vision of the beholder.

Q-11. Would this instrument enable photography of the aura?

A-11. Enable photography with colored photography, but it would have to be attached to both characters of machines, see?

Q-12. Will you give a description of the arrangement of the lenses in the end of the scope?

A-12. These are only glass, and set or so arranged that they will meet the needs of the beholder, see? So that they focus as *one* vision and not as looking with just one eye; for, as indicated, each individual's two eyes are not *exactly* set the same. Some have astigmatism, some have *more* astigmatism than others, some have the retinae in its rotary astigmatism and others have no change necessary. Hence these in the end will necessarily have to be set so they may be altered somewhat, but will only require very little change—but set at the angle so that the focus makes for the vision seen as single and not double.

Q-13. What is the shape of these lenses?

A-13. Well, you would make them rather oblong—to fit rather the scope or the character of the scope that is set for the vision, see?

Q-14. Can you give the correct division between the Y axis as shown on Figure 3?

A-14. As set, the figures here are all wrong! But the distance from the axis or from the vision through the color glass (or clear, depending upon how far it is turned, see) to the plain glass would be six to nine inches.   440-6

Q-18. You mentioned obtaining the blue color of the crystal for the aurascope from this stone [lapis]. There are many shades of blue present.

A-18. Use that shade which will come as near being that through which the light may pass in the same manner as it does through the yellow and the red. Of course, the white or the crystal will be that change where, with the rotation of the aurascope prisms, that place where there will be the beginnings of the colors coming into vision as it is slowly turned. Hence to have too deep or too pale a blue (for the blue will be opposite the crystal)—the others then, of course, opposite each other—the yellow, the red. So that in their rotation this becomes as a harmonious effect of *all* color, as they are formed to the retinae or vision of individuals in the order as they will come from this natural setting.   440-12

Sound

Sound is the third of the manifestations of solar force to be taken up in this book. It is of a lesser dynamic degree of vibration than color. It is, however, a powerful influence, and acquaintance with its effects is important for utilizing it thoroughly.

Music of the Spheres

How completely sound surrounds us can be apprehended by considering "the music of the spheres." Most people do not consciously hear this mighty rhythm, composed of the vibrations of natural objects. However, since the spiritually developed being does, every one of us may anticipate the possession of such a sensitivity. That the music of the spheres affects us is a conclusion deduced from the injunction of the readings to draw closer to nature and share in this pulse of life.

These [abilities] are limited only by what spirit of creative energy the entity entertains. For thy body is indeed the temple of the living God . . . Embrace Him, while ye may, in music, in art. Faint not because of oppositions, but do keep the music of the spheres, the light of the stars, the softness of the moonlight upon the water as upon the trees. For nature in its song, as the birds, as the bees make music to their Creator, contributed to man.   5265-1

This [experience] also gives the abilities for music, of a nature that arises from the activities of nature, of individuals, of things, as they sing or as they are in harmony with that office performed.
Think, for a moment, of the music of the waves upon the shore, of the morning as it breaks with the music of nature, of the night as it falls with the hum of the insect, of all the kingdoms as they unite in their song of appreciation to an all-creative influence that gives nature consciousness or awareness of its being itself. And harmonize that in thine own appreciation, as to bring music akin to the song of the spheres.
                                                                    2581-2

Q-7. Through what specific school and course would I obtain a closer insight into the study of the forces or music of the spheres?
A-7. The lower electrical vibrations to life!   933-2

. . . the influences as seen in that of Mercury, has brought for the entity most of the music, and especially the symphony—or the chords of the spheres; for, to the entity, the beautiful evening, or the moon and the planetary relationships, are ever a wonder—yet mean more to the entity than to most. The beauty of nature in its activity, the clouds, the lightning, the thunder, all of the voices of nature, answer and find within the entity those of a stabling [stabilizing] influence that is oft hard to be understood by many who have not experienced, nor found favor in the grace of that whom the entity serves.
                                                                    1716-1

In the present abilities we find the latent and manifested urge for the love of outdoors, of nature—as in voice, as in sound; whether the waves upon the seashore, the wind in the pines, the song of the birds, or the music as of nature and the spheres combined.   2450-1

Then enter into meditation, in the wee hours of the morning, when the world at large is quiet—when the music of the spheres and the morning stars sing for the glory of the coming day . . .   440-4

The entity then in the name Ah-Hai. In the present experience we find while the music of the spheres and those of the mysterious nature are as that that finds expression most, that as impelled the call to worship in that period carrying much of that as sounds in the deeper notes, finds the better expression under the entity's activities.   933-1

The entity came for the purpose, then, of making more manifest in the experiences, in the lives, in the hearts of those that are weak and distressed and stumbling as in the dark, seeking the light, those beauties that manifest themselves in music as of the spheres, in the art as of the enlightenment that enraptures the soul into becoming one with that in nature, in love, in harmony, in grace, in hope, in faith, which lifts up the *inner* man to the more perfect at-oneness with Him who gave, "A new commandment I give, that ye love one another, even as I have loved you; forgive them, they know not what they do."
                                                          827-1

Thus may there again be the effect and the beauty of those things wrought during that period of activity, through the efforts of the entity in following those things in nature.

As there is the music of the spheres, there is indeed the music of the growing things in nature. There is then the music of nature itself! There is the music of the growth of the rose, of *every* plant that bears color, of every one that opens its blossom for the edification, for the sanctification even of the environs thereabout!

In the study and in the meditation of such, then, as it unfolds itself to the spiritual awareness of the influences that may bear upon man in the present, the entity may bring help to the many—individually oft; yea, to masses and to the groups of many natures, through help of the very nature that was given during that experience.

How, you ask then, may the entity so attune self?

By looking on the beauty of a sunset, of a rose, of a lily, or any of those things in nature, and—by the very nature of the mood that these create in self—arouse or bring forth those melodies upon the instruments of the day; the piano, the organ, the reed or even the stringed instruments; to express the nature of these as they express themselves in their unfoldment.

And gradually may the entity so enter into the accord with same as to in self *attune* self to that unfoldment, that beauty, that nature to which it adapts itself for the healing forces necessary for man's awakening to his relationships to the Creative Forces.   949-12

180

One that has been endowed with an understanding of a peoples known as the Indian, that may by grunts, incantations, or in the various forms of expression...convey that which is being sought of the relations of one to another, is not understood by one who has been endowed with an understanding of the other environs; as in France or in the U.S.A. Not understood, no; but when that language that bespeaks of faith, hope, kindness, love, is manifest it expresses, it conveys to the heart and soul of all a *universal* language; as does music, as does the beauty of a rose, as does the music of the spheres partake of that which is the closer to that relation as the soul, whether occupying this or that body, has with that Creative Force from which it emanated.

294-155

The song of the angels seems to be part of the music of the spheres.

For, as is oft expressed, the angels sing—and the music of the spheres, as in color and relationship—this becomes the means or manner that is universal in its activity upon the minds and souls of men.

1938-2

In music the entity finds *much* solace, much that bridges those distances—whether of the mental or of the spiritual forces. In same the attunement of self may be brought the nearest to the applications of the innate *forces* of self, and to the *entity* the strains of same—whether in that of the deep vibrations, of those that raise up and up—or those of the higher chords that bind—carry for the entity the *attunement* of self in the sphere or element, or *phase* of experience the entity seeks apace. Well were *this* developed to a more acuteness *in this present* experience, for the acumen of experience to the entity is gained *much* more in a manner that may become concrete ensamples of the attunement of a soul with the heavenly, or the happy, choir.

115-1

Before that we find that the entity was in the beginning, when the sons of God came together to announce to matter a way being opened for the souls of men, the souls of God's creation, to come again to the awareness of their error.

The entity then, as indicated from those experiences, was among those *announcing* same.

Hence as the music of the spheres, in the voice of nature itself, we find that expression; in the laughter of the entity, in the sound of its voice, in the look of its eye, in the movement of its body, in the patter of its feet; giving expression in a manner that brings to the minds and consciousness of those who seek to know God and God's ways with the children of men, a manifestation, an expression of same.

2156-2

The entity was among those that were of the hill country about the land of Bethlehem when there were the shepherds that heard the voices, the halleluiahs proclaiming to them the birth of their King, of their Savior.

The entity was aroused first by those very shouts of joy nigh unto the city or the town of Bethlehem; the entity then in the name Jocsice, though called Josie.

In the experience there came that great overshadowing desire within the entity to become attuned, as it were, to the heavenly song, the heavenly music, the vibrations as it were of the spheres when all nature proclaimed the joyous event into the experience of man!   1487-1

Then . . . the herald angels sang . . .

All were in awe as the brightness of His star appeared and shone, as the music of the spheres brought that joyful choir, *"Peace on earth! Good will to men of good faith."*   5749-15

And as there was followed the receding of His star, and the flight into Egypt through the devious ways and manners in which there came the news through word of mouth, yet in awe and quiet kept, it made for that in the experience of the entity—when it sits alone in the twilight, and there is almost again felt the music of the spheres, the singing of the morning stars, as the earth is quieted—there enters oft again that peace, that is only troubled by the cares of a workaday world.   1152-3

The music of the spheres continues on in Arcturus, Polaris and the outer sphere.

. . . as long as an entity is within the confines of that termed the earth's and the sons of the earth's solar system, the developments are within the sojourns of the entity from sphere to sphere; and when completed it begins—throughout the music of the spheres with Arcturus, Polaris, and through those sojourns in the outer sphere.   441-1

Man's Music and Its Uses

For those who do not hear this music of the spheres as yet, that made by man's musical instruments is important.

One of the references given under "Color" suggests that not only should purple and lavender be kept around a particular deranged person but also *harmonious music* of the type of "The Spring Song" and "The Blue Danube" should be used to restore her normalcy, mental and physical. (2712-1) Those suffering from nervous disorders, shell shock and weariness can also be helped by music.

In music should the entity excel, in the stringed instruments, harp or piano, and such music should be used for the applications in healing, or as part of the entity's endeavor to reclaim individual entities that are disturbed by nerve or shell shock or long weariness in the out-of-the-way places.

3908-1

The relation between music and harmony is repeatedly stressed.

Do learn music. It is part of the beauty of the spirit. For remember, music alone may span that space between the finite and the infinite. In the harmony of sound, the harmony of color, even the harmony of motion itself, its beauty is all akin to that expression of the soul-self in the harmony of the mind, if used properly in relationship to body. Not that music is to be made the greater portion of thy life, but let much of thy life be controlled by the same harmony that is in the best music, yea, and the worst also; for it, too, has its place. But cling to that which may be experienced by listening and watching a mother sing the lullaby of Brahms, and it will mean much throughout thy life. Catch something of the note that is indicated in the love and in the emotion of the body as it may sing the song of songs, or the pure true notes of "the songs my mother sang to me." These would come to mean much and ye will not lose them when ye, too, may give them meaning to those of thine own body in the earth.   3659-1

As has been indicated, music becomes . . . a means of expression that bridges much of that which may bring beauty and harmony into the experience . . . and it is then one of the channels in which and through which the entity may bring to self much of the beauty and harmony that has been lost by the turmoils of the minds of men about the entity. For they take hold upon the ways of the world, and He hath given that the *world* cannot know—it is not ready; only those who listen to that voice within where He hath promised to meet those who know the beauties of the more abundant life.   412-9

Music itself is a means or a manner of expressing the harmonies of the mental self in relationship to spiritual ideals and spiritual concepts. Hence—as is the very nature of rhythm or harmony in the expression of tone or sound—it is to arouse, does arouse the natures of the hearers to activity, either for uplifting the soul or the mind to activity or otherwise—in the directions that are indicated by the harmony itself.   949-13

. . . each home, each hall, each edifice, has—and there is felt the vibration in such a place. Some are in harmony, some are at disharmony . . . As this is brought in thought by or through music . . . and thus used as the channel, the means of approach to that necessary for individual conditions.   2881-3

Those ill in body as well as mind may be helped by music.

. . . sounds, music and colors may have much to do with creating the proper vibrations about individuals that are mentally unbalanced, physically deficient or ill in body and mind . . .   1334-1

Do give the entity then, a background of not too formal a nature, but the musical education, that there may be the better vibrations in the keeping of the anatomical structures in the body for its health's sake.   5263-1

In the one [incarnation] before this, we find in that period when divisions arose in the land now known as Egypt. The entity then chief among the musicians of the period, furnishing to the peoples that of the first according of vibratory forces in nature to the healing of forces in physical ills; or the first ability of the physician in charge of the institution of learning, toward the application of mental and of material conditions for the welfare of the human race, to gain the knowledge of the nerve vibration in the body from this entity's application of stringed and horned instruments as applied to vibratory forces set in various diseases of the mental and physical body. The urge as seen from this experience, the love of music—of harmony—yet that innate unsatisfied desire to be able to minister to the physical ills of individuals, and the entity has often, and does often feel the urge to be a physician; yet not knowing what branch, what field, to express self in. Find and express same in the harmony of stringed instruments with the varied ills of the human family as respecting to certain diseases; for from this entity's ability much of that as has become of material rather than of spiritual impulse arose the chants (that are so often heard) to drive away the varied impulses in the human heart.   4609-1

From a reading for a five-year-old girl who was unable to hear properly due to birth injuries:

Q-2. Just what kind of music, and in what manner may it be used?
A-2. Especially those tones or chords that will be found to be pleasing, and will find response in the emotions of the body. This should be a part of its training . . .   2527-1

For a woman of twenty-three who could see nothing out of her right eye and just a little sunlight and color out of her left:

Q-2. Is it advisable for the body to study music, or any other subject, or would it tax her mind and strength so as to retard her improvement?

A-2. Study of music would assist, for there is much music in the make-up of the body, and those vibrations of music would assist the body in regaining sight and use of sound forces, which is seconded to the vision, see?   4531-2

Do get the note vibrations in music to which the body will respond and continue to interest the body in same whenever treatments are given.   3401-1

The entity lived to be a ripe old age, for with the regenerations of the Priest—these were brought in greater part by those activities of the entity itself in making for those incantations which raised the influences of the spiritual forces above the secular or the material things.

Thus the entity lived to be what would be called today the years of two hundred and fifty-four (254.)   949-12

Music can influence the soul, also.

The influences through Venus as well as Uranus and Neptune make for the ability of the entity to play upon stringed instruments, especially the viola or the cello, that have been or may be channels through which the entity may find an outlet for its moods of ecstasy, either emotional of the body or of the soul, in the airs of same that partake often of the mysteries of nature and its influence upon the souls as well as the minds of men; as well as an outlet for the periods of sadness or depression.   1904-2

. . . the entity in the present may enter into that manner of expression in music which will *best* bring *healing* and strength to the body, to the desires towards spiritual things.

These be the channels through which the entity may gain the most.   949-12

. . . music is that which appeals to the latent and creative force within the entity. For music alone may span that sphere from the spheres of activity to the realms of the divine.

Music is . . . as a destructive or creative force, dependent upon that to which it appeals in the influence of individuals.
                          3509-1

The entity's music may be the means of arousing and awakening the best of hope, the best of desire, the best in the heart and soul of those who will and do listen. Is not music the universal language, both for those who would give praise and those who are sorry in their hearts and souls? Is it not a means, a manner of universal expression? Thus may the greater hope come.   2156-1

Moods can be affected by music.

And whenever there are the periods of depression, or the feeling low or forsaken, play music; especially stringed instruments of every nature. These will enable the entity to span that gulf as between pessimism and optimism.   1804-1

Here in music, as in other vibrations, individuals have various needs.
A musician had specialized as a harpist. She was told how to select pieces that would have a healing effect on her body.

Q-19. Give pieces, and composer of same, for the harp, that would have the most elevating and healing influence on my body.
A-19. These had best be developed with the various moods and the temperament of the body, under the varied experiences.   275-31

In a later reading it was made clear that the harpist had first developed her skill in the lifetime when, as a Libyan princess, she came under the influence of Ra Ta in exile.

Hence the entity became among the first users of the harp, or the lyre—as was later called, of the instrument.   275-33

The lute may be soothing.

Thus the lute, as well as the stringed instruments, become those that act more as the soothing influence, as well as those in which the entity may in its dance interpret the better; rather than the brass instruments.   2700-1

The piano, organ and song are suggested as a means of being a channel of blessing to others.

Hence music, beauty, joy, harmony, even song, should be a part of the unfoldment. Learn sorrow, learn joy; but let that expressed in "I walked in the garden with Jesus" be as the light in thy composition of song, yea, in thy melody upon the musical instrument in which ye may give voice. Practice the more upon the organ. Let that be a means or way of expression, as well as upon the piano . . .
Make *music*—the piano, the organ, song—thy life's work; as a concert artist, as a teacher, as a director in choir or the like.

186

These will bring to the entity the opportunities for ever being a channel of blessings, and bring peace into the soul of the entity—which brings happiness and gladness under every circumstance.   3234-1

The banjo, also, has its place.

Q-8. Should he study a musical instrument; if so, which instrument would be preferable?
A-8. Music should be a part of each soul's development. There's not a great deal of music in this entity, except of certain natures. The piano would be well, or the banjo, for this entity.   2780-3

In the reference from 1904-2, previously given, the viola or cello is cited.

... the ability of the entity to play upon stringed instruments, especially the viola or the cello, that have been or may be channels through which the entity may find an outlet for its moods of ecstasy, either emotional of the body or of the soul ... as well as an outlet for the periods of sadness or depression.
                                                                      1904-2

Reed instruments instead of stringed ones were recommended for one person.

The instruments of music ... should be of the reed nature, rather than the stringed instruments; though these—the stringed instruments—should be a part of the training ... but the *activities* should be rather in the reed instruments.
                                                                      1566-3

The use of the reed or flute in very early days is brought out in a reading for a woman who had lived in Arabia at the time that the priest Ra Ta was active in Egypt. This person was the first to tame the animal kingdom. She did it not by force but by love, expressed by music of the flute or reed. It also made the hearts of men merry and could do so again.
    The picture given is clearly that of Pan, the Greek god of flocks and herds, of all woodland creatures, who pipes to both wild animals and his followers, the satyrs. Just as Ra Ta appears to have become the Egyptian god Ra, so Valtui seems to have been immortalized as Pan. Since there was an influx of Grecian people into Arabia following the Ra Ta period, the story of this legendary character could well have been carried to Greece itself.

The entity's activities . . . had to do with the domestication and use of the wild animal life and also those that later became the servants with and of man in his activity; and brought about much that had to do with the raising of the horse from the smaller or pigmy animal to the charging steed; that had to do with the using of the wolves and the wild things for the closer companionship to man . . .

In the conscious use of these same influences, with being directed by those that had found . . . the relationship between the Creative influence and the creature and its brother, the creature and its Maker, the entity so applied self as to bring harmony into the *kingdom* over which the entity ruled. Not as ruled by might, rather by love. Hence the instruments used were of the reed or flute, that is known in the present, and made the hearts of many merry; not as of those that would gratify the satisfying of carnal forces, but rather that as awakened within each those abilities for the expressing of—in its physical body—the music of the spirit in its activity in and through the body. So in the present, as the experiences of self that go to make up its abilities to quell within the breast of many a tortured soul or many a tortured body that wars within itself with the spirit that is willing and the flesh is weak with its own desires, that as may be given by the entity in word or by the music will bring something to each of the vision that came to those that were under the entity's supervision or kingdom in that sojourn.   276-6

Singing and humming to oneself are also recommended.

Then, sing a lot about the work . . . Hum, sing—to self; not to be heard by others but to be heard by self.   3386-1

A human being has real need of music and may become soul- and mind-sick without it.

For music is of the soul, and one may become mind- and soul-sick for music, or soul- and mind-sick from certain kinds of music.   5401-1

The foregoing stresses that music can be destructive as well as constructive, a point already brought out in the reference from 3509-1. Constructive music results when the intent is spiritual and the desire to help one's fellow man and glorify the Creator, paramount. Music should not be used to gratify the body or the bodily emotions *alone.*

Q-9. *Is there any spiritual advice that I should have for my benefit at this time?*
A-9. As the emotions of the body are raised to their activities through that which *impels* the body in its desire and in its

desire of expression in voice or song, see that which is ever of a *constructive* nature to others, and it will be more constructive to self!   622-1

Just as the individual who has by practical application gained the correct pitch, correct tone in a musical composition. This may be as a soul expression or a mechanical expression; and only when it is in the true accord, as from the soul, is it perfectly understood.   281-31

Q-8. Give specific directions for approaching this study of music under present conditions.
A-8. As has been given all along here, again and again—see the rhythm in the activities of every nature; whether in viewing the scrubwoman or the artist in giving expression— see the timing of same necessary to make the activity *valuable* and of a *spiritual* nature in its essence!   949-13

... this is the basis—the interpreting, the ability to interpret most to the types or classes of music. So, begin with this. Get this thoroughly, and begin with the simplest, but of ever interpreting the emotions of the body, the mind, the soul. And we will come into symphonies then, to be sure. For these are those upon which the greater interpretation of the soul and mind may attune the body to the infinite.   3053-3

Remember ... music is the one element which may span the distance between the sublime and the ridiculous. That which may arouse violent passion, which may soothe the beast of passion, as that which may make for thoughts of home, of heaven, of loved ones, the laugh of a baby, the tears of a beautiful woman, the arms of a loved one, the jeers of the crowd; and the entity is capable of depicting these in manners in which they would become unusual and give the opportunity for the entity to not only give out, but to find in helping others, in bringing more and more of the thoughts of good, thoughts of home, thoughts of heaven, thoughts of mother, thoughts of those things which bring at times sadness, at times joy, but always helpful influences into the experiences of individuals. For as ye pour out self, in a way to be of help to others, ye are the greater help to thyself.   5253-1

... let thy prayer ever be ... "Let me, O God, in my music, in my heart, give that which is as helpfulness to that in the lives of others."   5265-1

... an ever contributing factor to that character of music which indicates the hope, the desire, the purpose for which this America came into existence—and its place, its purpose, its position in the affairs of nations as a directing influence to the hopes of man, in its greater unfoldment of bringing peace on earth, good will to man.   5398-1

As has been indicated, do by sponsorship give help to those seeking in voice, in music, to find or to contribute something to the welfare of the people of the nation, or musical talent. Do help there.   5355-1

The entity then, as a daughter of the Priest . . . when there were greater activities of a spiritual nature, supplied the music that would span the distances between loneliness and crowds, that would make for the lifting of the soul in those periods even when operations were performed under the soothing strains of same. The entity perfected the stringed instruments. And when there was the roll of the organ in the ecstasies reached in the Temple Beautiful, again the entity supplied same.

Thus in music may the entity again unfold to that ability to sway those in distress, those that are fearful, those that are doubtful; as well as bringing those that are beset with doubts to the joyousness of a walk in the garden with Jesus.
                                              3234-1

Hence, as the attuning of music in the present makes or arouses emotions in the body to an unusual degree, well that there be choices made as to what the emotions are that are aroused by the character of music for the entity.

For there is a way that seemeth right to a man, but the end thereof taketh hold upon hell.

As to the experiences then that arise from same, choose that which is constructive in the experience, and know it must partake of that which brings peace to the soul and not gratifying of body or of an emotion of the body alone.
                                              1406-1

Q-4. Please define Temple music. How shall I proceed in developing it? and with what Temple should it be handled?

A-4. As may be indicated, in a manner, of how the entity may make himself more sought for by the public—as has been seen, there is that period through which the public is seeking an expression of the emotions through music. Hence called the jazz age in same. The entity also realizes through innate experience that there is a seeking by that same public for *some*thing that is much deeper, much more satisfying, much more contentment bringing, much more of an happiness producing from its association. The entity will find, apparently, some reverses from such a material change—but in the sincerity *of* purpose *of* the entity *so* give to the public, to the peoples, that which will *be satisfying* and *uplifting,* and of not only physical and mental but of *spiritual* assistance; for, with what verity of purpose, with what sincerity of purpose the entity presents self before a public, *that* sincerity will be returned as for the efforts *of* the entity, and *when* the entity presents self in any manner whatsoever that would attempt to be a laudation of self, of selfish interest, of selfish motives, of power, position, or what—then the security of position of the entity is already on the decline. Then, in that—*not* that there should not be given those of jazz, those of light music, those of the satisfying—but ever should there be tempered with same more of those abilities of the entity with the instrument, or instruments, that is so capably handled by the entity, as to express that as is sought to be manifested *by* the entity in the expression of *self;* and in doing so, let this expression be to the *glorifying* of that the *entity* seeks to manifest of that force the entity seeks for, and let that glorification be to Him, the Giver of all good and perfect gifts. In a short while such an expression given by the entity *will call forth from* those in the worshipful places, in the temples of music, in the temples of service to man's spiritual body, to the temples where *mental abilities* are made the *criterion* of one's success, will the *entity* and his associates be called. This would be *not* too much at once, but tempered with the purposefulness, the abilities of the entity *to give* to others that *real* innate force, powerfulness, *in* self, to those in *every* circle—and let him that saveth a soul from destruction know that he hath covered a *multitude* of sins.   2897-2

Thus the interest in art, as well as music; not only the classic but the ragtime also, or the popular music—and of these beware. For, either the art or the popular music *may* tempt the entity oft . . .   3188-1

As the entity advanced through that experience, greater and greater became the activities. For the entity gained throughout that experience or sojourn. And as there were the preparations for the varied activities of the peoples as a nation, the entity developed that which later became the chant which to many would drive away what was called the evil eye, the evil influence. And, with their variations, many of those incantations of the savages of today, many of the beautiful martial pieces of music, many of the beautiful waltzes that give the rhythm to the body, many of the various characters of music used today have arisen from the efforts of *this* entity. Yet many, of course, were added to, many were defamed, many were carried into various forces not intended in the beginning.

But the entity in the present may enter into that manner of expression in music which will *best* bring *healing* and strength to the body, to the desires towards spiritual things.

These be the channels through which the entity may gain the most.   949-12

How Music Affects Man

Just how does music affect a human being? The brain acts upon the nervous system, thereby releasing vibrations. (We have learned that the vibrations are slightly different for every person.) These vibrations, rhythmic in nature, initiate electrical forces in the body. Music which vibrates in the same way as does electrotherapy of the short wave (with low amplitude and high frequency) has a creative effect and can, therefore, help to set up the proper electrical forces for all of us.

Persons whose brains have been injured and who, therefore, cannot entirely avail themselves of these processes may be helped by having music of the proper characteristics set in motion the vibrations that are lacking, which, in turn, trigger the electrical forces. Also, direct application of electricity may achieve the same effect.

Q-7. Through what specific school and course would I obtain a closer insight into the study of the forces or music of the spheres?

A-7. The lower electrical vibrations to life!

Q-8. What is meant by the rhythmic side of my development and experience, and how may I gain the proper understanding of this?

A-8. This is indicated in that we have given for the consideration in the *material* things, see? that the *rhythmic* vibrations of the body, as to music, set the electrical forces in the physical body. As: an activity of the brain upon the nervous system makes for the releasing of vibration. Hence the study of music as related to electrical vibration and electrical applications for the human body, or as a technician in same, brings *both* to bear upon that which will make for the greater understanding by the entity.

For many an individual that has had a brain wreck might be aided by electricity and music to a revivification of those cells, of those atomic forces that need their coercion and their regeneration by their absorbing one into another—rather than being separated and fighting its own self, or lack of proper coagulation of the cellular forces in the blood and brain forces; as in some forms of dementia, strained by great religious fervor or excitement that makes for the separation of that which is the *spiritual* and the *material* application *through* the vibratory forces of a physical body.

Q-9. Are there any books or studies or courses recommended for me to aid in my development?

A-9. As indicated, begin along those lines first in the preparatory forces of physics, biology, pathology, and the application of the musical vibrations to same.   933-2

From a later reading for the same person:

The innate ability as the musician should and will exert itself. More often the entity should turn to that natal and natural ability in music, when there are those periods of indecision, periods of loneliness, periods of wonderment, to find that quieting influence.

For, it has been truly said, music alone spans the sphere of spiritual and mental attainment.

Then, rather than in those applications that are as rote, as found in biological studies—prepare self more for the application of helpful experience in same; as of music—that vibrates to the body in the same manner as electrotherapy of the short wave, of the high vibration—for it is the lowest form of vibration electrically that gives creative forces, rather than the highest. It is the high vibration that destroys.   933-3

Personalized Music for Healing

It had been suggested in a reading for a music professor that he use music and higher vibrations of electrical energies in healing work. He asked how he should do this.

He was told that every disease or dis-ease creates in the body a vibration opposite to one of those the body needs. If the proper vibration is introduced, it will in some cases counteract the undesirable vibration, in other cases bring about a change (or the desirable vibration). [1861], who was obviously somewhat psychic, was to try to develop within himself a vibration in rhythm to the general or composite vibration of the person who needed healing. He was to practice doing this with associates, with his pupils, with his wife. Sometimes a mood might change the vibration of the person under study, but if the professor persisted, he would be successful in ascertaining what the body-mind responded to, not just what it liked or disliked but what struck a vibrant chord within its consciousness. He could then use this sound for healing of the individual or the dissipating of the undesirable vibration(s) that had been held fast by the patient's consciousness.

[1861] inquired whether there were any sounds specifically useful in healing and was told that R, O and M are vibrations which are in keeping with the central forces of the body itself. If these three are used, what is necessary will be supplied. However, continued use of such sounds with persons who are not in immediate need of such healing may be distracting to them. In other words, a well person may be overstimulated by therapeutic measures of value to an ill person.

The professor was admonished to put some of this information to use before seeking more.

Q-9. How may I use music and higher vibrations in electrical energies for healing, as suggested through this channel? [See 1861-4, A-2]

A-9. Every individual entity is on certain vibrations. Every dis-ease or disease is creating in the body the opposite or non-coordinant [coordinate] vibration with the conditions in a body-mind and spirit of the individual. If there . . . [are] used certain vibrations there may be seen the response. In some it is necessary for counteraction, in some it is necessary for changes.

Then, the better way is to first develop in thine own consciousness, with the various individuals, or thine own pupils, or thy associates or thy companion, that vibration which is in rhythm with the vibration of that body.

To be sure, moods often apparently change this vibration; yet by study, by practice and by application, the vibration of the body may be ascertained.

Thus there are the needs for the aiding in using such for healing, of the dissipating—that is, the dissipating of suppressions. And that's what we need for your own companion, and it's a very good one to practice on! [2072]

Q-10. What means of application can be used?

A-10. As just indicated, the finding of that to which the body-mind responds; not just what it likes, or dislikes, but that which strikes a vibrant chord within the consciousness of the individual, see?

Q-11. Any specific compositions that can be used for healing?

A-11. R and O and M are those combinations which vibrate to the center forces of the body itself. In any compositions of which these are a part there will be found that necessary for the individual. What might be healing for one might be distracting for another, to be sure.

Q-12. Should further information on same be sought through this channel?

A-12. Well, put some of it in use first, if you're going to seek further information! If you don't, you won't find any!

1861-12

Chants

Chants as used in ancient Egypt at the time of Ra Ta have a powerful influence on humans. Since those participating in such chants need to purify and prepare themselves in special ways in advance and work at this as a *spiritual service,* a complete discussion of this subject is not in order here. Those who wish to pursue the matter further should get in touch with a healing prayer group. A person who is uninstructed and who attempts to harness the forces involved may suffer dire consequences.

Then, as ye begin with the incantation of the Ar-ar-r-r-r— the e-e-e, the o-o-o, the m-m-m, *raise* these in thyself; and ye become close in the presence of thy Maker—as is *shown* in thyself! They that do such for selfish motives do so to their own undoing. Thus has it oft been said, the fear of the Lord is the beginning of wisdom. Wisdom, then, is fear to mis-apply knowledge in thy dealings with thyself, thy fellow man.

281-28

It is, however, of interest to note that such incantations raise the forces of the body above the material.

. . . for the voice nerve center is the highest vibration in the whole nerve system . . . 341-4

The entity lived to be a ripe old age, for with the regenerations of the Priest—these were brought in greater part by those activities of the entity itself in making for those incantations which raised the influences of the spiritual forces above the secular or the material things.

Thus the entity lived to be what would be called today the years of two hundred and fifty-four (254). 949-12

[275]: Now you will have before you the entity [275], present in this room. You will give complete description in detail of the music used in the Temple Beautiful and Temple of Sacrifice, in the Egyptian incarnation of [275], in connection with the healing of the body, mind and soul—bringing in the tone, range, the structure and keys of the scales, the meters, the tempos. Answer all questions.

Mr. Cayce: In giving that which may be helpful to those seeking to understand the nature of the healing of the body, the mind, the soul, and the music of the day, in rhyme, in tempo, in structure—these would be rather at the extremes, were one to consider same even as it is today when one considers that which is resounding to the awakening of the I AM within, and that which may be of such natures as to be destructive to that which has set itself as an animation of movement or force in a physical body, such as is in the healing influences.

Do not misconstrue that which was accomplished by thine own understanding in that experience. Turn for the moment, then, to thy service in the Temple Beautiful. Here we have those incantations that are as but the glorifying of constructive forces in all of their activity within the human emotions that may be known in the present day; for glory, not of self, not of the ability of self, but the glory of the oneness of purpose, of the I AM of the individual for the glorifying of that creative energy within self that may keep the whole body, whole body-individual, whole body as of the group, the whole body as of those within the sound as it ranges from the highest to the lowest of the incantations within; following that known in thine own present as i-e-o-u-e-i-o-umh.

These as they make for the raising of that from within of the Creative Forces, as it arises along that which is set within the inner man as that cord of life that once severed may separate, does separate, that balance between the mind, the body, the soul; these three, as accorded within the human forces, are the activities that were carried on by thyself in movement of body in its *every* motion that made for the lifting up, the intoning in of self within; that there might come, as it were, the sound as of many waters; or as the morning stars in their circuit about the earth may sing with the glorious coming of the light into the experience of man to raise same to his at-oneness and his attunement with those beauties of the coming of the sons of men into the earth that God in His Oneness of Purpose may bring those activities with the sons of God as an at-onement in their purposes in the earth. The glorifying of Him in the dealings and associations with the fellow man, and these find *their* attunement in each chord as it rings one with another in all the music that may be heard from every sound that follows in eeiu-u-u-ummmm in its *forms,* through that attunement along the pineal to the source of light within the self to make for the emotions of glorifying alone.   275-43

Q-21. What is the note of the musical scale to which I vibrate?
A-21. As we have indicated, Ah—This is not R, but Ah—aum, see? These are the sounds. Those that respond to the centers of the body, in opening the centers so that the kundaline forces arise to that activity through those portions of the body. Sound these, and ye will find them in thyself. They are the manners or ways of seeking.

For as ye have understood, if ye have read Him and His conversation with His friend, His disciples as respecting John—John was a great entity, none greater. And yet the least in the kingdom of heaven was greater than he. What meaneth this manner of speech?

They that have wisdom are great, they that have understanding as to the manner to *apply* same for the good of self *and* others—not for self at the expense of others, but for others—are in the awareness of the kingdom.

Thus, as to the note of thy body—is there always the response to just one? Yes. As we have indicated oft, for this entity as well as others, there are certain notes to which there is a response, but is it always the same? No more than thy moods or thy tendencies, *unless* ye have arisen to the understanding of perfect attunement.

When a violin or an instrument is attuned to harmony, is it out of tune when struck by the same motion, the same activity? Does it bring forth the same sound?

So with thy body, thy mind, thy soul. It is dependent upon the tuning—whether with the infinite or with self, or with worldly wisdom. For these, to be sure, become the mysteries of life to some—the mysteries of attuning. What seek ye? Him, self, or what?

He is within and beareth witness.

The tone, then—find it in thyself, if ye would be enlightened. To give the tune or tone as Do, Ah-aum—would mean little; unless there is the comprehending, the understanding of that to which ye are attempting to attune—in the spiritual, the mental, the material.

There *is* music in jazz, but is there perfect harmony in same?

There *is* harmony in a symphony, as in the voices as attuned to the infinite—a spirit and a body poured out in aid or the search for the soul.

There is no greater than that as may be expressed in that of, "O my son Absalom, my son, my son Absalom! would God I had died for thee, O Absalom, my son, my son!"

To what is this attuned? What *is* the note there?

That as of the realization of the lack of training the mind of the son in the way of the Lord, rather than in the knowledge of controlling individuals.

This, then, is indeed the way of harmony, the way of the pitch, the way of the tone. It is best sounded by what it arouses in thee—where, when, and under what circumstance.

2072-10

Q-5. What is the correct way of sounding "aum"?
A-5. That of attuning self by your own vocal cords—not tuning like you are giving vocal orientations.   1861-18

...part of the entity's activity, that establishing of the chants that aided in *healing*—and in bringing the mental attributes of those who had determined to become as channels through which there might be the spiritual expression in the Temple Beautiful.   2584-1

For the entity identified as Ruth, sister of Jesus:

Such then the entity finds necessary, in giving forth in song, in the harmonies of same. Just as has been indicated through this channel for many, the entity will find that there are the combinations of that ye call the scale—or those harmonies set to the Ar-ar-r-r-e-e-e-ooo-mmm—that awaken within self the abilities of drawing that love of the Father as shown to the children of men in the experiences of His own, through their activities in the earth.   1158-10

The Use of Song in Raising Heavy Structures

How the Great Pyramid in Egypt was built has long been a matter for speculation. According to the Cayce readings this particular pyramid along with other buildings was erected at the time of Ra Ta. The readings tell us that song was one of the motive forces in its construction.

Hence there began the first preparation for what has later become that called the Great Pyramid, that was to be the presentation of that which had been gained by these peoples through the activities of Ra Ta ...   294-151

For there was not only the adding to the monuments, but the Atlanteans aided in their activities with the creating of that called the Pyramid, with its records of events of the earth through its activity in all of the ages to that in which the new dispensation is to come.   281-43

Q-2. Are there urges for music and art?
A-2. Just as indicated in the building of the pyramids, the house of records as well as the chamber in which the records are built in stone [in the Great Pyramid]—these were put together by song. This the entity [Ajax-ol] learned—as he did the chants upon the river.   2462-2

Q-3. By what power or powers were these early pyramids and temples constructed?
A-3. By the lifting forces of those gases that are being used gradually in the present civilization, and by *the fine work or activities of those versed in that pertaining to the source from which all power comes.* [Author's italics. This appears to be a reference to chants.]   5750-1

There is motive strength in song and chants when developed in a special way.

The Effects of Sounds in Languages

It is generally recognized that people of various nationalities show slightly different personalities. That the differences may be partially attributed to differences in language and its sounds is a concept usually not taken into consideration. Yet the readings aver that such is the case.

Few people have gathered the import of what the variation would make to an individual to speak French or to speak Japanese, or to speak Sanskrit, or to speak pidgeon-Spanish—or as would be in those various lands. For these have their vibrations, these have their movements as to the motivating influences. And as the entity itself is, through its astrological as well as material sojourns, moved by emotions, it becomes a positive experience in the entity. And for such things, in giving expression of same to others, may the entity gain a great deal in the present.   706-1

The Effects of the Sounding of Names

When the tone of a language can have so much effect, it is only natural that the sounding of an individual's name over and over during his lifetime should be of the greatest importance. A basis for numerology is firmly established by the readings.

With reference to use of a name chosen numerologically:

It is well with this entity that in the sounding of the name, in the writing of same, it always all be included. The vibration, the harmonious effect of same becomes almost as a shield in the entity's experience; as well as in the numerological effects and their vibrations upon those the entity may approach.

And this is ever a part of the entity's experience as an emissary or messenger to others. Hence it is well that in its own mental and material and spiritual self there be kept that balance.   1770-2

Q-8. Just how would entity benefit by changing his name from [452] to John?

A-8. How did Abraham benefit by the changing of the name from Abram to Abraham? How did Paul gain by the change from Saul to Paul? How was there difference in the names of the Hebrew children in their varied surroundings? There is builded about each name that which carries its own meaning or significance, that gives rather the impelling of—and the lifting up to—meeting such conditions. So does the changing or the altering of a name set about varied environs or vibrations, that makes for the conduciveness of changed surroundings.

452-6

Q-12. What is the meaning of names? I have been told that Martha should be my real name. Is there a reason why?

A-12. This comes rather as to the minds and purposes of those who give names to their offspring. Names, to be sure, have their meaning, but as given by the poet, a rose by any other name would be just as beautiful or just as sweet. So may such be said of these. Yet, as given by Him, names have their meaning, and these depend upon the purposes when such are bestowed upon an individual entity entering the earth's plane.

Have ye not understood how that in various experiences individuals, as their purposes or attitudes or desires were indicated, had their names henceforth called a complete or full name meaning or indicating the purpose to which the individual entity or soul had been called? So, all of these have their part. They are not *all,* as indicated. For, *all* is one. One is all, but each individual is impressed by the various phases of man's consciousness in materiality. These . . . have varying degrees of effect upon the consciousness . . . of individuals.

For, "My Spirit beareth witness with thy spirit" is complete in itself.

Q-13. Do names have a spiritual influence on people?

A-13. As has just been given.

Q-15. When would it be best to choose a name for the child?

A-15. When ye have determined as to the purpose to which ye hope, and which ye will, which ye are willing to dedicate same.

457-10

Q-3. Why is this body so often referred to as David[his middle name] rather than as Edwin [his first name] in psychic readings given by Edgar Cayce?

A-3. The development of the entity is rather in that vibration of David than of Edwin, for these two conditions are with the vibration in names: Edwin [first name], meaning that of a peacefulness, defender of peacefulness, carrying both the condition and implied forces from same. David, rather that of the gift from the higher forces, or a Son of the Father. One, especially, endowed with gifts from the higher forces.

137-13

Q-9. Should [1650] and [1523] change their names? If so, what names would be suggested?

A-9. They each are significant of that they have to meet in each other. Hold that thou hast! [Joint reading for married couple.]

1523-6

The body would do well to change its name, with those things which we may give for the body here, from Carl to Michael . . . and then start over again and do more lecturing and living up to that.

5023-2

Q-4. Please explain what was meant in reading of Oct. 28, regarding the "relative" connection of Name in the Lord's Prayer with the pineal gland.

A-4. This might occupy a whole period of several hours, if the full conclusion were to be given; but each must reach this. There is a Name to each soul. For He hath called His own *by name!* What name? All the names that may have been as a material experience through an earthly sojourn, or all the names that may have been through the experience of an entity in that environ or those relative associations of Venus, Mars, Jupiter, Uranus, Saturn, Sun, Moon, or what! Or a Name that is above *every* name!

Then as has been indicated this becomes relative, as is signified in the indication as given to the number, which is of John's own. But as has been given, every influence—you see—

is *relative!* Hence the name is relative to that which is accomplished by the soul in its sojourn throughout its whole experience; whether in those environs about this individual sphere or another—this individual sphere meaning thine own sun, thine own planets with all of their attributes (Does an earth mind comprehend such?) and it carried through with what is its *relative* force to that which has been or is the activity of the entity-soul (not a body now at all!) toward Constructive Force or God, or God's infinitive force to that integral activity of the soul in its sojourn. Hence it becomes *relative.* And for the finite mind to say Jane, John, Joe, James or Jude would mean only as the *vibrations* of those bring the *relative* force or influence to which, through which an entity's sojourns have brought the concrete experience in any one given or definite period of activity!

Was one named John by chance? Was one named Joe or Llewellyn by chance? No; they are relative! While it may be truly in the material plane relative because you have a rich aunt by that name, or relative because an uncle might be named that—but these carry then the vibrations of same; and in the end the name is the sum total of what the soul-entity in all of its vibratory forces has borne toward the Creative Force itself.

Hence each soul has a definite influence upon the experiences through which it may be passing. This ye have illustrated in thine own secret organizations, in thy papal activities in the religious associations, and in each vibration. For when ye have set a vibration by the activity of thy *soul's* force, ye are then either in parallel, in direct accord, or in opposition to constructive force—whatever may be the position or activity of the soul in infinity. For ye *are* gods! But you are becoming devils or real gods!   281-30

Q-1. Please interpret the 2nd Chapter, 17th verse of Revelation. "To him that overcometh will I give to eat of the hidden manna, and will give him a white stone, and in the stone a new name written, which no man knoweth saving he that receiveth it."
A-1. In giving the interpretation of this particular portion of the Revelation, it must all be kept in mind that, as has been indicated, while many of the references—or all—refer to the physical body as the pattern, there is that as may be said to be the literal and the spiritual and the metaphysical interpretation of almost all portions of the Scripture, and especially of the Revelation as given by John.

Yet all of these to be true, to be practical, to be applicable in the experiences of individuals, *must* coordinate; or be as one, even as the Father, the Son and the Holy Spirit.

In the interpretation of the Name, then: Each entity, each soul, is known—in all the experiences through its activities—as a name to designate it from another. It is not only then a material convenience, but it implies—as has been given, unless it is for material gain—a definite period in the evolution of the experience of the entity in the material plane.

Then as each entity under a given name makes its correlating of that it does about the Creative Forces in its experience, it is coming under those influences that are being fed by the manna—which is a representation of the universality as well as the stability of purposes in the Creative Forces as manifested to a group or a nation of peoples.

So it becomes that as the Master gave, "Ye shall not live by bread alone but by every word that proceedeth from the mouth of the Father."

That indeed is the holy manna which each entity, each soul in each experience must make a part of its mental and spiritual self. Thus it becomes as is indicated, in that the name—as in each experience—bears a relative relationship to the development of the individual entity in each experience.

Then in the end, or in those periods as indicated, it is when each entity, each soul has so manifested, so acted in its relationships as to become then as the new name; white, clear, known only to him that hath overcome. Overcome what? The world, even as He.

For what meaneth a name? John, Jane, Peter, Andrew, Bartholomew, Thaddeus, Rhoda, Hannah? All of these have not only the attunement of a vibration but of color, harmony; and all those relative relationships as one to another.

Then as has been asked, and has been indicated in another portion of Revelation, all those that bear the mark, those that have the name, those that have the stone—these are representatives then of the same experience in the various phases of an individual experience for its activity.

Then the interpretation is that they *have* overcome, they *have* the new name, they *have* the manna, they *have* the understanding, they *have* their relationships as secure in the blood of the Lamb!   281-31

From these last two references it can be deduced that a person's name generally indicates a stage in his development as a soul. When this soul finally overcomes the earth or completes its development here, it receives a new name, which is the sum total of what the soul-entity in all of its vibratory forces has borne toward the Creative Force itself.

Numerology

Let us reexamine a statement just noted from 281-30, "this becomes relative, as is signified in the indication as given to the number, which is of John's own." How do the vibrations in sounds, the vibrations in names correspond to numbers? How can a numerological interpretation indicate the meaning and

202

effect of a name? The readings explain that there are numbers which break or form combinations in nature itself or that in man's response to the conditions in nature there are recurrent conditions or circumstances in certain numbers. Possibly the best understanding of these numerological values may be obtained from the Talmud, the readings continue.

The Talmud comprises Jewish law. The Cabala is the mystical interpretation of Jewish thinking. (Cabala means "received.") Therefore, the Cabalistic system of numerological interpretation would seem to be what the readings point out as the most accurate one. This is very reasonable because according to the Cabalistic system similar sounds have the same numerical value. Since these sounds must be translated from Hebrew to English for our purposes, we may find different values ascribed by different teachers to certain letters. However, the general system may be illustrated. One exponent of the Cabala gives a, i, j, q and y one numerical value; f, s, u, v and x another one; t (and only t) another; etc.

Reading 5751-1 explains that the sum of the values of the letters in a name gives a number that is significant for the individual. If the letters in a person's first, middle and last names have the values 1, 6, 3, 1, 5, 9; 2, 2, 7, 7, 2, 5; and 2, 1, 3, 3, 1, 2, 4; these may be totalled to 25, 25 and 16. Since only integral numbers are considered, the next step is to add the parts of every sum, making 7, 7, and 7. These, in turn, are added, making 21. Further addition gives 3. The final number, 3, is meaningful for the person. The sums secured along the way may have some significance, also.

The alternate method of arriving at an applicable number according to this same reading will now be illustrated. It is first necessary to secure the birthpath. We shall use a birthday of February 6, 1913. This reduces to 2, 6, 1913; then to 2, 6 and 5; and finally to 4.

We now have the birthpath as 4 and will use it along with the values secured above. Since they ultimately totalled 3, 3 will be added to 4, making an overall 7.

It is possible, however, to be even more exact and ascertain current trends. 75 is the number of years assigned to a full life span. We count the number of letters in the first, middle and last names as given above and find they total 6, 6 and 7; eventually 19. 19 is then divided into 75 to see how long the effect of every letter persists. It is 3.947 years. If this person is 62 years old now, he would divide 3.947 into 62 (answer 15.7) and find that he had gone through the influences of the first 15 letters of his name and was nearly through the 16th. The 16th is 3. Further figuring would disclose exactly when the person would be under the influence of 1, 2 and 4. After reaching 75 years of age, he would start through his name again.

The reference to this method in reading 5751-1 is "the numbers as applied *to* each individual letter *in* the name."

The significance of the various numbers as presently conceived are dealt with in the following extracts.

We note that 3 contains both weakness and strength but on the whole indicates strength. 4, on the other hand, shows the greater weakness in all its associations and powers. Even numbers are always the weaker while the odd numbers show strength. (137-119)

Now, as concerning an outline for information concerning or regarding numerology—many have approached the subject from various angles, and since there have been regular radio programs concerning same a great deal of speculation has been brought in the minds of many.

To approach the subject from the viewpoint as to make same worthwhile in the lives of individuals is the *purpose* of this discourse.

Then, as there is the necessity then of looking at the matter from more of a statistical or scientific standpoint, then let each apply same according to the dictates of their individual consciences or developments.

As may be surmised from the fact that the ancients in all lands have and did place the interest in numbers, these indicate that individuals under different circumstances gave to numbers certain valuations, principally according to the *influences* same were *supposed* to have upon the ritual or the form of individual worship in some manner or another. Hence we see that under varying circumstances there were attributed certain powers to certain numbers, according to the form or ritual of that individual group. As to whether these actually exist or not depended much upon the confidence or faith of the subjects in that ritual, that rite, that belief; yet when one looks about them they may see that in a scientific manner there are numbers that break or form combinations in nature itself, or that in man's response to the conditions *in* nature there are the recurrent conditions or circumstances in certain numbers. As we find in music, that the scale itself is composed of so many tones, tone values, and that those numbers that are half pitch or half tones are those that in most of the formulas given are the breaking points or divisions in numbers. The same may be seen in color combination, that when certain tones or the valuation of tone in color, that in the combination of certain numbers these begin to alter or change much in the same manner or way as they do in tones in music. The same may also be illustrated in the elements themselves, when there is the division of those elements these same numbers, same conditions, are seen in the elements in their variations themselves. Then, is it any *wonder* that the ancients—or even the students of the mystic, of the mental or occult forces of today give credence or valuation to numerology, or numbers?

Then, what form, what force, has given the most perfect illustration of *how* numbers—either in individual life or individuals' experiences in life—affect individuals; or the numbers themselves, and as individuals, or 1, 2, 3, 4, 5, 6, 7, 8, 9, 10, 11, 12, *or* whatnot—how do the *numbers themselves* value? Possibly the best authority on such is that of the Talismanic, or that obtained from the Talmud—which is a combination of the ancient Persian or Chaldean, Egyptian, Indian, Indo-China, and such.

One is the beginning, to be sure. Before *One* is nothing. After *One* is nothing, if all be in *One*—as *One* God, *One* Son, *One* Spirit. This, then, the *essence of all* force, *all* manners of energies. All activities *emanate* from the *One*.

Two—the *combination,* and begins a division of the Whole, or the One. While *Two* makes for strength, it *also* makes for weakness. This is *illustrated* in that of your music, of your paintings, of your metals, of *whatever* element we may consider!

Three—again a combination of One and Two; this making for strength, making for—in division—that ability of Two *against* One, or One against Two. In *this* strength is seen, as in the Godhead, and is as a greater strength in the whole of combinations.

Again, in *Four,* we find that of a division—and while a beauty in strength, in the divisions also makes for the greater weakness—as may be illustrated as in the combinations seen in metal, or numbers, or music, or color.

Five—as seen, a change—as may be seen in a comparison of any of the forces outlined.

Six—again makes for the *beauty* and the symmetrical forces of *all numbers,* making for strength;

As does *Seven* signify the *spiritual* forces, as are seen in all the ritualistic orders of any nature; as seen in the dividing up of conditions, whether they be of the forces in nature or those that react to the sensual forces of man in any character.

Eight—again showing that combination in strength, also a combination in weakness;

Nine making for the *completeness* in numbers; yet showing not the strength as of Ten, nor yet the weakness as of Eight, yet making for that termination in the *forces* in natural *order* of things that come as a change imminent in the life.

In *Ten* we have those of the completeness as of numbers, and a strength as is found in *few*; yet these are as a combination in the forces as are manifest.

In *Eleven* is again seen . . . the *beauty* of numbers, yet that weakness as was signified by those of the betrayal in the numbers.

Twelve—as a *finished* product, as is given in all forces in nature; as was given in all forces as combined to those of the ritualistic forms, those of the mystic forces, those of the numbers as related to those of a combination; for as of the voices of *Twelve* requiring Twenty to even drown same, or to overcome same. The same as may be seen in all of the forces in nature. *Twelve* combined forces brought those strengths into the world as . . . [were] necessary for a replenishing of same.

Now, how may we apply same to our daily lives? How—or what is *my* number? How do numbers affect me?

Numerology, or numbers, may be termed as one of the *non*-essentials to those who feel or know that same cannot affect them, unless they allow same to affect them. Just so with any other force as in nature, will there be set within self that which is as to be combative against every other force *that* force may affect little or none at all, dependent upon the activities of that being guarded against or guarded with. So, in approaching or reaching the effect of numbers:

The period of the year—dependent, of course, upon that point reasoned from. The numbers, or the name—these give the significance to the numbers of the individual. These may be reached either by adding the numbers of the letters as signify the name, or the numbers as applied *to* each individual letter *in* the name. These will give the sum total of that which applies to the individual.

How do they affect the individual? It will be found that one, then, that is of a given number—from the name given—is under those influences that have been indicated by the influences of numbers in the forces, or among the forces, in nature itself. These may be reached by the various forces or various manners in which individuals have *classified* same.

In applying same, use them for the *benefits*—and not for the destructive forces! We are through.   5751-1

Remembering, however, that these numbers—and numbers as a whole—only give that as is the *relative* activity of the *mind* of man concerning same, and it is not infallible! for *man* may change his *mind* as respecting *any* condition, and may therefore upset *any* factor as would be the criterion of the dates, month, or year, as taken as respecting any individual stock. But each number, then, has its *own* vibration. All emanating from one, even as is shown in that only those of integral numbers are considered—for when one is one, ten is the one again, see?

One, then, the whole number—divisible by that of the various parts as may be taken up to make the whole. One always being then, a basis for a start—for division—for building—or for disintegration; shown by the relationship of other numbers as respecting same, as may always be seen that when one and one are two—*Two* then the weaker number. *Always,* in the division, the even numbers—as two, four, six, eight—are the weaker, while the odd numbers are the strength—each having its variation from the vibrations as are naturally created by such. One, then, the Unit.

Two the division, and ready for a change.

Three, again with strength, with the activity of both one and two.

Four, again a weakness—slowing either in the up or down direction.

Five always active—and double the two, and one—or three and two, which it is the sum of. Hence, as is questioned here, no factor is more active than would be that of a five—fifth division—or five-eighth division, or five-sixth division, or five *any* division—in any activity! Five being the *active* number!

Six again showing a weakness, or a strength again—the multiple of three, strength—yet showing either weakness *or* strength, dependent upon the relationship of the day, month, or year, or stock—according to the conditions as are added in same.

Seven again becoming strength—with the added activity of five and the weakness of two showing its relation.

Eight, also, that of the double weakness of four—and no one, any, remaining at any given place.

Nine is as of the finish.

These are as the conditions as come with numbers or numeral forces—and these added in the way and manner as is outlined here, in that as is given, why we will see these will give the correction of these forces as respecting numeral numbers, relating to stocks, bonds, places, individuals, or *any—according to* the relationship of one to another. 137-119

Q-18. Are there any further suggestions or advice for this body at this time, or any further recommendation as to a change in any of his activities?

A-18. There's a lot here to think about! Much advice might be given as respecting this numerological working out of things.

Take that which is of the easier form, knowing ever that this is as the basis of all activity: These are only as *signs* when worked out in the most. But one source, one power, one influence, as may be had within self and turning to the within will be not as hunches, but as the influence made erect from within self through making self in *every* manner as one with Him. For He has promised to guide, to guard, to direct. And as ye put into application those suggestions, ye will find more and more there will come—in those periods that thou dost set aside for thine own meditation upon problems of self, problems as related to individuals—the voice as from within.

Q-19. Are there books from which one may study numerology?

A-19. *Numbers* of same! But best study as you would your own A.B.C.'s. One—the all power. Two—divided. Three—the strength of One and the weakness of Two. Four—the greater weakness in all its associations and powers. Five—a change imminent, ever, in the activities of whatever influence with which it may be associated. Six—the strength of a Three, with a helpful influence. Seven—the spiritual forces that are activative or will be the activative influences in the associations of such an influence. Eight—a money number. Nine—the change. Ten—back to One again. These in their correlated influences as you will find in your own experience, and we will see these are but signs. Study in some of these, but turn most to the influence of the force of the One within self.

261-14

Q-1. Can the entity's psychic faculties be expressed or developed through numerology?

A-1. As we have indicated oft, astrology and numerology and symbology are all but the gateways or the signs of expression.

As for this entity, as we have indicated, the symbols of numerology may be developed; but the *intuitive* forces that arise *with* same make for rather the safer, the saner, the more spiritual way, with the less aptitude of turning to forces from without.

For, as we see in numbers, or numerology:

One indicates *strength,* power, influence; yet has all the weaknesses of all other influences that may be brought to bear upon any given activity in which same may be indicated. But it is *known* as strength and power; even as the *union* of self with the Creative Forces that express themselves in the activity of matter, in *any* form, is power.

Two makes for a division; yet in the multiple of same, in four, it makes for the greater weaknesses in the divisions. In six and eight it makes for the same characterizations, yet *termed* more in these that one is power, two is weakness, three is the strength of one with the weakness of two; four being more and more of a division and weakness; six being the changes that have been made in the *double* strength of three. Seven is the spiritual number. Eight indicates the commercial change. Nine indicates strength and power, with a change.

These, then, are as *indications;* and *not* other than the *signs* of things, that may be altered ever by the force or factor from which they emanate.

Hence *intuitive* force is the better, for in this there may come more the union of the spirit of truth with Creative Energy; thus the answer may be *shown* thee, whether in Urim, in Thummim, in dream, in numbers, in *whatever* manner or form. For He *is* the strength of them all, and beareth witness *in* thee and through thee—if ye but do His biddings.

Q-2. If so, how can they be used through this method for the benefit of others?

A-2. As indicated, there are many channels, many manners— as we have just given. These are as free in themselves; the numbers, see?

As related to individuals these each vibrate to certain numbers according to their name, their birth date, their relationships to various activities. Then when these appear, they become either as strengths or as losses or as helps or as change, or as the spiritual forces. But, as indicated, they are rather as the signs, or the omens; and may be given as warnings, may be given as helps, may be given in any manner that they may be constructive in the experience of the individual.

Q-3. Any other advice that will be of help at this time?

A-3. There are many authorities (so called) upon numerology. Study same, if ye would know same; yet rely upon the spirit of truth, ever, that may make itself manifest in its own way unto thee.

Does the beauty of the rose excel the beauty of the violet or of the other flowers? Each in its own manner has its own appeal; yet who giveth the beauty of these? It was *ordained* that these might be as signs, as omens, as knowledge, unto man; that he might make himself—through the desires, through the longings, through the application of these beauties—at-one with the Source, through the expression of gentleness. As He gave, "A cup of water given in my name loseth not its reward." Just as the beauty of the rose expressed loseth not its preciousness in the sight of the Maker, though it be trampled underfoot by a disappointed personage.

So in thine application of thy abilities, of thy influences in thine experiences, make the applications in the *spirit* of helpfulness, hopefulness. Not of exhortation, not of aggrandizement of self nor for the laudation of self; but that His beauty, His joy, His peace, His glory, may be through thy efforts taken account of, taken thought of, be experienced by those ye meet day by day.   261-15

From the last reference it is apparent that numerology is but one of the many aids given to man in his search for at-one-ment. The only sure source of information, however, is found in personal intuition.

CYCLES

It is evident that if man were equally affected all of the time by all of the influences and forces we have been considering, the effect on him would be devastating. To obviate such a state of affairs and at the same time to give each entity the benefit of all these influences and forces, a system of cycles exists.

The word "cycle" comes from the Greek for "ring" or "circle." A cycle occupies a particular interval of time and in it a course of events recurs in the same order in a series.

All matter passes through a cycle.

For, as has been in the experience, and as is partially understood by the entity, everything in motion, everything that has taken on materiality as to become expressive in any kingdom in the material world, is *by* the *vibrations* that are the motions—or those positive and negative influences that make for that differentiation that man has called matter in its various stages of evolution into material things. For it enters and it passes through. For—as is the better understood, and as will be proclaimed (and the entity may be able to aid in same)— all vibration must eventually, as it materializes into matter, pass through a stage of evolution and out. For it rises in its emanations and descends also. Hence the cycle, or circle, or arc, that is as a description of all influence in the experience of man. And very few do they come at angles!   699-1

The cycle of the seasons is well known. The significance of it is brought out in the following excerpt, which also touches on certain cycles of animal life and of man.

Hence the necessity; hence the judgment; hence the mercy, the justice shown by the All-Wise Creative-Force—that is so beautifully illustrated in the spring, the summer, the fall, the winter—the returning again and again of the body of man for its purification.

211

Has not man demonstrated how that the elements in the earth are purged of the dross by the fires of the furnace for their purification? Have not the weaklings in the flock or the unhealthy plants been made sturdy in their relationships of beauty in nature, by purging, pruning, and making for those advancements again and again. And yet some deny that the All-Wise, the All-Merciful Father would be so gracious to the sons of men who have erred in this a little thing! What hath the Maker of the heavens and the earth said? They that are guilty of the least are guilty of them all! 262-81

The need for and value of cycles is brought out clearly in what the readings have to say about day and night.

Day and Night

Again, in the figurative sense, we find that light and darkness, day and night, are represented by that termed as periods of growth and the periods of rest or recuperation, through the activities of other influences in those forces or sources of activity condensed in form to be called matter, no matter what plane this may be acting from or upon. 262-55

For as nature itself opens in the day, it spreads out for life, in the night it opens its petals, it bursts its bonds from the shell or from the plant. 5148-2

It is of interest here to note that in his book *My Ivory Cellar,* Dr. John Ott, pioneer in time-lapse photography, records that apples grow during the day and relax during the night. This was shown in his sequence of photographs.[20]

Is the Day significant of the life that is a span experience or existence in a sphere of activity when an entity, a soul, becomes conscious of that activity in or about self, or self's own associations during such an experience?
Is Night the rest from such an activity? Or, as manifested in the material world, is Night only a change from one realm of a source of consciousness to another?
Such questions have been sought since the foundations of the world.
Or, does Day and Night present that experience sought in every soul that is given expression to as in days of yore, when it was said, "If a man die, shall he live again?" Live, or give expression, or manifest?
From whence came man into the consciousness of Day and Night?

[20]John Ott, *My Ivory Cellar,* Twentieth Century Press, Inc., Chicago, 1958, pg. 101.

What makes for the awareness, in the experience of each soul, of a change?

Are such questions merely answered in the heart of each, as: "The sun goes up, the sun goes down," and "There will be a big night tonight"?

These are questions. These are basic truths.

What thinkest thou?

What will ye do with presenting these and all phases of that through which man, and the soul of man, passes in his experience of a consciousness in a material world?   262-54

Then, in the mental plane, what becomes Day and Night? That which separates the one from the other. Or, as illustrated, the Day becomes the first day or the consciousness of separation from the forces which the power, or the activity, is in action. And there ... [are] set then in the materiality, or in the plane in which the physical activity begins, those that represent time or space. So we have the *rulers* of the light, or Day, and the rulers of the Night.   262-56

The need for periods of growth and others of rest requires no explanation.

Cycles Based on Numerals

In Combination with Astrological Cycles

Since the planets revolve about the sun, their effects on particular individuals recur in cycles as has been previously noted. The combination of astrological cycles and those of numerals can be rather involved.

In the application of will's force as respecting those elements of influence, these we will find will have much to do with the developments for the entity, for under the influence of Mars with Uranus these may become very erratic, even to where destructive forces may be made manifest, especially through arms, firearms, or temper as exercised by the body, or in that of erratic actions in speech towards others. These influences occur in the cycles when 7, 9, and their multiples are in the activities of those forces that are manifest both through the astrological and numerals, or numerical forces as come in every influence. In those as are seen in Uranus with that of those in the Mercurian, these have more to do with the physical and the care that will be necessary to prevent the overtaxing of the nerve and mental forces to the extent that anemia will prevail in the physical actions. These as warnings, especially in the 23rd, 29th and the 34th years. These coming again as multiples, or numbers, in the life, as well as influences astrological. These may be met by those conditions as are ever active through the application of will in self as respecting those of astrological, or even physical conditions for the body.   4248-1

Then the astrological aspects, as intimated for this entity, will come rather as in cycles or periods. As has been seen by the entity, those periods when the greater emotions were manifesting in the material experience of the entity, as from desires in spiritual directions or of creative influences, were in the seventh, fourteenth, twenty-first—and will be in the twenty-eighth—years.

Hence the entity will find in this present year, or part of this year—of course, this begins about the middle of May and will extend until along in July of 1939—there will be great emotional changes; as there were at the age of twenty-one.

These periods lap over from one year to the next, you see; not just exactly one year, but months and days and weeks lapping over at the beginning or ending of each cycle change.

But these for this entity are rather definite, and will be seen if there is the analysis of the determining factors the entity has chosen in its activities in this experience . . .

In Venus, as well as in Jupiter, we find there are the abilities in the directions for drawing, writing of the natures that would be a description to the entity of what he would *like* or would *not* like life to be. In the writing of such we find that the abilities would be the *extremes,* or in those highest ideals or those farthest from what the entity would desire to attract to itself.

These arise *innately,* and—as has been indicated—periods of sevens will be the cycles when these activities would better be undertaken, or changes made in activities, associations or relations.   1574-1

As to the sojourns in the earth, not all of these may be indicated. With the cycles under which the entity has manifested, and as it is in the midst of a cycle, we will find more than the ordinary influences upon the entity in the present; owing to what may be called—in astrological parlance—the closeness of the entity's entrance to a divided influence, or to the cusps.

These, however, are indicated rather in the experience of the entity under the variations; as in the combination of material experience and the astrological sojourns.   3175-1

Thus there is quite a variation as to how the reflexes react with the body. For there come certain cycles. All portions of the body come under varied cycles as changes are wrought. For the body fully and completely changes in seven years. Yet this is something continually going on, and various portions change at various reflex periods. And from astrological

214

aspects (so called) it might be said that it gets about all the good there is in it. For various individuals, under various cycles of course, are subject to changes as they pass through the various periods of the zodiac.   3688-1

The complexity and potential value of this system of cycles is indeed beautifully pointed out in the above excerpt. The following one is a supplementation with a thought contained in it which is constantly echoed in the Cayce readings.

For with each cycle of seven years there comes the passing from one realm of activity to another, through the various urges according to that tempered by the consciousness in other realms. Thus has been builded a theory of astrological aspects. These take little into account of will. For there is no urge that surpasses the will of an individual entity. Hence it depends upon how well such urges are cultivated or applied, or resisted, or done nothing about and letting them take their course. To be sure, all of these have an effect upon the mental urges. For mind is ever the builder.   3412-2

With Reference to Body, Mind and Soul

Numerical cycles were repeatedly mentioned with reference to body, mind and soul.

As to the appearances of the entity in the earth, and those influences that will bear upon the early experiences—we find that these, as may be seen, should be changed in the seventh and in the fourteenth year. These are as cycles of impressions and changes; and activities in the developing of the body, the mind, the soul.   1788-3

As is understood by some, thought by many, there . . . [are] within each physical being the elements whereby the organs and their activities and functionings are enabled within themselves to supply that needed for replenishing or rebuilding their own selves.
This may be done, as comprehended, in a period of every seven years. Thus it is a slow process, but it is a growth in the energies of the body and thus necessitates there being kept a normal balance in the chemistry of the body-force itself. For it is either from potash, iodine, soda or fats, that each of these in their various combinations and multiple activities supply all the other forces of the body-energies. Yet in each body there is born or projected that something of the soul-self also. 3124-1

Thus we will gradually more and more bring about the normal conditions . . . for this body. [8-year-old girl]

It must be near to the second cycle, as indicated, and this is only a small portion of fourteen years—but it will be worth it!
3117-2

Note in the reference above that the particular treatment had to be undertaken at a special time in a special cycle to be effective.

It will be seen, as we find from the records here, that varied experiences of the entity in its developments through the cycle of its experience will be altered by the variation in the cycles of development; and that as may be given in the present as having the greater influence will during its seventh to fourteenth or fifteenth year be changed—as when it is twenty-one and twenty-eight; and *then* it will be determined as to whether it is to be the material or the mental and spiritual success to which this entity may make for its experiences in the present sojourn.
1332-1

As there was in the entering of the entity's inner forces into this physical body, the first [change] will come at the age of seven, at fourteen, at twenty-two—these will be decided changes, or one will so lap over the other—but may be said to be periods when changes will come to this entity; for there was some lapse of time (as time is counted from the material) between the physical birth and the spiritual birth.
566-1

For the body renews itself, every atom, in seven years. How have ye lived for the last seven? And then the seven before? What would ye do with thy mind and thy body if they were wholly restored to normalcy in this experience? Would these be put to the use of gratifying thine own appetites as at first? Will these be used for the magnifying of the appreciation of the love to the infinite?
3684-1

Q-4. What has caused the apparent division of my life activity into four-year cycles? How can I best use the urges resulting from this experience?
A-4. Today, if ye will hear His voice, as He hath given, is the acceptable day of the Lord. Work while it is day.
That these are divided, or apparently have been, indicates that they are as stepping-stones, unfoldments that have come. While apparently they have taken different directions at times, are they not now ready to be coordinated into one specific effort?
And these as we find are the better manners in which these may be applied in the present experience.
2787-1

As to the appearances in the earth, and the effects these have upon the characteristics and the latent and manifested abilities in the entity's present experience—not all may be given, but these are indicated in the urges at present, and for the next two or three cycles—this meaning periods of seven to ten years each . . .   1664-2

Hence little of astrological influence (so-called) has a part in the experience of the entity, until after it has completed its third cycle—or until the entity in earth years has passed its seventeenth year.   2779-1

Those influences that have to deal with great numbers of people, those desires that find expressions in being associated with large groups are a part—not as a herd but rather as a part of the experience of the whole—all of these become as a portion of the entity's inner self. And these have found, these do find their expressions in the material or earthly sojourns as from these—that influence the entity in the present; and we will find that in seven to ten years *others* will become a part of the entity's experience, when duties, obligations, the setting of self in the various activities in which it may find itself producing and making for the varied environmental forces become under other urges.   1243-1

While all the appearances may not be given, these we find have an influence in the experience through the next two cycles of the entity's unfoldment, or in those periods of preparation the entity would make for its place among its fellow man. And let this ever be the purpose: The place where thou art, the corner in which ye may shine, may it ever be better for your being in it. Give something of self rather than demanding of others. Contribute to the welfare of thine own household, thine own community . . . and as you apply self in these various phases of the experience you will find self—and the abilities of self—unfolding.   3203-1

As is understood by many, in the earth manifestation and the cycle of time much repeats itself; and those in authority, in high and low places, have the opportunity for individual expression—that wields an influence upon those who are directed in body, mind or thought or spirit by the activities of those manifesting in the earth.   3976-26

One that will have strong body after reaching the second cycle from the present.   4353-4

For each *cycle* is as a grade in the experience of an entity or soul, and as application is made does the material experience become an urge in the present influence or force.   1703-3

This last reference brings out clearly that the system of cycles constitutes a school. It appears from the foregoing material that an entity passes through general cycles in periods of seven years unless special circumstances modify this.

In Respect to the Physical Body

The details as to effects of cycles on the physical body are of great interest.

How a cycle of vibrations can bring strains to the body is brought out below. Apparently the cellular producing or produced portions trigger the situation.

In the nerve tissue and centers we find much of this strain comes, for this is involved in the circulation and the dissimulation [dissemination] of those forces, as an element in the system brings these strains on the various portions of that governed by the circulation in its course through the system, and attacking those portions that are weaker or as the cycle of vibrations change in the cellular producing or produced portions of the body for the use in the physical forces.

4517-1

However, the body constantly replenishes itself. Those portions which are channels for changes, rebuild more quickly. The digestive forces of the body or the lungs, liver, heart, digestive system, pancreas and spleen change almost seven times during the usual 7-year cycle.

Remember, the body rebuilds and replenishes itself continually. What portion would be the more active in its changes than those that *are* the channels for these very changes—the *digestive* forces of the body; the lungs, the liver, the heart, the digestive system, the pancreas, the spleen? All of these change the more often, so that when it is ordinarily termed that the body has changed each atom in seven years, these organs have changed almost *seven times* during those seven years!

796-2

There may be great regularity in recurring physical conditions.

As in most conditions of the nature of migraine or so-called headaches, the cause is in the colon—where there are patches of adhesions of fecal forces to the walls of the intestine, causing activities that come in general cycles. These may come at times regularly, almost so that you could set this by your clock at times; for it is as the regularity of the system itself.

3630-1

Both teeth and thyroid glands may be affected by calcium administered during the change of the cycle for teeth.

Cycles change for the teeth during the second year of each cycle. During that year take... to supply calcium to the system, and it will aid not only the teeth but all the activities of the thyroid glands.   3051-3

The cycle of the eyes is completed in slightly over six weeks.

Q-4. How often should [this] body have eyes examined?
A-4. At least every six weeks. That's near a cycle for the eyes, see?   758-13

The eliminating systems require twenty-eight days to complete a cycle. Is it possible that the flow of liquid involved in elimination is affected by the pull of the moon?

Q-3. Should the treatments be continued daily?
A-3. They should, for at least another twenty-eight days. Why twenty-eight days? for this is a cycle of functional reaction with the eliminating systems, and with the changes as should be inaugurated, in the character of eliminations set up, and changes made by the change of vibratory forces in the use of same, this should require at least that period, and then this could be judged by the reactions as have taken place.
5522-2

An explanation is given for night sweats. During the day the body is especially concerned with upper circulation or that needed for physical activity. During the evening the circulation is directed toward building the body trunk. If the circulation is unbalanced, the operation of this cycle and the force of nerve plexuses are in conflict. Increases in respiration and perspiration are more likely.

Q-3. What causes the night sweats?
A-3. In the whole system of a human individual, we find as this: There are cycles of functioning of organs of the body. The natural tendency then of system is upper circulation, or plain activity during the day, and of body building through trunk circulation during evening. These are natural cycle conditions. Then, the lack of the equalized circulation produces the overstimulation to mental forces, of the blood attempting to form this cycle operation going, as it were, against nerve plexuses, [and] with the improper incentives, create[s] the too full capillary circulation. Hence the inclination towards respiration increased, or perspiration increased in sleeps.   4520-4

219

The difference in vibration of the tissues of different organs is responsible for the length of time these organs take to complete their different cycles.

Q-9. What are the length of the cycles which come to this body?
A-9. Each organ has its own cycle; the cycle as given here is the period of seven years, as time is reckoned from the physical plane. The cycles for the organs vary in their development.   47-1

It has long been confirmed that the body in toto renews itself in ever so many periods, or so many cycles of change. It is seen that not all portions of the system move in the same cycle, for the vibration that is necessary to create that tissue which will replenish a heart cell, or a ventricle, will not move in the same cycle as one that replenishes the glands of digestion, whether it be the salivary glands themselves or those of the lactice, or lacteal glands, or mammary glands, or the adrenal gland, or the thyroid gland, or those of the ducts as in the gall duct, or the pancreas, or that of the spleen in itself. *All* of these, in *this* particular case, are self-evident that there has been left in system such conditions as that at various stages of their cycle of replenishing or of resuscitating, have the various functionings of organs, or glands, or ducts, suffered at times under the strain put upon same by non-coordination in eliminating system.   108-2

The cycle of activity of each organ is dependent upon its relationship to sympathetic and cerebrospinal reactions.

As we find, there are disturbances preventing better physical functionings through the body. These come rather periodically, or as the various cycles of the body-functioning are involved in changes that take place gradually and continually, as in everybody. For the cycle of activity for each organ is dependent upon the relationship of that functioning system to the vibration of the sympathetic and cerebrospinal reactions.   3644-1

Physical treatment in conjunction with cycles should not be commenced for oneself or a child unless the effort is to be a continuing one.

Each atom may be changed within seven years. If there are those interested in contributing to this, *begin.* If you are not interested in doing it for fourteen, don't commence!   3117-1

Remember there are gradual changes that take place in a body, and especially in a developing body, a growing body. The whole anatomical structure is changed in each cycle—or every seven years.

Unless this suggested treatment is to be continued—not altogether continuously but very persistently—until the second cycle for this body, don't begin it—just put it away and forget it. 3236-1

However, real application of effort will bring results. Weaknesses persist only when left to do so.

These may be called contributory causes. But the body—remember—renews itself at each cycle of seven years. Why should these, then, *now* cause disturbance—save where scar tissue has formed or where structural portions are unaligned? They have produced weaknesses; and if there has not been and is not the proper application and the keeping of a balance in the body-building, then they become chronic. 1620-3

Such conditions need not be expected to be cured in a day, a week, a month, or a year. For, as has been and is—or should be known, it requires seven years for resuscitation, change, or eliminations.

This is not to discourage, but rather to encourage; if there will be the keeping close to those suggestions, diets, activities, rubs; for there will come the gradual change. 1710-10

For the blood supply is added to three times each day if meals are taken, else we would never recuperate or change a whole body every seven years; it is a *constant* growth. No condition of a physical nature should be *remaining* unless it has been hamstrung by operative forces or strictures or tissue that may not be absorbed; and even this may be changed if it is taken patiently—and persistently—in *any* body! 133-4

While it would require *persistent* application (and, of course, it can be overdone!), there may be added that in the system in such a manner as to aid in rectifying the ends, so as to take away the natural wall built up in the nerve ends—and be the more helpful. This would require almost seven years for a change. 783-1

For, while from a pathological standpoint there are nerve ends destroyed, we find that these *can* be replenished or rebuilded. For, as is recognized, the body changes continuously. And through a cycle or period the body may have rebuilded or replaced itself entirely. To be sure, nominally this is termed inconsistent with the findings of many. Yet there are those abilities within self, through the application of spiritual truths, as well as in making application of the physical conditions to supply and replenish same, to bring this about. The attitude, then, is the more important. 3038-1

Q-1. Are the nerves of motivation dead?
A-1. If they are, may they not be renewed? Isn't the body renewed at least once every seven years? Who is to renew it? Who is the giver of life? By pure coordination, pure faith, pure desire to be what God would have thee be. Ye have much work to do in this material plane. Don't become impatient with self, with others. Know ye are indeed the Lord's only as ye fulfill His commandments.

Read Psalm 119 under the section Tau. Also St. John 14, especially 1st, 2nd, 3rd, 4th, 5th, 6th, 7th, 8th verses and then those latter portions of the 15th chapter. Apply them to self. 5326-1

That nerves have been crushed, that they might be made to work against existent conditions, is rather crude—considered in the light of that given. It is self-evident that it will not be possible in the beginning to release those nerves that are pinched, where curvatures exist in the spine. But these may be *gradually* changed. For each cycle, every element, every condition must renew itself; else there becomes or is set up greater deterioration than creation. And each element, each organ, each functioning of the body throughout, is capable of reproducing itself. How?

Not merely from the ability of the glands to take from that assimilated those elements needed, but in each atom, in each corpuscle, is life. Life is that ye worship as God.

If God be with you, and you choose to use those elements in His creation that cause each atom, each corpuscle, to become more and more aware of that creative influence, there may then be brought resuscitation. May there not be created, then, health rather than disease, disorder, confusion? 2968-1

One sentence in the last reference invites elaboration. The sentence is, "It is self-evident that it will not be possible in the beginning to release those nerves that are pinched, where curvatures exist in the spine."

To many persons the term "curvature of the spine" represents a hunched back. However, a curvature of the spine may exhibit itself in other ways. Most people are right-handed. A right-handed person may use that arm and side largely to the exclusion of the left and eventually pull vertebrae in his back so badly that a curvature forms, exhibited in a sideways pull. This, also, can pinch nerves. The body is constructed in such a way that balance needs to be maintained. Right and left sides should be used equally insofar as it is practical, and the spine should not be pulled out of line in any direction.

If the spine has been pulled out of line, it is certainly good news to know that it may be pulled back with persistent care and treatment under a chiropractor or osteopath and that then the body can resuscitate the damaged areas.

This same reference points out that the Creative Influence we worship as God is in every atom. It, therefore, behooves us to have a creative attitude if we wish to conquer physical weaknesses. Spiritual progress brings mental progress which, in turn, brings physical progress.

While the body, [3165] should be able to respond to disturbances, and it will outgrow most of these conditions when there is the beginning of the 2nd cycle of changes in body, we find that—unless there [are] measures taken in the present for correction, these may take on other conditions that would become much more detrimental and may even become undermining to the physical well-being of the body. Hence there should be the setting of these in channels so that, as the physical body changes, the mental attributes, the ideals mental and spiritual, are set in those directions as to control the physical disturbances, or pathological reactions that occur in the present.   3165-1

Know, all that may be added to the body is only to enable each organ to reproduce itself in a consistent way and manner, and it will get rid of drosses with its reproduction. For, as in the spiritual life ye grow in grace, in knowledge, in understanding of the law of God, ye also in the mental life grow in unfoldment, in the awareness of thy associations with spiritual and material activities. So in the mental and spiritual, these throw off. For, have ye not heard how that constantly there is the change, and that the body has in a seven-year cycle reproduced itself entirely? No need for anyone, then, to have *any* disturbance over that length of period, if—by common sense—there would be the care taken. But if your mind holds to it, and you've got a stumped toe, it will stay stumped! If you've got a bad condition in your gizzard, or liver, you'll keep it—if you think so!

But the body—the physical, the mental and spiritual—will remove same, if ye will *let* it and not hold to the disturbance!
                                                         257-249

Here we find, at times, anxieties. Know, creative forces are eternal. The correction of the body-forces comes in cycles. And there are those corrections ever being attempted in a physical body. Add those material, mental and spiritual elements, and we may renew a body in any given period.

Then, keep creative in thought and purpose. Expect something, but do something about it. Use those abilities in the creative forces for helping others.   3096-1

Some Effects of Cycles on the Physical Body

It is important that nutrition scheduled for a special cycle of the body should be included during that time as otherwise the physical forces may suffer from a debility.

Those elements of gold and silver were lacking in those periods of gestation, which produced in the first cycle of activity the inability of the glands to create. **3100-1**

The application or ingestion of any *healing* substance should be made on a regular but intermittent basis. There are repeated instructions as to this in the readings with regard to all sorts of substances. This cyclic system brings stimulation to the body and then allows it freedom to take over itself.

Any application for a general condition or nature is better if applied for periods of three to four weeks (or less), as may be indicated, then rest a period allowing the system to adjust itself, for as is understood by the body there is every element in the active forces of the body (normal) for normal and proper development. Hence this gives these an opportunity to be secreted and become effective by assimilation for the blood stream and circulatory forces of the body in such way from the physical as well as the material applications as may be made from time to time. Thus the same is consistent with that where disturbances have been indicated in any portion of the body. **270-39**

Q-4. How often should this [Haliver oil with Viosterol] be given, and how many a day?
A-4. All such properties that add to the system are more efficacious if they are given for periods, left off for periods and begun again. For if the system comes to rely upon such influences wholly, it ceases to produce the vitamins even though food values may be kept normally balanced.
And it's much better that these be produced in the body from the normal development than supplied mechanically; for nature is much better *yet* than science!
This as we find then, given twice a day for two or three weeks, left off a week and then begun again, especially through the winter months, would be much more effective with the body. **759-12**

. . . in *every* character of application for healing of a body, there must be those periods for sufficient reaction to the impulses that are received from any character of application. **275-32**

224

Q-1. Should the body continue taking . . . internally?
A-1. The small portions, yes . . .

Take periods of . . . not continued every day but for a week every day, rest a week and begin again. These are more effective than continued, for *any* property. For this may be said to be the manner in which any outside influence acts upon not only this body but any body.

To continue the use of any *one* influence that is active upon the body *continually* is to cause those portions of the system that *produce* same to lose their activity or their significance, and depend upon the supply from without.

But to give stimulation to the system and then refrain from same tends to produce *in* the body that necessary reaction in the glandular system and in the functioning of organs. For the body (normal) produces within itself the necessary elements for its continual reproduction of itself at *all* times.   1100-8

Persons were often advised to carry out therapies at the same time of day. The following selection is taken from instructions on the use of a castor oil pack.

Have at least 3 to 4 thicknesses of old flannel saturated thoroughly with castor oil, then apply electric heating pad. Let this get just about as warm as the body can well stand, cover with oilcloth to prevent soiling of linen. Keep this on every afternoon or evening for an hour. Then sponge off with soda water. Do this for at least 7 days without breaking. One hour each day, same hour each day . . . If there are none [results] indicated, rest one day, then repeat for another 7 days, and we will find changes come about, unless there is undue exercise.
5186-1

Cycles Great and Small

One of the greatest cycles of which we know is that of the solar system. An entity can attain oneness in any of the many systems designed for such development, but if it has commenced the solar system cycle, it must complete this.

Q-7. . . . Is it necessary to finish the solar system cycle before going to other systems?
A-7. Necessary to finish the solar cycle.
Q-8. Can oneness be attained—or the finish of evolution reached—on any system, or must it be in a particular one?
A-8. Depending upon what system the entity has entered, to be sure. It may be completed in any of the many systems.
Q-9. Must the solar system be finished on earth, or can it be completed on another planet, or does each planet have a cycle of its own which must be finished?

A-9. If it is begun on the earth it must be finished on the earth. The solar system of which the earth is a part is only a portion of the whole. For, as indicated in the number of planets about the earth, they are of one and the same—and they are relative one to another. It is the cycle of the whole system that is finished, see?   5749-14

Among the smaller cycles experienced by man are those involving days of the week and months of the year.
Certain days and months may be fortunate or unfortunate for a person.

Tuesdays are the fortunate days for the entity, as in February the periods when the greater blessings come; and also from the middle of November to the middle of December the periods that bring disturbance.   1797-1

How the cycle for places operates is not clear.

Columbus, Ohio. Yes—one of the cities not a very good place to be born for some, and good for others—for it changes its place on the cycle at times.   3544-1

Personal Cycles

Each body has an individual cycle with a special vibration.

Q-2. *Does each body have its individual cycle?*
A-2. **Each body has its individual cycle and vibration.**
                                                              3329-1

In this cycle a person should be preparing for the next one. Completion of a cycle should bring the entity closer to the Infinite.

So has the entity found in its experience in such relationships that it must not look back, but ever forward; for that which has been must be again, if there will be the preparations in the *now* for its next cycle of activity. 541-1

Why ... is there in the third and then the tenth generation a reverting to first principles? (Remember, we are speaking only from the physical reaction.)
Because that period is required for the cycle of activity in the glandular force of reproduction to reassert itself. How is it given in our Word? That the sins of the fathers are visited unto the children of the third and fourth generation, even to the tenth. This is not saying that the results are seen only in the bodily functions of the descendants, as is ordinarily implied; but that the essence of the message is given to the individual respecting the activity of which he may or must eventually be

226

well aware in his own being. That is, what effect does it have upon you to even get mad, to laugh, to cry, to be sorrowful? All of these activities affect not only yourself, your relationships to your fellow man, but your next experience in the earth!
281-38

For, as the entity finds self, it is body-physical, mind-mental, and soul-spiritual; as the Father, the Son, the Holy Spirit. These are manifestations in the spirit world, in the mental world, in the material world. They are one. Thus as the manifestations are in the material in the present, they grow from an ideal or concept into the mind or purpose or aim *manifesting* in materiality.

Thus is the cycle or the growth of that which is purposed to do.

Hence mind is ever the builder, the way; as He, the ideal—in mind, in materiality, yea in spirit—is the way, the truth, the light.
2326-1

The purpose for each soul's entrance is to complete a cycle, to get closer to the Infinite, that it may know the purposes with the entity in the earth.
3131-1

Q-6. Is this the period of the great tribulation spoken of in Revelation, or just the beginning, and if so just how can we help ourselves and others to walk more closely with God?

A-6. The great tribulation and periods of tribulation, as given, are the experiences of every soul, every entity. They arise from influences created by man through activity in the sphere of any sojourn. Man may become, with the people of the universe, ruler of any of the various spheres through which the soul passes in its experiences. Hence, as the cycles pass, as the cycles are passing, when there *is* come a time, a period of readjusting in the spheres (as well as in the little earth, the little soul)—seek, then, as known, to present self spotless before that throne; even as *all* are commanded to be circumspect, in thought, in act, to that which is held by self as that necessary for the closer walk with Him. In that manner only may each atom (as man is an atom, or corpuscle, in the body of the Father) become a helpmeet with Him in bringing that to pass that all may be one with Him.
281-16

Particular past lives will have an influence in one cycle, others in another. The end of every cycle brings the entity to another crossroad.

In the personalities we find these (characteristics) more expressed or manifested from those material manifestations. While all of these may not be indicated here, those are given that have the greater influence in the experience of the entity

227

at this particular cycle of its consciousness or awareness of its
abilities, latent and manifested.   2902-1

As to the appearances or sojourns in the earth, we find that
not all are indicated or given at once—but those that in this
particular cycle of experience have the greater influence or
bearing upon the entity's opportunity for development.

For, as the very influences of the body are a growth day by
day, so is the spiritual development a growth. We are told that
in each seven years we are entirely new. Rather is it not true
that *some* portion is new each day? It is a growth! For it is
moment by moment, and not *wholly* cycle by cycle, that the
change comes.   1597-1

As to the appearances of the entity in the earth—all of these
may not be indicated here; for these alter according to the
application of the individual to the opportunities in the earth,
but with each cycle . . . [come] the various influences that are
apparent from sojourns in certain material environments.
These are given in the present, for the entity is in that stage or
state in which changes may be made, or may be wrought in the
activity of that chosen by the entity for its material activity.
                                                                     3132-1

*Q-3. Will you give my earth appearances, since the Crusade
period, and do any have a bearing on this earth life?*
A-3. These have no bearing in the present. This may depend
upon the application of self. There have been those that were
in and out, but *not* an urge such as to be active. It is as this: One
may be in an environ or an experience and yet not working at
or applying self in those directions, or not being aware of or
influenced by such. Thus those that have a direct bearing upon
the experiences in the present have been presented, now.
                                                                     1602-4

As to the appearances in the earth, not all of these may be
given. For these ye attain in thy varied cycles of unfoldment.
                                                                     3053-3

As to the appearances in the earth, these have been quite
varied. Not all may be given in the present, for with each cycle
there comes another experience as a part of the entity's
problems or help. Just as some set that each day or each hour,
as the earth passes from phase to phase of the constellations or
the signs of the zodiac, there comes greater impression.
Rather is it as the cycles. For it is admitted that the body
changes completely each seven years. Do you change your
mind that often? Not this body! What it knows it knows it
knows! and knows it!

In the experience then, apply those things. Be sure ye are

right, and no one will make you deviate from thy purposes and activities.   3637-1

Not all of the sojourns may be indicated at once, but those as we find that have their activity in the problems and experiences of the entity in the present.

Know that these change, as does the body, about every seven years; unless one becomes satisfied in body, mind and spirit, so that such have become atrophied.   2460-1

In giving the interpretation of the records as we find them, there is much from which to choose. It would be well if all the experiences that may be drawn upon in the present were fully understood. All will not be given but those that have the bearing of a great influence upon the entity in this present cycle of its experience in the earth. For there are changes indicated, as in body, so in tendencies, in urges; as the tenets or truths are applied in the mental self. For mind is ever the builder. One builds or destroys urges that have arisen from activities in the cycle of the interim or from the dwelling of the entity in a particular realm of activity in the earth.   4016-1

As to the appearances in the earth, not all will be indicated in the present but those having to do particularly with this individual cycle of the entity's experience. For know, all that the entity may know of law, of God, of international relationships, already exists in the consciousness for the entity to be made aware of same. Then, for this information to become knowledge or understanding there must be the application of self to those sources of material knowledge but with the faith and trust in universal knowledge. For as indicated by the lawgiver, think not who will descend from heaven that ye may hear or know; think not who will come from over the sea that a message may be brought; for lo, it is within thine own self. For the mind and soul is from the beginning. Thus there is to come within the entity's own consciousness the awareness of how the application is to be made.   5000-1

Q-18. Was I associated with Jesus Christ when He was on the earth as the son of Mary?

A-18. As this is to become a portion of the experience, this may best be given later.

You were!

This may not be wholly understood. It is as this: Individuals in the earth move from cycle to cycle in their own development, in their relationships with individuals and with the activities having to do with that which may be accomplished in a given experience. They have, as it were, taken this or that road in meeting certain conditions. And *one* experience at one portion of the life, then, is as a lamp or a guidebook. Then when they have come to the crossroads again, as it were, there is another experience or another lesson.

This might be illustrated in a very simple, yet a very direct way and manner as follows:

In training the mind in material things, that pertaining to the care of the body is not that used in meeting a friend; yet it is at times a *portion* of the same, see? Yet in meeting the friend, various portions of the development come to the forefront; as to what has been the manner of activity, the social custom, or the needs of the individual—whether friend or foe.

So, as that association is to be, as it were, the crowning of the efforts, the experiences of the entity in this particular experience or sphere of activity, hold fast that thou hast; and then it may be given thee.   993-4

As to appearances in the earth—these have been quite varied. All of these may not be indicated in the present, for—as given—each cycle brings a soul-entity to another crossroad, or another urge from one or several of its activities in the material plane. But these are chosen with the purpose to indicate to the entity how and why those urges are a part of the entity's experience as a unit, or as a whole. For, one enters a material sojourn not by chance, but there is brought into being the continuity of pattern or purpose, and each soul is attracted to those influences that may be visioned from above. Thus *there* the turns in the river of life may be viewed.

To be sure, there are floods in the life; there are dark days and there are days of sunshine. But the soul-entity stayed in a purpose that is creative, even as this entity, may find the haven of peace as is declared in Him.   3128-1

Even though we work out the problems of special lives *only* in this one, and are not concerned with our other lives now, there are general urges that remain with us as a composite outcome of previous earth lives and planetary interims.

All of the experiences in the earth are not indicated but those that are a portion of the experience in the present cycle. For as the body changes through each cycle, so do the urges change. For some are applied, some are retained, some are discarded. But the gentle and general urges, those indicated from the composite of the latent or manifested urges from sojourns and the interims between these, are predominant.   3685-1

An entity's development during a past cycle or cycles may bring a complete fulfillment such as birth at the stroke of noon or a return to earth on the same day of the year.

As to appearances in the earth, these have been disturbing, in a manner, in the present. These bring urges latent and manifested. Not all may be given, not all are visioned, but these we find as applying in the entity's particular second cycle of experience in this material sojourn . . .

Q-2. *Her birth at the stroke of noon?*

A-2. Just a complete fulfillment, as was the hour when the heavens rent the veil of the temple from top to bottom. 3621-1

For, the entity's departure and entrance in the present covered an earthly cycle, according to that accounted by those of Holy Writ. The entity departed on the 24th of August, 1876. It entered again the 24th of August, 1910. Thus a cycle . . .

Ye may ask—rightly—*why* such urges are in the experience so definitely as is being indicated. Because, as given, of a one cycle. For, remember—death in the material plane is birth in the spiritual-mental plane. Birth in the material plane is death in the spiritual-mental plane. Hence the reason that when those physical manifestations began to be impressed upon the brain centers—those portions of an individual entity that are a constant growth from first conception—there were the impressions to hinder rather than aid the memory of other experiences.

Yet here we find a manifestation where *this* entity, as indicated, should it choose or determine to do so, may see and experience (as it has in flashes) much of that experience now being interpreted here for the entity, as well as others. 2390-2

A cycle of time may be rounded out knowingly.

While the activity in the Armed Services would be galling at times, and offer opportunities for many forms of indulgence, we find that if ye will take it seriously, ye will have the opportunity in thy experience that will bring to thee by the 3rd day of January, 1945, the happiest day of thy experience in this life. Don't lose that opportunity, for it will be as a cycle of time, as in commemoration, as it were, of the blessings of the hand of the Master upon thee, if ye choose that day to give thy body, thy promises to a companion who may become a part of thy life on that day. Keep that body then, as it were, for that day . . . and when the opportunity is presented as for January 3rd, 1945, set that as thy wedding date.   5049-1

An entity may even enter under approximately the same astrological aspects as those of the last lifetime.

. . . we find in this particular entity, and oft—ones that enter an experience as a complete cycle; that is, upon the same period under the same astrological experiences as in the sojourn just before (that is, being born upon the same day of

[the] month—though time may have been altered); find periods of activity that will be very much the same as those manifested in the previous sojourn, in the unfoldment and in the urges latent and manifested.

Psychology, philosophy, reasoning, dramatic art, the dramatic critic—these will be the character and the temperament that [are] to be dealt with [in this entity].

For, in the appearance before this, the entity entered as Jean Poquelin, known as Molière the great French dramatist.

2814-1

Moliere's birthday was January 15, 1622; this person's was January 15, 1942.

The time of return depends upon what the entity has accomplished in its cycle through the solar system.

When an individual incarnates in the earth, he has *possibly* passed through all the various spheres, either once, twice, *many* times—yet the changes bring those same conditions about for an understanding of each relationship in its *magnified* sphere. In the earth alone do we find them *all* in *one!* for man has taken on a bodily *form* in matter, or in nature. In the others we find in the *varied* forms, dependent upon that to which it has builded for *its* sojourn—see? Now, as to one's incarnations in the earth—then we find they *do not* come at *regular, given,* periods—but more as cycles, dependent upon what the individual, the entity, *has* done, or *has* accomplished through *its* cycle of the earth's passage *through this* solar system . . .

311-2

Even the position of the organs of the body and right- or left-handedness stem from past development. Whether an individual is material- or spiritual-minded also comes from this. The left side of the body is associated with the spiritual by many, the right with the material. Could it be that the habitual use of the left denotes a spiritual-minded person?

Then, these are the influences that have to do with the emotional life or experience of the entity, as well as the mental or dream or psychic life of the entity in this sojourn.

These we term as astrological influences, for the want of better terms. For, the activities of an individual through such interims are interpreted according to the phases of accredited influence in this particular sphere—or this solar system.

Hence these correspond with the emotions and oft with what may be termed cycles of activity.

It is not (if the student is interested in these phases) merely coincidental that there are seven days to the week; but the seven centers and seven phases of experience and of reactions of sojourns of the entity in environs produce what may be termed a cycle of urge or experience.

Just as it is not perchance that the entity has physical activities that are not the ordinary or the usual—as to the position of the organs in the body (as the heart), and the use of the left instead of the right hand. But it is rather from the experiences in the earth, as will be seen, that now find expression in the physical as well as emotional forces of the body itself.   2594-1

As the soul and spirit entity takes its form in the spiritual plane, as the physical body takes form in the material plane, it is subject in the spiritual plane to those immutable laws of the spiritual plane. The spiritual entity of the individual is composed, then, of the spirit, the superconsciousness, the soul, the subconscious body, as the body is prepared for the entity in the spiritual plane, taking then the position in the universal force, or space, that the entity has prepared for itself, and goes through its development in that plane, until ready again to manifest in the flesh plane, and sow that degree of development toward that perfection that would make the entity in its entirety perfect, or one with the Creator. This is the cycle, or development, or condition, of the entity in the earth plane, and in the spiritual plane, whether developed to that position to occupy that it occupies, with its relative conditions left in the environment, and giving, partaking, or assisted by such conditions in its completion of development. As this: We would find the ever-giving forces, as long as not given to becoming in that sphere that would bring the entity into the perfect conjunction with the universal force, the entity depending, whether in spiritual plane, or physical plane, upon its relation with the sphere to which it is the closer attracted. Hence we have those conditions as expressed in the earth's plane; those individuals of a spiritual nature, those individuals of the material nature; the nature not changing in its condition, save by the environment of development.
                                                        900-20

If an individual has not completed his cycle satisfactorily, eventually he will be blotted out as an entity. The author's understanding is that the forces of the individual return to the general reservoir of force.

As indicated in the certain periods, remember—as has been given—it is not because ye were born in May, or on the 4th of May, that such and such happened to thee. For, as a corpuscle in the body of God, ye are free-willed—and thus a co-creator with God. Thus the universe stood still, as it were, that ye might manifest in a certain period that ye had attained by thy activity in the earth. For, as He hath given in all places, *time*

must be full. An individual entity's experience must be finished before the entity may either be blotted out or come into full brotherhood with the greater abilities, or the greater applications of self in the creating or finishing of that begun.
3003-1

Cycles of Group Manifestation

In addition to all the influences stemming from personal development which draw a soul back to earth living, there is the very considerable one of sharing in a group cycle. Those who have been engaged in some special work together return at certain times to further perfect it or make their part in it more meaningful.

As to the appearances in the earth—these we find quite varied. Not all would be given in the present, for—as indicated—different groups come to choose manifestation at varied cycles. And as indicated the entity is entering what might be called the sixth cycle in the present, for there is the using of the entity in the application of those tenets or truths, those inclinations that arise from the urges and the sojourns in the earth. For, those sojourns are as lessons, as grades, as activity of which, in which and through which the entity may use or abuse within the experiences of self. 3226-1

At the present time many persons active in the Atlantean scientific culture are returning. It can be readily understood that since the fall of that civilization, there has been no real chance to "try again," to choose once more between true spiritual development and the emphasis on technical achievement and preoccupation with self. The Atlanteans were highly developed mentally, and their influence today is the potential that can determine whether our civilization meets a similar disaster or whether it rises to the point of making mind subservient to soul.

Q-1. About how much time have I spent in reincarnation up to the present time?
A-1. Almost in all the cycles that have had the incoming from period to period hast thou dwelt. Thine first incoming in the earth was during those periods of the Atlanteans that made for the divisions. Hence, counting in time, some twenty thousand years. 707-1

As many who entered this cycle of 1910 and 1911, or during this cycle, the entity is an Atlantean. 2428-1

234

... more and more the reincarnating of the Atlanteans in the present experience, these bring a union of energies in the activities of those that sojourned there.   528-14

Another Atlantean, who will make the world better *or* worse for his having been in same, dependent upon the manner of application of the abilities that are latent, and may be made manifest under many varying circumstances.

For, as we have indicated, in those cycles especially of '09, '10 and '11, many, many Atlanteans were incarnated into the earth experience. And through their formative *and* active experience in materiality many changes are in the formation in the earth, as to nations, as to powers that are to bring into the consciousness of man in many spheres of activity the awareness of the Creative Forces and Influences.   1776-1

. . . as we have oft indicated, the Atlanteans are all *exceptional.* They either wield woe or great development. And their influences are felt, whether the *individual* recognizes it in himself or not.   1744-1

For, as we find, Uranian and Mercurian influences that are indwelling in the earth during these cycles of experience, from 1909 to 1913 inclusive in their ends, have been Atlanteans in their sojourns in the earth, and the wiles that may be made for such an activity of emotion, such an activity of mental abilities, such an engorgement of the carnal influences in the experiences of others. For, self-indulgences by so many in that land, in that experience in Atlantis, must make in these periods in the earth's sojourn the opportunities in the mental attitudes of individuals respecting what are constructive and what are the basic influences for the activities upon the souls of men when *these* souls may—as may be said—rule or ruin man's association in the earth during their sojourn in the present.   518-1

Another group incarnation occurring now, though on a much smaller scale it would seem than that of the Atlanteans, is the one coming from the Egypt of Ra Ta's day. It was then that the first concerted attempt was made to purify body and soul. Since Ra Ta reincarnated as Edgar Cayce, it is natural that those persons active in furthering the Priest's ideals and teachings at that time should today be interested in making Edgar Cayce's psychic discourses available to the world.

These in their divisions, then, made for what may be seen as a *real* representative of the conditions that are arisen in the earth in the present period, when there is the drawing near to that period of a change again, which is as a cycle that has brought about that period when there must be the establishing of that which is in the present the representation of that experimentation for the advancement of those various groups in that particular period.   294-147

Q-31. *How can the Egyptian history be completed?*
A-31. Finding those as would be necessary to complete same, which would run into many, many numbers. The Egyptian history should be especially correlated for the benefit of those attempting to carry on the work at the present time; for with these correlated influences, much is being attempted at this time, even as during that experience. Time is used here only figuratively. Or again the cycle has rolled to that period when the individual entities again in the earth's experience gather together for a definite work, with their various experiences as cause and effect through the various forms of the effect upon the environmental and hereditary conditions; yet these studied aright, any given fact may be worked out, even mathematically, as to what will be the response of an individual towards any portion of same. Hence this should be particularly interesting to those desiring to make the success of this at this period.
Q-32. *Should a history be attempted of any other period?*
A-32. Should of all periods, for they will be seen to come in cycles. This, then, will give the antipode to the various phases of continuity of existence; for, as in energy, there is seen the relativity of space and force as is begun, and as same continues to vibrate, that one law remains. Whenever it vibrates in the *same* vibration, it shows as the same thing. That's deep for you, yes. But when time, space, and the effect of thought and the activity of same—same was given aforetime through the Master, in this: "Your law says he that committeth adultery shall be stoned, but *I* say he that looketh on a woman to *lust* after her has committed adultery already." Now here we have relativity of force as applied through the mental body. Here we have as in application of same to the various experiences in the earth's plane and application of, when taking thought, or building by the mental body, this contributed or detracted from the soul of the individual.   254-47

This last reference particularly emphasizes the purpose of cycles. They provide a means by which an entity can meet a situation again. He will, thus, be tested more and more keenly. He who has resisted the act of physical adultery will have an opportunity to reject that of mental adultery.

In addition to the cycles running full term for Atlanteans and those in Egypt at the time of Ra Ta, there is another cycle evolving today, of paramount importance to us all. That is the cycle of the Master's return.

The position of the North Star with relation to the southern clouds indicated the beginning of the Piscean age at the time of Jesus' birth. We are now in the beginning of the Aquarian age. The cycle has come full term for the return of the Master. A way is being prepared for a new race, new experiences of man, all as a prelude to the Master's coming. It is only in the times that He has walked and talked with man, that the various stages of development have occurred.

Yes, we have the entity here, Thomas Sugrue, with the desire and the purpose for the understanding and knowledge of the physical experience of the Master's in the earth.

In those days when there had been more and more of the leaders of the peoples in Carmel—the original place where the school of prophets was established during Elijah's time, Samuel—these were called then Essenes; and those that were students of what ye would call astrology, numerology, phrenology, and those phases of that study of the return of individuals—or incarnation.

These were then the reasons that there had been a proclaiming that certain periods were a cycle; and these had been the studies then of Arestole, Enos, Mathias, Judas, and those that were in the care or supervision of the school—as you would term.

These having been persecuted by those of the leaders, this first caused that as ye have in interpretation of as the Sadducees, or "There is no resurrection," or there is no incarnation, which is what is meant in those periods.

In the lead of these, with those changes that had been as the promptings from the positions of the stars—that stand as it were in the dividing of the ways between the universal, that is the common vision of the solar system of the sun, and those from without the spheres—or as the common name, the North Star, as its variation made for those cycles that would be incoordinate with those changes that had been determined by some—this began the preparation—for the three hundred years, as has been given, in this period . . .

In these signs then was the new cycle, that as was then—as we have in the astrological—the beginning of the Piscean age, or that position of the Polar Star or North Star as related to the southern clouds. These made for the signs, these made for the symbols; as would be the sign as used, the manner of the sign's approach and the like.   5749-8

. . . the change between the Piscean and the Aquarian age. This is a gradual, not a cataclysmic activity in the experience of the earth in this period.   1602-3

For as has been indicated, now, in the next few years, there will be many entrances of those who are to prepare the way for the new race, the new experiences of man, that may be a part of those activities in preparation for the day of the Lord. 3514-1

Rather giving self to seeking, day by day to *know* the will of the Father as was manifest in Him, and may be manifest in thee, for He will not leave thee desolate, but will come to thee— but not unless invited; for, as in the periods, as we find, when He walked with men as the Master among men, or when as Joseph in the kingdoms that were raised as the saving of his peoples that *sold* him into bondage, or as in the priest of Salem in the days when the call came that a peculiar peoples would proclaim His name, He has walked and talked with men. Or, as in those days as Asapha . . . in those periods when those of the same Egyptian land were giving those counsels to the many nations, when there would be those saving of the physical from that of their own making in the physical; or in the garden when those temptations came, or as the first-begotten of the Father that came as Amilius in the Atlantean land and allowed himself to be led in ways of selfishness. Hence, as we see, all the various stages of developments that have come to man through the ages have been those periods when He walked and talked with man.

In this, then, when—as we find—that those periods began in a like period from that of Joseph to Joseph, or Jesus, then again we see the cycle when perfected in body, overcoming the world in the body of man, will He appear in those *varied* experiences; for He tarries not, and the time draws near.

364-8

The time draws near. Those who have helped Jesus in His work on earth before are undoubtedly gathering to help Him again. Yet this is a work in which we all may share. Every one of us may place himself—body, mind and soul—in the service of the Master. By utilizing our understanding of universal law and of the many wonderful things provided "to meet the needs of man," we may the better prepare ourselves for this mission which lies ahead. Because of our knowledge we may go more surely along the path, the spiritual path that leads back to God the Father.

BIBLIOGRAPHY

Allen, Eula, *Before the Beginning,* A.R.E. Press, Va. Beach, Va., 1966.

Beal, James B., *Electrostatic Fields, Electromagnetic Fields, and Ions—Mind/Body/Environment Interrelationships,* presented at the Symposium and Workshop on "The Effects of Low-Frequency Magnetic and Electric Fields on Biological Communication Processes" and the 6th annual meeting of the Neuroelectric Society, Vol. 6, February 18-24, 1973, Snowmass-at-Aspen, Colo. (Publisher) The Neuroelectric Society, 8700 West Wisconsin Ave.,Milwaukee, WI 53226, reference 15, pg. 5.

Bircher-Benner, M., M.D., *Food Science for All and a New Sunlight Theory of Nutrition,* translated and edited by Arnold Eiloart, B.Sc., Ph.D., The C.W. Daniel Co., London, 1939, pp. 59-61, 66 and 110.

Carlisle, Norman, "The Moon and You," *This Week Magazine,* November 17, 1968, pg. 12.

Cayce, *The Edgar Cayce Readings,* as referenced.

Cayce, Edgar Evans, *Two Electrical Appliances Described in the Edgar Cayce Readings,* A.R.E. Press, 1965.

Collier, Barnard Law, "Inventor Races Time at Age 100," *Parade,* January 14, 1973.

Friedman, Herbert, "The Sun," *National Geographic,* November, 1965, pp. 717, 721 and 740.

Gammon, Margaret H., *Astrology and the Edgar Cayce Readings,* A.R.E. Press, Revised Edition, 1973.

Goldman, M.C., "Should We Plant by the Moon?" *Organic Gardening and Farming,* March, 1965, pp. 58-60.

Henderson (N.C.) Daily Dispatch, "Sunpower May Be Solution to Future Energy Crisis," issue of December 20, 1971.

Ott, John, *My Ivory Cellar, the Story of Time-Lapse Photography,* Twentieth Century Press, Inc., Chicago, Ill., 1958.

Ott, John N., *Health and Light,* The Devin-Adair Company, Old Greenwich, Conn., 1973.

Scott, Cyril, *Music, Its Secret Influence Throughout the Ages,* Rider & Co., London, Revised Edition, 1958, pg. 145.

Sutton, John H., Ph.D., "The Tuaoi Stone, an Enigma," *The A.R.E. Journal,* January, 1974, pp. 20-34.

Turner, Albert E., "A Study of Color, Part I," *The Searchlight,* August, 1963.

—— "A Study of Color, Part II," *The Searchlight,* November, 1963.

Tushnet, Leonard, M.D., *The Medicine Men,* Warner Paperback Library, New York, 1972, pp. 59 and 60.

Virginian-Pilot, Norfolk, Va., "Sun Storms Rake Earth, Blackout Possible," issue of August 6, 1972, pg. A15.

Weschcke, Carl, "Gardening by the Moon," *1974 Llewellyn's Moon Sign Book and Daily Planetary Guide,* Llewellyn Publications, St. Paul, Minn., 1973, pp. 290-300.

Winston, Shirley Rabb, *Music as the Bridge,* A.R.E. Press, 1972.

INDEX

What Is A.R.E.?

The Association for Research and Enlightenment, Inc. (A.R.E.®), is the international headquarters for the work of Edgar Cayce (1877-1945), who is considered the best-documented psychic of the twentieth century. Founded in 1931, the A.R.E. consists of a community of people from all walks of life and spiritual traditions, who have found meaningful and life-transformative insights from the readings of Edgar Cayce.

Although A.R.E. headquarters is located in Virginia Beach, Virginia—where visitors are always welcome—the A.R.E. community is a global network of individuals who offer conferences, educational activities, and fellowship around the world. People of every age are invited to participate in programs that focus on such topics as holistic health, dreams, reincarnation, ESP, the power of the mind, meditation, and personal spirituality.

In addition to study groups and various activities, the A.R.E. offers membership benefits and services, a bimonthly magazine, a newsletter, extracts from the Cayce readings, conferences, international tours, a massage school curriculum, an impressive volunteer network, a retreat-type camp for children and adults, and A.R.E. contacts around the world. A.R.E. also maintains an affiliation with Atlantic University, which offers a master's degree program in Transpersonal Studies.

For additional information about A.R.E. activities hosted near you, please contact:

> A.R.E.
> 67th St. and Atlantic Ave.
> P.O. Box 595
> Virginia Beach, VA 23451-0595
> (804) 428-3588

A.R.E. Press

A.R.E. Press is a publisher and distributor of books, audiotapes, and videos that offer guidance for a more fulfilling life. Our products are based on, or are compatible with, the concepts in the psychic readings of Edgar Cayce.

We especially seek to create products which carry forward the inspirational story of individuals who have made practical application of the Cayce legacy.

For a free catalog, please write to A.R.E. Press at the address below or call toll free 1-800-723-1112. For any other information, please call 804-428-3588.

> A.R.E. Press
> Sixty-Eighth & Atlantic Avenue
> P.O. Box 656
> Virginia Beach, VA 23451-0656

P.

8 "SOUL AND ITS COMPANION, WILL"

9 IMORTALITY & MIND OF THE SOUL

14 !

5.

8